Gender and Migration

Gender and Migration

Caroline B. Brettell

polity

First published in 2016 by Polity Press

Polity Press
65 Bridge Street
Cambridge CB2 1UR, UK

Polity Press
350 Main Street
Malden, MA 02148, USA

ISBN-13: 978-0-7456-8788-9
ISBN-13: 978-0-7456-8789-6 (pb)

A catalogue record for this book is available from the British Library.

Library of Congress Cataloging-in-Publication Data

Names: Brettell, Caroline, author.
Title: Gender and migration / Caroline B. Brettell.
Description: Cambridge, UK ; Malden, MA, USA : Polity Press, 2016. | Includes
   bibliographical references and index.
Identifiers: LCCN 2016003546 (print) | LCCN 2016005764 (ebook) | ISBN
   9780745687889 (hardcover : alk. paper) | ISBN 0745687881 (hardcover : alk.
   paper) | ISBN 9780745687896 (pbk. : alk. paper) | ISBN 074568789X (pbk. :
   alk. paper) | ISBN 9780745687919 (mobi) | ISBN 9780745687926 (epub)
Subjects: LCSH: Women immigrants--United States. | United States--Emigration
   and immigration--Social aspects. | United States--Emigration and
   immigration--Government policy. | United States--Emigration and
   immigration--Economic aspects. | Immigrants--United States--Economic
   conditions. | Women immigrants--United States--Economic conditions. |
   Immigrant families--United States.
Classification: LCC JV6602 .B74 2016 (print) | LCC JV6602 (ebook) | DDC
   304.8/730082--dc23
LC record available at http://lccn.loc.gov/2016003546

Typeset in 11 on 13pt Sabon by Servis Filmsetting Ltd, Stockport, Cheshire
Printed and bound in the UK by Clays Ltd, St. Ives PLC

For further information on Polity, visit our website: politybooks.com

Contents

Preface

In 1972, between my first and second years of graduate school, I spent the summer in the field with Portuguese immigrants in Toronto, Canada. I found an apartment in the attic of a three-story house in the heart of Kensington Market, a neighborhood that had always been an immigrant receiving area. At the time, the Portuguese were the most recent residents. Two Portuguese families, one from the Azores and one from mainland Portugal, lived in the building. The man from the mainland told me his story of having worked in France for a while and then, hearing that life was better in Canada, he returned to Portugal and with his wife and child moved to Canada. Both he and his wife were working in Canada, although his wife had never migrated with him to France. And yet they talked about other Portuguese women who were migrating to France as they were to Canada. This is how I first became interested in Portuguese migration to France, a migration that I thought might permit more back and forth movement between the country of emigration and the country of immigration than for those in Canada. But as I talked to the two Portuguese women in the household I also realized that to date little was known about female migrants and an idea for a dissertation topic – on Portuguese migrant women in France – began to brew in my mind.

Louise Lamphere, one of my professors, had already sparked my interest in feminist anthropology, and in gender as a critical but under-examined category within anthropology more generally.

At the time, she and her close colleague Michelle Rosaldo were beginning to formulate a framework for studying the lives of women in different cultural contexts, and two years later they published their path-breaking edited volume *Woman, Culture and Society* (Rosaldo and Lamphere 1974). It made sense to me to put the broader questions of feminist anthropology together with my interests in migrant populations. With funding from the Social Science Research Council and the Social and Humanities Research Council of Canada I went to Paris for a year (1974–1975), followed by six months of research in northern Portugal to launch a study of Portuguese migrant women and of the impact of male migration on women who remained behind. After completing my dissertation, I published two monographs, *We Have Already Cried Many Tears: The Stories of Three Portuguese Migrant Women* (1982; 1995), and *Men Who Migrate, Women Who Wait: Population and History in a Portuguese Parish* (1986). With a sociological colleague, Rita James Simon, I also coedited a book titled *International Migration: The Female Experience* (1986), which at the time was pioneering in drawing attention to women who were movers rather than stayers.

These were early works problematizing and theorizing the role of women in the migration process and the relationship between gender and migration. By the 1990s research in this area began to proliferate as migration itself became increasingly "feminized" and globalized. Growing numbers of women, single and married, were mobile for both shorter and longer distances. South–south migrations began to coexist with south–north migrations. From the perspective of the second half of the second decade of the twenty-first century, a question that had not even been posed in 1972 is now well addressed and we know a good deal about migration as a gendered process that impacts both women and men in meaningful ways. Personally, I moved on to other questions about the migration process, but I have always kept my eyes on the anthropology of gender broadly speaking and on the research that has illuminated gender and migration. This book is a product of these sustained and continuing interests.

I dedicate this book to all the scholars, many of them women, who have brought the gendered dimensions of migration to the forefront in the period since I first explored the issue. The research of many of them is discussed and cited in what follows. But above all, I dedicate this book, with gratitude, to Louise Lamphere. Not only has she been an inspiring mentor and leader, but also a very good and lifelong friend.

Caroline B. Brettell
Dallas, Texas

Introduction:
Engendering the Study of Immigration

Beginning in the 1970s, and emerging from the broader development of feminist analysis, scholars in several disciplines began to
formulate a gendered approach to the study of population mobility, both internally and internationally. Although the geographer
and statistician E. G. Ravenstein (1885) had observed gendered
differences in migration patterns (women participate more heavily
in short distance moves while men appear in greater numbers in
longer distance mobility) toward the end of the nineteenth century,
these differences were not rigorously documented or considered
and women in particular remained largely invisible in studies of
migration. And even as a new generation of scholars, many of
them women, began to highlight the significance of gender and the
role of women in migration, they were, as Pierrette Hondagneu-
Sotelo and Cynthia Cranford (1999: 105) point out, met with
hostility. As late as 2003, anthropologist Patricia Pessar (2003), a
well-known scholar of gender and migration, was writing about
the marginalization of panels on gendered and family issues at
major conferences on migration and immigration. Yet, despite
the resistance along the way to gender as a significant analytical
category, by the second decade of the twenty-first century it is
well established as vital to a full understanding of the migration
process.

Some of the earliest research was focused on correcting the
omission of women as subjects and hence documenting their
participation as social actors in the migration process. In the

European context, one can point to a pioneering volume edited by Annie Phizacklea (1983) that emphasized migration and female labor. In the United States, one might note the volume that sociologist Rita James Simon and I edited titled *International Migration: The Female Experience* (1986), as well as the book edited by historian Donna Gabaccia titled *Seeking Common Ground* (1992) in which essays addressed how different disciplines were approaching the topic of migrant women. Like much feminist scholarship of this period, this first phase of gendered migration research was characterized by a "women only" or "just add women" approach. It offered any number of descriptive analyses of women who were mobile, some of them in their own right, in pursuit of employment. Even if women were moving largely as dependants, the interest was to hear their voices about the decisions they made and how it impacted their lives. An effort was made to move away from the assumption that whatever migrant men experience is equally characteristic of migrant women.

This "women only" emphasis is perhaps best represented by an important 1984 special issue of the *International Migration Review* edited by Mirjana Morokvasic (1984) that was titled "Women in Migration". One article in this issue included a statistical "first look" at female predominance among immigrants who had entered the US since 1930 (Houston et al. 1984); another, from a more historical perspective, explored the emigration of Irish women to the US before and after the famine of 1845 to 1849 (Jackson 1984); another addressed women, migration and development in the South Pacific, examining not only women as migrants but also the impact of migration on non-migratory women (Connell 1984); while another focused on stress and distress among Turkish immigrant women in Denmark (Mirdal 1984). The volume, which was divided into five sections, included several census-based quantitative analyses of female immigrants and labor market characteristics in a range of host societies including the United States, Australia, and Canada. Another section contained articles based on theories and survey research of migrant women in the labor market and included case studies of Dominican women in New York, undocumented Mexican women in Los Angeles, and

Turkish women in Germany. The final section included studies of female rural to urban migration in Asia and Africa.

From these impressive and empirically substantive early beginnings, scholarship moved rapidly to a more theoretical approach that considers how gender fundamentally structures the migration process and the immigrant experience for both men and women. Gender refers to the social construction of differences between men and women and how such constructs of difference are played out in daily practices. It encompasses ideals and expectations within particular social and/or cultural contexts regarding men and women and hence ideas about masculinity and femininity – something often referred to as gender ideology. It addresses not only how gender ideologies vary from one cultural context to another, but also through time and in relation to differential processes of change that may occur over time and across space. Thus, to view migration through a gendered lens means to focus on how men and women relate to one another in theory and in practice, how their experiences might differ, and how gender roles (i.e. the particular activities and tasks that are assigned to men and women), which vary from one culture to another, might both affect and be affected by geographic mobility. It also means that we can highlight how gender is constructed by the state in relation to the laws and policies that regulate and control migration as well as processes of exclusion and inclusion that are often associated with the extension or withholding of the rights of citizenship. Thus, understanding gender relations is vital to a full explanation of both the causes and the consequences of migration. Gender must be considered in both sending and receiving contexts, not only in relation to families but also in relation to global labor markets and the wide range of institutions with which migrants interact in places of origin and places of destination.

Ironically, bringing gender fully into the study of migration, as anthropologist Jason Pribilsky (2012: 325) has emphasized, has enhanced our understanding of male migrants. Men have overwhelmingly been the focus of research on migration, but their gendered lives were rarely considered. Sociologist Chad

Broughton (2008: 569) argues that what is often omitted from economic and social demographic studies of migration is how individuals make sense of the migrant experience and "how their strategic responses to economic dislocation are shaped not just by instrumental calculation but also by a knotty set of gendered cultural considerations: prevailing normative expectations and standards, social roles and obligations, and shared understandings relating to family, work, and place." Based on his research with Mexican male migrants, Broughton reveals three masculine stances by which they can be characterized: the traditionalist, the adventurer, and the breadwinner. Broughton suggests that these men "orient gendered understandings and adopt gendered practices increasingly in relation to the specific material forces accelerated by Mexico's neoliberal turn." They are, like women, gendered actors in the migration process.

Gender is about inequality, specifically the inequality between men and women and hence about power and prestige differences that are gendered. Sometimes for example, women face double discrimination not only as a migrant but also as a female because gender ideologies that are rooted in patriarchy may be transported if not sometimes even enhanced in the immigrant context. Further, immigrant men, who may feel more disempowered in the public sphere or in jobs in which they have clearly experienced downward mobility, may try to exercise more control over their wives and children in the private sphere. These are just two possible outcomes in relation to issues of gender and power that can characterize the migration process and the immigrant experience. As the research on the gendered dimensions of immigration has accumulated it has become increasingly apparent that gender ideologies and the unequal distribution of power associated with them serve the interests of capitalist enterprises as well as private employers looking for domestic helpers. Both seek a docile labor force willing to work for low wages. Women immigrants often fit this bill and hence the theoretical question of whether geographical mobility is empowering, must in fact be determined empirically and is subject to variation in relation to a host of different variables and contexts.

Thus, as thinking about gender as an analytical concept has developed, attention has increasingly been paid, theoretically, to the intersections among gender, race, class, and religion (often referred to as intersectionality) as these define and influence the unequal distribution of power and the construction of difference (Brah and Phoenix 2004; McCall 2005). Researchers may choose to explore how the unequal distribution of power impacts processes of oppression or discrimination as these are experienced by men and women of various social, economic, religious, and ethnic or racial backgrounds. They might explore how class distinctions mediate the relationship between professional women of the middle and upper classes and their domestic servants. Also of significance is the question of how immigrant men are constructed as sexualized, threatening, and other in relation to their religion or ethnic background. In other words, the overarching theoretical concern, one that is taken up in this book, is how gender identities interact with other social identities in shaping the experience of immigration.

Another important theoretical consideration is the relationship among structure, agency, and gendered migration. Writing about John Higham's early book on US immigration history, *Strangers in the Land* (1955), Deirdre Moloney (2012: 271) remarks on how women in particular were portrayed:

> As was common in pre-1970s historiography, women lacked the agency to decide to immigrate, to participate in the work force, to mobilize politically, or even to shape their communities. In contrast, men are active: they appear as legislators and government officials, immigrant laborers, labor leaders, elites, eugenicists, writers, and nativists.

A generation of feminist history has corrected this omission. Today, for immigrants of the past and the present, we ask questions such as: To what extent can men and women who migrate be viewed as independent social actors pursuing their own goals and strategies? Do men and women make different decisions about migration (do they have different reasons for moving, for example)? How are these decisions shaped respectively for men and women by economic and political structures that are local, national, and/or global? What autonomy do women in particular have in relation to geographical mobility? Are their remittance behaviors the same? As sociologist Chad Broughton (2008: 569) has phrased it, are the strategic responses of migrants "to economic dislocation . . . shaped not just by instrumental calculation but also by a knotty set of gendered considerations: prevailing normative expectations and standards, social roles and obligations, and shared understandings related to family, work and place?"

Embedded in Broughton's question is the assumption that the entire migration process is gendered in both its causes and its consequences. If we accept this assumption, we may find that what are identified as economic motives for migration may not be strictly economic or may be something else entirely. Thus, Dianne Walta Hart (1997) quotes the Nicaraguan woman who is at the center of her book *Undocumented in LA* stating that what really drove her to leave her country was "lo que dirán" (gossip), something that also drove one of the Portuguese women discussed in my book *We Have Already Cried Many Tears* (Brettell 1995) to leave her village in Portugal for France in the 1970s. This point about the complexity of motives for geographic mobility is further reinforced by sociologist Helma Lutz (2010: 1659) who has recently argued that "any effort to exceed economic reductionism in theories of migration needs to make perceptible migrants' gender, their gendered obligations, care responsibilities, loyalties, family ties and the like. This may include submission to dominant gender orders as well as their modification and transformation."

The shift from women to gender in all its theoretical complexity is captured in another special issue of the *International Migration Review*, published twenty-two years after the first and titled "Gender and Migration Revisited." As the co-editors observe, the contributors to this issue demonstrate that "gender analysis is no longer exclusively limited to the analysis of families, households or women's lives . . . Scholars now analyze gender in the lives of both female and male migrants, in the politics and governance of migration, in the workplaces of immigrants, in neoliberal or welfare state policies toward migration or foreign-born populations, in diasporas, and even in the capitalist world system" (Donato et al. 2006: 6). The essays in this special issue are written by scholars from a number of disciplinary perspectives: anthropology, geography, history, law, political science, psychology, sociology, and queer studies. These essays not only explore the bridging from one disciplinary perspective to another that occurs but also the mixed methodologies that permit aligning quantitative data (statistics) with more qualitative data (from interviews and surveys) that accesses the subjective experience and agency of migrant actors. Further, they outline how formulations of space, place, and scale on the one hand, and time and periodization on the other (the business of geographers and historians respectively) enhance understandings of "the fluidity of gender as migrants move through time as well as across space" (Donato et al. 2006: 15). Collectively, the essays indicate that in some disciplines (anthropology, history, sociology) gendered analysis of migration is well developed, while in others (law, political science, psychology) it is less extensive. The limitations to research in some fields have to do with the nature of the questions asked (what is considered important), as well as with methodologies that emphasize quantitative methods exclusively and hence sex (not gender) as a dichotomous variable. Collectively, the editors of this special issue and their contributors are calling for a more interdisciplinary and collaborative approach to migration studies broadly speaking and to the gendered dimensions of migration more specifically.

Gender and migration has become a subject in its own right and hence this book.[1] While the research on gender and migration is global, encompassing a range of both sending and receiving societies, the empirical emphasis here is on the gendered dimensions of migration to the United States from any number of sending societies. However, occasional references are made to research on other global flows where I have determined that a few cross-cultural comparisons help to illustrate the broader theoretical issues being discussed. While the focus of this book is on post-1965 migrations to the US, I do include an historical perspective in most chapters; specifically, to compare the gendered dimensions of migration from the mid nineteenth and early twentieth centuries with more recent flows. Finally, the focus in this book is on international not internal migration. While some scholars have recently challenged the intellectual and theoretical divides between these two forms of geographical mobility, I find it useful to keep them distinct, particularly in relation to discussions of the laws and policies that impact movement across international borders and that explicitly construct who is an insider and who is an outsider. I leave it to the reader to think about how some of the issues addressed, such as feminized and masculinized labor markets or changing gender ideologies, might equally impact intra-national (internal) movement.

This book is divided into four chapters. The first chapter deals with the gendered demography of migration. It explores similarities and differences in the male and female composition of migration flows over time. It addresses, for example, the contrast between family migrations (the Jews who came to the US in the late nineteenth and early twentieth centuries, for example) and gender-biased migration streams (Mexican braceros or single Irish women, for example). Where appropriate, the narrative of the US experience is set into a global context – that is, brief comparisons are drawn between migrants who came to the US at a particular period and those who may have moved elsewhere. This demographically informed historical overview not only interrogates the theoretical debate about the so-called "feminization of migration", but also helps to lay out a range of issues that then become the focus of subsequent chapters – immigration and citizenship laws and policies, labor markets, exclusion and inclusion – as well as myriad factors that may either constrain or encourage the migration of men and women (individual characteristics such as age, marital status, reproductive status, education; and sociocultural factors such as gender norms and ideology).

The gendered dimensions of migration are heavily influenced by immigration laws and policies of both sending and receiving societies as well as by the labor markets and opportunities of societies of immigration. Chapter 2 deals with the first issue and Chapter 3 with the second. Recently, any number of scholars (for example, Salcido and Menjívar 2012) have observed that immigration laws, and by extension citizenship laws, are hardly gender neutral although they often claim to be. Rather, they reflect the social, political, and cultural context, including the hierarchies of power and inequality, within which they are formulated. Chapter 2 discusses the legal framework of gendered immigration into the United States from the mid to late nineteenth century to the present. It also addresses issues of gendered citizenship and, by extension, the exercise of political rights once citizenship is accorded. The significance of the intersectional theoretical approach is well-illuminated in this discussion, as are the legal structural constraints that differentially impact male and female immigrants. Chapter 3 takes up the question of gendered labor markets and labor force participation among immigrant men and women. It explores the sectors of the economy and the occupational niches that have been differentially filled by foreign-born men and women in the US, both in the past and at present. Are there gendered labor recruitment strategies that influence the formation of these gendered sectors of employment? Among the topics addressed in this chapter are global care work, sex trafficking, and immigrant entrepreneurship. National contexts other than the US are occasionally introduced largely to illustrate that segmented labor markets and their impacts on migrants are a global phenomenon. Other theoretical frameworks brought to bear on this discussion are the international division of labor and agency and resistance.

Chapter 4 turns a gendered analytical lens on the immigrant family. Among the critical theoretical questions explored are: is migration disempowering or empowering to men and/or women within their families; how are gender roles and gender ideologies (ideas about masculinity and femininity) changed in the immigrant context; and what impact does migration have on social and intimate relationships in the domestic sphere? The chapter also focuses on the gendered dimensions of transnationalism. How are the gender relations and gender ideologies of transnational migrant families impacted and altered? And how does transnational migration itself impact the social and cultural constructions of gender in sending communities? The chapter demonstrates that studying migration from a gendered perspective necessitates bringing the home society and the host society into a single field of analysis. In the conclusion I summarize some of the theoretical and empirical arguments as well as point to some areas for future research.

1

The Gendered Demography of US Immigration History

Beginning in the mid nineteenth century, when whale oil was a valuable commodity and a source of fuel for light, whaling ships used to depart from Massachusetts ports. They would make their way to the Cape Verdean and Azorean Islands, Portuguese overseas territories situated in the Atlantic Ocean. There they would pick up all-male sailing crews. After a few months of whaling, the ships would return to New England, including ports like New Bedford, Massachusetts. There the male crews would spend the winter. Some returned to the ships in the spring while others found alternative occupations. It was through whaling that a Portuguese immigrant presence was established in New England and that New Bedford gained its name as the Portuguese capital of the United States.[1] Eventually women and children joined the settler population and by the dawn of the twentieth century the Portuguese represented 16 percent of New Bedford's inhabitants. But by this time the whaling industry was no more and the Portuguese, men and women, had found work in factories, fisheries, and the cranberry bogs of southeastern Massachusetts and Cape Cod.[2] In Providence, Rhode Island, Portuguese men, including Cape Verdeans, could be found working in coal and brick yards, as longshoremen and dockhands, pork packers in slaughter houses, and as operators in oyster and screw companies. Portuguese daughters found employment in lace factories, cotton mills, and laundries.[3]

More than a century later, with the Immigration and Nationality

Act of 1965 and the re-opening of the United States to immigrants, a new generation of Portuguese arrived in New England. This migration brought families, largely from the Azores, who found work in the still-operating textile mills. These immigrants made the transition from being rural agriculturalists to industrial wage workers. Wives took work outside the home to supplement the low wages earned by their husbands. In comparing this more recent migration experience with that of the beginning of the twentieth century, anthropologist Louise Lamphere (1987) describes a shift from working daughters to working mothers. This shift had a direct impact on the division of labor within the family, with men contributing more to childcare and other domestic chores.

The history of US immigration is often told through the lens of particular immigrant groups – the Portuguese, the Irish, the Jews, the Italians, the Chinese, the Vietnamese, the Mexicans. But how do we tell this story through a gendered demographic lens? In one sense the tale has already been told, largely based on the uninvestigated assumption that in the past the majority of immigrants were men and that if women moved it was as the dependants of men. However, once the question of how precisely women might be involved in migratory movements was directly posed, and data more closely examined, it quickly became apparent that women and girls accounted for close to half (47 percent) of all international migrants as early as 1960 and that by 2000 the proportion was 49 percent (for a total of 85 million female migrants and 90 million male migrants). By 2005, the proportion had risen to very close to 50 percent and in 2006 the United Nations reported 94.5 million international female migrants (United Nations 2006). In developed countries female migrants made up a larger portion of migrant stock (51 percent) in 2000 than in the developing world where they comprised 46 percent (Zlotnik 2003; see also Sharma 2011). These data, demonstrating that women as well as men are on the move globally, have generated debates about the "feminization of migration" (Castles and Miller 2009; Morrison et al. 2008; Zlotnik 2003) in the late twentieth- and early twenty-first centuries.

Characteristic of this process of "feminization" is an increasing number of women, both married and unmarried, who migrate by themselves or with other unrelated migrants. This is distinctly different from historical migrations where women primarily moved for marriage or as part of a family reunification process (United Nations 2006: 22). The so-called feminization of migration has been explained by a range of factors including the absence of opportunities for paid work in sending countries; the awareness of, if not recruitment for paid work in receiving societies; the desires of women for more independence and autonomy; marital instability, including political violence, divorce and separation, that often leave women as sole breadwinners for their families; and a relaxation in the restrictions that are placed on the geographical mobility of women, whether within families and communities (in accordance with changing gender ideologies) or by sending states.

Despite a label that suggests dramatic change, some scholars have argued that an increase from 47 percent to 50 percent in the proportion of female migrants among all migrants seems minimal (Donato 2012a; Moya 2012), leading them not only to propose the phrase "shift toward gender balance" as an alternative to "feminization" (Donato et al. 2011), but also to delve more deeply into the historical record to render a more accurate assessment of the gendered demographics of population mobility (Donato and Gabaccia 2015). The result is not only a reconsideration of statistician Ernest George Ravenstein's (1885) original and famous formulation of the gendered nature of short (more female-dominated) versus long (more male-dominated) distance moves (Alexander and Steidl 2012), but also new evidence of wide variations in the proportions of men and women who have participated in migration across time and space.

Historians Donna Gabaccia and Elizabeth Zanoni (2012) offer a useful and more nuanced typology by which to categorize gendered migration flows in demographic terms (Table 1.1). They argue that the shift to more gender-balanced flows for some migration streams most likely occurred before and not after 1960. They also point us to the right kinds of questions to ask of any migration flow in relation to gender: "how international

Table 1.1   Typology of Gendered Migrations

Types of Gendered Migrations	Proportion of Females in the Migration Flow %
Heavily Male Dominant	25
Male Pre-dominant	25–47
Gender Balanced	47–52
Female Pre-dominant	53–75
Heavily Female Dominant	75

Source: Adapted from Gabaccia and Zanoni (2012)

migrations have been gendered, when transitions in the gendering of migration have occurred, why they have occurred, and what their consequences may have been" (p. 199).

What then is the story of the respective participation of men and women (the gendered demographics) of international migration flows to the US over time? In the middle of the nineteenth century, just over 40 percent of immigrants to the United States were female, while for the rest of the nineteenth century the proportion dropped to approximately 38 percent and to 30 percent in the first decade of the twentieth century – thus verging on being heavily male dominant.[4] Table 1.2 presents the gender ratio of immigrants to the US between 1870 and 2012.[5] After 1930, a period when immigration was restricted as a result of the National Origins Quota Act of 1924, the proportion of female immigrants began to rise. In the 1940s in particular, the proportion of women among US immigrants rose to over 60 percent, impacted no doubt by the 1945 War Brides Act which made it possible for non-Asian spouses and children of American military personnel to enter the country. Historian Suzanne Sinke (2006b: 300) points to this period as the greatest female majority immigration in US history, but also emphasizes that the War Brides Act actually reinforced the gendered intentions of immigration policy which have always tended to classify women as dependants. I return to the issue of policy in the next chapter. However, it is worth noting here that the 1940s was also a time when overall immigration was

Table 1.2 Males/100 Females Ratio among Immigrants to the US, 1870–2012

YEAR	Males/100 Females	YEAR	Males/100 Females
1870	117	1950	103
1880	119	1960	96
1890	121	1970	84
1900	120	1980	88
1910	131	1990	96
1920	123	2000	100
1930	117	2010	96
1940	112	2012	95

Source: Adapted from http://www.migrationpolicy.org/programs/data-hub/ charts/males-100–females-ratio-among-immigrants-1870–present

low, something that would statistically impact the proportion of women in the immigrant population.

By 1960 and through until 2000 women comprised more than half of the foreign-born population in the US – 53 percent in 1980 and 51 percent in 1990. While in 2000 there were an equal number of immigrant women and immigrant men, thereafter the figures have hovered just over 50 percent.[6] In 2008 women were granted 54 percent of all the green cards issued in that year and accounted for 56 percent of all naturalizations. In that same year there were almost 19 million immigrant women (18.9 million) in the US, comprising 12 percent of all women in the country. Close to eighty percent (78.2) of these immigrant women were of working age – between eighteen and sixty-four – compared with 82.5 percent of foreign-born men but there were more foreign-born women over sixty-five than foreign-born men. The comparable working age figures for native-born women and men were 59.8 percent and 61 percent. Twenty-seven percent of the immigrant women in the US toward the close of the first decade of the twenty-first century were born in Mexico. Of the 19.1 million immigrant men in the country at that time, 33.5 percent were from Mexico. The median age of foreign-born women (forty-two years) was higher than that of native-born women (thirty-seven) and higher also than foreign-born men and native-born men. Finally, foreign-born women over age twenty-five were less likely to have a bachelor's degree than foreign-born men (9.5 percent compared with 12.6 percent) but slightly more than two-thirds (68.4 percent) had a high school degree compared with 66.6 percent of foreign-born men (Batalova 2009: 2–4).

In summary, the story of the gendered demography of immigration to the US is one of change over time, moving from patterns that were male-predominant to almost heavily male dominant, to female pre-dominant to gender balanced. Such changes over time are worthy of further exploration and explanation. One explanation can be found in late-twentieth-century immigration policy rooted in family reunification. Thus, Linda Gordon (2005: 806) observes that the "trends and levels in the gender ratio of the US immigrant population are now determined in large part by the spouse categories, specifically spouses of citizens (who may enter without numerical limitation) and lawful permanent residents (who are subject to an annual ceiling)."[7] Another explanation can be found in labor markets, something discussed in a later chapter. Gendered mobility patterns are also influenced by the economic and political conditions in the homeland, by marital status, and by gender ideologies and the overall status of women in both sending and receiving contexts (Tyree and Donato 1985; Donato 1992, 2010; Kanaiaupuni 2000). These too are issues that will be explored more fully later in this book. However, demographically, it is important to address the impact of national origins on the proportion of males to females (the gender ratio) in specific migration streams.

Migration, Gender Ratios, and National Origins: Then and Now

Scholars have observed that if Mexican migration to the US toward the end of the twentieth century were removed from consideration, the analysis of the overall composition of the immigrant population would look decidedly more "feminized" than gender-balanced (Donato et al. 2011). In the nineteenth century, as today, the gender ratios of immigration and hence of immigrant populations have varied by national origins. For example, the absence of opportunities in their home country resulted in high rates of outmigration for single Irish women, who went to England or America. While only a third of Irish emigrants in the period between 1815 and 1844 were women, in the aftermath of the Great Famine (1845–1851) women left in numbers equal to those of men. "Famine created an environment that marginalized women economically and reduced their status in society. The virtual ending of partible inheritance, the eradication of the poorer classes among whom female labor was particularly important, the spread of arranged marriages and the dowry system, and the reduced opportunities for female wage earning combined to spur emigration" (Mageean 1997: 96).[8]

By the end the nineteenth century women made up more than half of all Irish emigrants. Between 1885 and 1920 close to 700,000 young and mostly unmarried Irish women left their homeland (Nolan 1989). "They were the only significant group of foreign-born women who outnumbered men; they were the only significant group of women who chose to migrate primarily in female cliques. They also accepted jobs that most other women turned down" (Diner 1983: xiv). Historian Donna Gabaccia (1994: 30) has observed that in 1910 only 17 percent of Irish women came to the US with nuclear families. In fact, it was common for young unmarried Irish women to be sponsored by a female sibling and then, when they had saved up enough to marry, to in turn send passage for another sibling or relative to emigrate to America.

Women came to represent 52.9 percent of the Irish immigrant population in America. By contrast, the Jews who were pushed out of Eastern Europe and Russia by pogroms and other forms of discrimination and persecution were more likely to leave in nuclear family units, although men still outnumbered women. During the first decade of the twentieth century, women comprised 43 percent of all Jewish immigrants to the US (Joseph 1914). For these Jews, their departure was permanent and their goal was to build a new life in America. The writers Mary (Mashke) Antin, author of *The Promised Land*, and Anzia Yezierska, author of *Hungry Hearts* and *The Breadgivers*, offer good examples of these family migrations. Antin was born in a shtetl in what is now Belarus to a well-to-do family of Jewish shopkeepers. In 1891, when she was nine years old, and in the context of the pogroms in Russia, her father left for Boston. His family joined him three years later. Yezierska, born in 1885, came with her family to the US from a shtetl in Poland. They settled in the lower East side of Manhattan in the early 1890s. She was sent to work in a sweatshop but eventually earned a scholarship to Columbia University.

By contrast with an Irish migration that verged over its history on being female predominant, and with a Jewish migration that approached gender-balance, the Italian migration stream to America in the late nineteenth century was heavily male dominant – between 1880 and 1910 approximately 80 percent of Italians entering the US were men. In the period between 1911 and 1920, the proportion of Italian women rose to 31 percent; from 1921 to 1930 the proportion was 39 percent. When Italian women emigrated it was generally as followers and dependants (wives, daughters, sisters) rather than as independent single women. Historian Miriam Cohen (1992: 39) has labeled the migration of Italian women to the US a "delayed migration" – they arrived, if they arrived at all, on average fourteen months after the men. For Sicily in particular, women and children comprised less than 15 percent of all migrants prior to World War I. "Sicilian women sailed overseas in greater numbers than women from Calabria, Greece, or Spain, but even they never made up more than one-third of the emigrants who left before 1925" (Reeder 2003: 5).

Italians were economic migrants who often left their homeland with an expectation of return; hence, the initial decision was to leave their families behind. Their wives, known in Sicily as "white widows" (Reeder 2003), assumed the management of the family farm and experienced a repositioning of their status in civil society.[9] It has been estimated that as many as 1.5 million Italian immigrants returned to Italy in the period between 1900 and 1914 (Caroli 1973: 41). One historian has noted that unlike the Russian state, which permanently expelled particular national minorities (like the Jews), the Italian state worked hard to retain the allegiance of nationals who were abroad by encouraging temporary migration, fostering ties with families left behind, and facilitating remittances and return (Friedman-Kasaba 1996). But as the twentieth century began to unfold more and more Italian men, husbands and fathers, abandoned the idea of return and began to encourage their families to join them.

On the West Coast, a parallel case of a heavily male-dominant migration stream can be found among the population of Indians from the Punjab region who arrived toward the end of the nineteenth century to work on the farms of California, in the lumber mills of Oregon, as well as in railway construction. In 1930, there were 1,572 Asian Indian men per 100 women in California (Leonard 1997: 41). Many of these early Indian immigrants, particularly in the Imperial Valley of southern California, married women who were of Mexican ancestry. "Unable to bring their wives and families from India because of the restrictive immigration laws, those who wanted a stable family life in the United States married predominantly Spanish-speaking women, producing families known locally as 'Mexican-Hindus'" (Leonard 1997: 47).

The Filipino immigrant population at this time was also heavily dominated by men. Filipinos were not affected by the Asian exclusion laws of the United States that impacted immigrants from India, China, and Japan. Many young single Filipino men entered the US during the first three to four decades of the twentieth century to work in agriculture (including in the sugar industry in Hawaii) and other forms of manual and service labor. According to geographer James Tyner (1999), 87 percent of the 102,000 Filipinos who were recruited to work on the Hawaiian plantations were men. In addition, beginning in 1903 the US Navy began to recruit Filipino men who eventually came to represent 5 percent of its manpower. Between 1910 and 1930, the Filipino population in California rose from 5 to over 30,000. During the 1920s, 93 of every 100 Filipinos who migrated to California were males and 80 of these men were between the ages of sixteen and thirty (Espiritu 1995).

Finally, the Chinese immigrant population in the West Coast was also almost exclusively composed of young Chinese men who first arrived in California at the time of the Gold Rush. In 1851 there were 2,716 Chinese in the US. During the 1860s, 64,301 Chinese immigrants arrived, many of them recruited to work on the building of the transcontinental railroad. In the 1870s the figure rose to 123,201. Most of these young men never intended to stay and many returned home having sent remittances to their families in China; but some remained to establish businesses and build the Chinatowns that we still see today in the cities of the West Coast. The nineteenth-century Chinese migration to the US was short-lived, largely as a result of the increasing racism that eventually culminated in the Chinese Exclusion Act of 1882 which suspended all further immigration from China.

In the late twentieth century, a similar variety of gendered demographic patterns can be found in the migration streams from different countries of origin (Grieco 2003). As mentioned above, the Mexican migration to the US has been male predominant if not heavily male dominant, although over time it has shown some variation. This pattern of men migrating alone, leaving their families behind in Mexico, was to some extent shaped by the Bracero Program of the period between 1942 and 1964. This guest-worker program brought over four million temporary agricultural laborers, most of them male, to the US while it was in effect (Cohen 2011; Snodgrass 2011). Toward the end of the first decade of the twenty-first century, the gender ratio among the Mexican foreign born was 126 males/100 females (Batalova 2009). However, while in 1985 women comprised only 41 percent of Mexican immigrants entering the US, in 2000 they were 60 percent. The Immigration Reform and Control Act of 1986, which made it possible for many Mexican men who had entered the country without documents to legalize their status and then bring their families to join them, had an important impact on the gendered composition of this migratory flow. Katharine Donato (2010: 82) cites a host of research documenting that women's "representation among legal and undocumented migrants grew from the early 1980s to the late 1990s (from 48 to 59 percent and from 26 to 33 percent, respectively)." However, more holistically, Mexican immigrants in 2008 were a third of all immigrant men while Mexican women represented only a quarter of all immigrant women (Batalova 2009).

Three forces that have shaped the gendered migration patterns of Mexicans to the US have been identified: social norms in Mexico that impact the social behaviors of men and women, including migration; "institutionalized economic roles and structural characteristics of the labor market that contribute to the financial dependence of women"; and finally the immigration policies of the United States (Kanaiaupuni 2000: 1317). Particular emphasis has been placed on Mexican gender ideologies – that is, ideas about masculinity and femininity that have promoted the migration of men and restricted the migration of women. However, migrants "as gendered subjects defy a simple dichotomy of regulated females and liberated males" because men's actions can be controlled by the US state, just as many women who are left behind gain a certain degree of independence (Boehm 2008b: 20).

Sociologist Douglas Massey and his colleagues (Massey et al. 2006) take these issues a step further by comparing five different Latin American countries along a gender relations continuum from matrifocal (mother and children are the basic family unit and men come and go) to patriarchal (formal authority over wives and daughters is invested in a male head of household). Nicaragua and the Dominican Republic fall at the matrifocal end; Puerto Rico is in a middle position combining characteristics of both systems; and Costa Rica and Mexico fall at the patriarchal. These authors write: "Whereas most women in Mexico and Costa Rica live in a husband-wife household, most women in the Dominican Republic, Nicaragua, and Puerto Rico do not" (p. 73). They then proceed to argue that these differences in gender relations impact the composition of migration streams. While Mexico and Costa Rica have low rates of female outmigration compared with that for men, especially if a woman is in a formal or informal union with a man, in the two matrifocal countries the migration of females often exceeds that of males. They further find that in the matrifocal societies the migrant status of a partner or having relatives in the country of immigration has less of an impact on female migration than it does in patriarchal societies. Another finding is that unattached women are more likely to migrate in matrifocal societies than in patriarchal societies and at times their rate of migration is even greater than that of unattached males in matrifocal societies. Finally, they find that in patriarchal societies cumulative causation (a theory that explains how once a migration flow has begun it is perpetuated)[10] is more driven by men while in matrifocal societies it is more driven by women. The significance of this research, in juxtaposition with what has already been discussed, is clearly that the economic and political conditions and gender ideologies in both sending and receiving societies impact the gendered demographics of migration flows.

Using the same data set, Katharine Donato (2010: 89) adds a consideration of legal status to the equation, arguing that the "male-led process of undocumented migration from Mexico ... differs sharply from the female-led process of documented migration from the Dominican Republic." In the Puerto Rican case, male and female migration streams are roughly equivalent because legal status is not relevant – Puerto Rico is a US territory and hence population movements are unrestricted.

Although at the other end of a human capital continuum (that is, among migrants with higher levels of education, a greater command of the English language, and a higher earning potential in largely white-collar positions), Indian immigrants also show a slightly male-biased pattern of mobility. At the end of the first decade of the twenty-first century there were close to 2 million Indians in the US, making them the third-largest immigrant population after the Mexicans and the Chinese. The gender ratio in 2011 was 111 men/100 women, with Indian men therefore representing 53 percent of the total population and women 47 percent (Whately and Batalova 2011). Although in earlier periods (for example between 1985 and 2000) the proportion of women was closer to 50 percent, the opportunities for education and for employment on H1B high-skilled employment visas (primarily in technology and engineering sectors) promote the migration of greater numbers of young Indian men by comparison with young Indian women. Some of these men, if married, may be accompanied by their wives and children, who enter on H4 dependent visas and are hence not entitled to work. Others may migrate to pursue an education, acquire legal residence, and then return to India to marry, whereupon the new wife joins her husband.

One exception in the Indian case – that is where a woman may be the "lead migrant" – can be found among nurses who come from the province of Kerala in southwestern India (Sharma 2011; Walton-Roberts 2012, Walton-Roberts and Rajan 2013). Thirty-eight percent of Kerala nurses work in the United States, 30 percent in the United Kingdom, 15 percent in Australia, and 12 percent in the Gulf (Lum 2012). They are often the primary breadwinners for their families, sometimes living abroad on temporary work permits while their spouses remain at home with children – particularly the case in the Gulf. Alternatively, and this is characteristic of those in the United States, husbands and children migrate as dependants (George 2005).

Other countries of origin where male migrants outnumbered female migrants (a gender ratio above 100) at the turn of the twenty-first century were El Salvador (110) and Haiti (109) (Grieco 2003). By contrast, those countries with low migration gender ratios (below 100) and hence where females outnumbered males were Germany, South Korea, the Dominican Republic, the Philippines, and Japan. In the case of the Philippines, the sex ratio was 71, marking a sharp contrast with the gendered demographics of this migration flow in the early decades of the twentieth century that were discussed above. However, as geographer James Tyner (1999: 672) points out, the gendered demographics of Filipino migration varies by destination country: flows to the Middle East, Africa, and Oceania are male-dominated; those to Western Europe, North America, and Asia are female-dominated.

Filipinos comprised 1 percent of the US foreign-born population in 1960 but were 4 percent by the end of the first decade of the twenty-first century. Women were 60 percent of the Filipino immigrant population in 1960 and more than 18 percent of these women worked in nursing (Storey and Batalova 2013). While labor opportunities in the health care sector can explain the gendered dimensions of the Filipino migration stream, it is also important, as with Mexico, to consider homeland culture and society. In the Philippines, daughters are expected to contribute to the household economy; thus, sending a single daughter overseas, whether to America, to Hong Kong, or to Italy, to take a position as a nurse, in domestic service, or in home health care is common (Constable 2007; Parreñas 2001b). Direct recruitment plays an important role in this process, but equally significant are the economic and structural changes in the Philippines that have made it possible for Filipino women to pursue educational and occupational credentials in fields (such as nursing) for which there was a global demand (Tyner 1999). According to the 2006 United Nations Report on women immigrants, over 65 percent of the nearly 3,000 Filipinos who left their country each day in 2005 for work or residence abroad were women. Like the nurses from Kerala, some Filipina women who are married take positions abroad, leaving their husbands in the Philippines to take care of the children.

Young Filipino men are also migrants, but often they find work on cruise ships or in construction (McKay 2007). By 1974, the Philippines was pursuing a labor-export strategy to take more advantage of changing global opportunities and to relieve the pressure of increasing unemployment at home, some of it the result of the deliberate expansion of agribusinesses that displaced rural populations. Demand for Filipino male laborers was high in the Middle East during a phase of massive construction, but once the large-scale infrastructural projects (hospitals, hotels, etc.) were completed (by the late 1980s) the demand for service workers to sustain them increased and the Filipino labor flow to this part of the world shifted from being male-dominated to being female-dominated (Tyner 1999).

Local gender ideologies also shape the other well-known female predominant, if not heavily female dominant, migration flow – that from the West Indies. In many parts of the West Indies, female-headed households are not unusual and women are major breadwinners. These responsibilities at home and the opportunities abroad influence their decisions to migrate, including the decision to leave their children behind in the care of extended family members. In the United States, in 2009, there were 3.5 million West Indian immigrants, of whom 75 percent entered the US between 1980 and 1999. Within this population, 29 percent were from Cuba, 23 percent from the Dominican Republic, 19 percent from Jamaica, 15 percent from Haiti, and 6 percent from Trinidad and Tobago (McCabe 2011). Over half (53.7 percent) of these immigrants were women (compared with 50.1 percent for the foreign born overall). However, this gender imbalance was greater for the populations from Trinidad and Tobago, the Dominican Republic, and Jamaica (56 percent female in each case) than it was for Cuba where the gender ratio was more balanced with 50.5 percent of the population male.

This predominance of women was not always the case. During the late nineteenth and early twentieth centuries it was primarily men who migrated to Panama (to help build the canal) and other countries of Central America as well as to other islands in the Caribbean. The Cuban sugar industry employed large numbers of Jamaican men, although Jamaican women also migrated to Cuba to find employment in a variety of service occupations including domestic service. Even the flow to the US at that time was heavily male. And the male-dominant pattern also characterized the large migration to Britain in the period following World War II. In the period between 1952 and 1954, approximately 70 percent of migrants from the Caribbean region to Britain were men and the proportion in 1955 and 1960 was 60 percent. This is not to suggest that Caribbean women did not migrate to the United Kingdom but in smaller numbers relative to men until 1961 when net arrivals of West Indian women began to exceed those of men (Foner 2009).

Since 1967, West Indian women have migrated to the US in greater numbers than have men. At this time it became easier for women to qualify for labor certification because of the demand for domestic labor and for nurses. Fifty percent of the total Jamaican workers in 1968 were listed as private household workers and between 1962 and 1972 a third of legal Jamaican immigrants who were classified as professionals were nurses (Foner 2009: 8). This trend continued, with the Immigration and Naturalization Service recording, for the period between 1990 and 1992, that 29 percent of the Jamaican-born professional and technical immigrants were nurses. This predominance of Caribbean women in the migratory flow is equally characteristic of Canada – they comprised 57 percent of those arriving in Canada between 1961 and 1996 (Foner 2009: 10).

In 2010 African immigrants, at 1.6 million, constituted 4 percent of the foreign-born population in the United States. Among African migrants to the US, the majority of whom have entered since 1990, men outnumber women. In 2010, 53 percent of the African immigrant population in the US was male. The highest gender ratios were among Senegalese immigrants – 284 males/100 females (Batalova 2009).[11] The United Nations 2006 report on immigrant women observes that 47 percent of the 17 million immigrants within Africa (that is, intra-African migrations) in 2005 were women, an increase from 42 percent in 1960. African women, particularly those trained as nurses, also began to migrate to Europe. But overall, the larger participation of African men in these migration flows outside of Africa is partially rooted in cultural attitudes toward male and female migration.[12]

For example, immigrants from Angola who had settled in Portugal were asked what they thought about the international migration of mothers as opposed to fathers. More than 80 percent of male respondents considered it "bad or very bad" for mothers to migrate abroad, while the largest proportion of women thought it was "neither bad nor good." But by contrast, 30 percent said it is bad or very bad for fathers to migrate, while more than 15 percent of men claimed it is good or very good (Grassi and Vivet 2014: 10–11). The authors of this study conclude that these results "help us to understand the common cultural values linked to the international migration amongst Angolan migrants and the gender division of parenting and household responsibilities, at least in the opinions and responses of our interviewees" (p. 11). It is important to note that while in 1999 Angolan men constituted 59 percent of the migrant population, by 2010 men were 49 percent of the population. This shift in just a decade is the result of the process of family reunification, thus indicating once more how important immigration policies are to the gendered demographics of migration. Indeed, other scholars have noted that during the first decade of the twenty-first century many migration streams from different parts of Africa are becoming feminized with both men and women participating in migration as a family strategy (Adepoju 2004a). Further, African women have begun to move independently, with their own economic needs in mind, rather than to simply join a husband or other family members. Finally, professional woman are migrating from certain African countries and leaving their husbands behind – this is characteristic of Nigerian nurses working in Saudi Arabia and Ghanaian nurses working in the United States or the United Kingdom (Adepoju 2004b).

While African economic migration streams to the US, from countries such as Senegal or Nigeria, tend to have higher percentages of men, African refugee streams, indeed refugee flows in general, tend to include more or equal numbers of women. Where women (and children) outnumber men, it is largely because the political violence that has generated the refugee flow frequently results in a high rate of male deaths. The United Nations High Commissioner for Refugees estimated that there were 16.7 million refugees (that is, people fleeing conflict and persecution) globally at the end of 2013, with the highest numbers in Asia and Africa. Another 33 million people were internally displaced. Since 1980, when the US Refugee Act was passed, the US has admitted over 3 million refugees. In 2008 when the annual ceiling for refugee admissions to the US was raised from 70,000 to 80,000, 60,108 refugees were admitted; 48.5 percent were females. In 2013, 69,930 refugees were admitted.

Since 1980 refugees have come to the US from places where the US has had geopolitical interests (Cuba, Russia, Vietnam, Laos, Cambodia, Afghanistan, Iran, Iraq) and from African trouble spots such as Ethiopia, Liberia, Somalia, and Sudan. In 2008 two-thirds of refugees were from Burma, Iraq, and Bhutan. In 2013, the top five countries of origin for refugees resettled in the US were Iraq, Burma, Bhutan, Somalia, and Cuba. Thus, the source countries for refugees are often different from those for economic migrants and generally refugees are composed of families travelling together, thus creating a more gender-balanced flow. This was as true of the families who came from Vietnam, Cambodia, and Laos in the 1980s as it is for the Burmese and Bhutanese today.

The Gendered Demographics of Migrants in non-US Destination Countries

The example of Angolans in Portugal discussed above provides some indication that variations in the gendered demographics of migration are equally characteristic of host or destination societies other than the US and that we need to explore the so-called "feminization" of migration in a global context. The 2006 United Nations report on women and international migration observes that in 2005 in all regions of the world with the exception of Africa and Asia there were slightly more female than male immigrants. But even within these regions there were particular flows dominated by women. Thus, by the mid 1990s approximately 800,000 Asian women were migrating annually to the Middle East and by 2000 approximately two million Asian women found employment in neighboring countries (United Nations 2006). Of the 15 million Indians who were reported by the Ministry of Overseas Indian Affairs to be residing in the United Arab Emirates in 2009, at least one million were women (Sharma 2011: 47–48). Central and South American women, who had been drawn to the US, were also migrating to other places in South America as well as to Spain and Italy. The foreign-born population in Spain was female-dominated in 1981 (53 percent) but a decade later women were 52 percent, and ten years after that, in 2001, they were 49 percent. France experienced the opposite trend, with women comprising 43 percent of the foreign born in 1962 and 48 percent by the last year of the twentieth century. By contrast, in the countries of the global south men tended to predominate in many areas, but in South Africa the proportion of women among the foreign born rose from 33 to 35 percent between 1996 and 2007. It also rose in Chile in 2002 to 50 percent; and similarly in Mexico in 2000.[13] Thus, the data on global trends show a shift "toward more women among both immigrant populations and in populations emigrating from many, but not all, parts of the world. Despite considerable variation by region/national origin since 1960, migration streams worldwide have become increasingly female. One exception is international migrants from African countries, where men's share has increased since 1960" (Donato et al. 2011: 513).

A few examples will suffice to better illustrate these patterns of gendered mobility in destinations other than the United States. Sociologists Jorge Durand and Douglas Massey (1992), in relation to the Mexican migration to the United States, have described stages of a migration process. In early stages, local communities send young men who often migrate illegally without families. However, as migration streams mature and develop, more wives and children begin to participate, joining husbands and fathers abroad. This gendered and staged migration described for the Mexican case aptly fits the case of the Portuguese who migrated to France in the decades following World War II, but with a twist.

At the end of the nineteenth century and during the first three decades of the twentieth century, when the majority of Portuguese were migrating to Brazil and to a lesser extent the US, the proportion of men within this population was always above 70 percent and often higher. Thus between 1868 and 1877, men were 92 percent of Portuguese migrants; between 1901 and 1911, 80 percent; and while they were 70 percent between 1912 and 1920, in the succeeding decade (1921–1930) the proportion rose to 78 percent. Beginning in 1930 the proportion of men dropped to 65 percent (1931–1950) and between 1951 and 1960 it dropped further to 60 percent (Serrão 1974). It was in this latter period that the emigration of Portuguese workers to northern Europe, and particularly France, began. The countries of northern Europe turned to southern Europe for labor to fill jobs that their own countrymen would no longer fill and to assist in the reconstruction of countries devastated by war. In 1950, 314 Portuguese immigrants entered France; by 1970 the figure had reached 110,615. In the mid 1960s, 71 percent of all foreign workers in France were from the Iberian Peninsula, and by 1975 the total foreign worker population in France numbered approximately four million.

The early years of this migration of the Portuguese northward to France was dominated by men who found work in construction and manufacturing. Many of these men left their country clandestinely (illegally), because emigration was only "approved of" by the Salazarist Portuguese state within certain limits. This clandestine flow was enhanced after 1961 by the escalation of the colonial wars in Portuguese Africa. Many young men simply chose emigration over military service. Further, a rigid set of regulations was put in place to limit the legal emigration of young men who wished to leave Portugal before reaching the official age (eighteen) for military conscription. This is the twist. Portuguese policy fostered a population of emigrant male "draft dodgers." The rigidity of these laws and of others that impacted a broad segment of the Portuguese population, as well as the time that it took to secure a passport, steered more and more potential male emigrants of all ages in the direction of clandestine departure. Paralleling the figure of the *coyote* characteristic of undocumented Mexican migration flows to the United States, was the figure of the *passador* (guide) who was paid to help the Portuguese make "*o salto*" (the leap) across the borders of Portugal and Spain and into France.

Initially, clandestine emigration was not considered safe for women and hence as late as 1968 the proportion of women among Portuguese immigrants in France was only 9.1 percent. However, by 1973 this proportion had risen to 21.2 percent. Women began to join their husbands abroad, and single and unmarried women began to depart Portugal to find work in domestic service, in private homes or with cleaning companies. By the mid 1970s close to 50 percent of Portuguese women in France above the age of fifteen were actively employed and the figure of the Portuguese *concierge* (porter) living in the small apartment on the ground floor of the Parisian apartment building had become well-known across the city (Brettell 1995). While employment opportunities drew more Portuguese women beginning in 1965, an explicit shift in French immigration policy at this time, which facilitated procedures for naturalization and for the introduction of families (family reunification) also played an important role.

Capturing a more recent migration flow within Europe, Hofman and Buckley (2013) explore how a pattern of feminized migration developed and gained social acceptance in the Republic of Georgia. Georgia has had a long history of men moving to other parts of the former Soviet Union as part of construction brigades. With the collapse of the USSR, the destinations for emigrants from Georgia shifted to Europe, the Middle East, and North America. These destinations offered opportunities for migrant women that were not available before. Whereas prior to 1993, 76 percent of migrants were men and 24 percent were women (thus heavily male dominant), in the period between 2004 and 2008 women comprised 41 percent of migrants. And increasingly these women were leaving in search of work rather than in search of education or as "tied" migrants. Hofman and Buckley argue that not only have changes in local and global structural factors shaped this change in the gendered demographics of migration, but also the process of "cognitive adjustment and cultural reframing" (p. 530) has made female migration more acceptable. "Cultural beliefs stigmatizing women migrants can be renegotiated as female migration grows framing women's migration within normative gender approaches to caregiving and self-sacrifice and providing pathways for cultural maintenance" (p. 530). From this perspective, they argue, the feminization of migration may in fact be self-reinforcing: "Once women's migration begins, gender norms in the original society become more egalitarian, thereby facilitating the emigration of more women" (p. 512). Of course, this is not always the case. In some contexts the departures of women may result in a retrenchment of patriarchal gender norms (Parrado and Flippen 2005).

What is evident is that women have been actively involved in contemporary intra-European migration flows, not only as a result of family reunification, but also in relation to expanding labor markets. In addition, by the 1990s women had also become an important minority of asylum seekers within Europe "although their specific experiences and claims for refugee status do not receive adequate attention in general reviews of European asylum and refugees" (Kofman 1999: 270). Legal scholar Eleonore Kofman challenges some of the temporal sequencing of gendered migration flows, particularly if they place too much emphasis on women following spouses, but ultimately each flow must be studied independently to develop an understanding of how it has evolved.

Conclusion

This chapter has focused on the gendered demography of migration. When and where have men outnumbered women in migration flows? When and where have migration flows been more balanced? What were the gendered patterns of migration in the past and how do they compare with those in the present? Theoretically, what do we mean when we talk about the "feminization of migration" and is this even an appropriate term? Some scholars have suggested a broader range of analytical concepts, spanning a range from heavily male dominant to gender-balanced to heavily female dominant, to capture more subtle variations in the gendered dimensions of specific migration flows across space and time. Of particular note is that the United States is the only industrialized country where the percentage of female migrants decreased in the period between 1980 and 2005 (from 53.2 percent to 50.2 percent) while globally it has increased from just over 47 percent to close to 50 percent. According to a Pew Hispanic Center report (Fry 2006), among adults, 58 percent of unauthorized migrants in the United States by the middle of the first decade of the twenty-first century were male and 42 percent were female. Among legal adult migrants, females were 52 percent and males 48 percent. Thus, it is the role of unauthorized immigrants to the US that has created this anomaly. This is in turn linked to gendered immigration policies and labor markets, but also to the gender ideologies in sending societies. It is these issues that begin to explain some of the "whys" of migration as a gendered process and it is to these that we turn in the chapters that follow.

2

The Gendering of Law, Policy, Citizenship, and Political Practice

During the summer of 2014 a crisis exploded in the US media. Large numbers of women and children were detained at the US border in Texas. They were Central Americans for the most part, fleeing criminal and political violence in their own countries and on their way to join relatives already living in the US. Many were unaccompanied children.

To handle the crisis, two detention centers were opened in Texas. A year later, in midsummer 2015, a judge (Dolly M. Gee) for the Federal District Court for the Central District of California found that these two centers failed to meet the minimum legal requirements for settling and housing children. These requirements called for placing children in facilities that are licensed to care for children and not secured like prisons. Those in Texas were being run by private prison contractors. One human rights activist commented: "I think this spells the beginning of the end for the Obama administration's immigrant family detention policy . . . A policy that just targets mothers with children is not rational and it's inhumane" (quoted in Preston 2015: A14). In addition to the Texas detention centers, there was one in Berks County, PA, and together they were holding 2,600 women and children. A *New York Times* story (Preston 2015) reported that in the beginning Homeland Security detained the families to send a message to others in Central America that they were not welcome in the US without legal papers for entry. But a federal court in Washington, DC, ruled that this approach was unconstitutional and officials ceased invoking deterrence as a basis for evaluating cases for asylum within this group. Despite this ruling, "many women and children remained stalled behind bleak walls and fences month after month with no end in sight. Mothers became severely depressed or anxious, and their distress echoed in their children, who became worried and sickly" (Preston 2015: A14).

The experiences of these Central America women is quite different from that of a young Indian woman, whom I call Anjuli, whom I met very soon after she arrived in the US in the summer of 2002. Anjuli had been recently married. Her husband had been working in the US on an H1B skilled worker visa and had returned to India to marry her. After waiting in India for a few months, Anjuli was able to join him in the US, entering the country on an H4 dependent visa. Although Anjuli was well-educated and had been working in a multinational bank for several years in India, according to the stipulations of the H4 visa, she was prohibited from seeking employment in the US. After acclimatizing herself to her new life, including finding an Indian grocery store in the city of Dallas and the Hindu and Jain temples, Anjuli began taking some courses at the local community college. Her husband, whom I call Sudeep, began the process, with his employer, of applying for a green card. After a year, Anjuli and Sudeep bought a house in one of the suburbs of Dallas but a year or so later Sudeep accepted a job in Seattle. His new company took over the green-card process and eventually both Sudeep and Anjuli became legal permanent residents. Anjuli was able to work for a short time but then she became pregnant with her first child and cut back on her hours. Anjuli and Sudeep have relocated several times over the years I have known them and two more children have arrived. All their children are US citizens, and they are thinking about naturalization for themselves. Sudeep is certain about it; Anjuli less so.

Migration policies and laws of citizenship, while proclaiming to be gender-neutral, are, as the cases described above suggest, in fact imbued with gender (as well as class and racial) inequalities that influence migration patterns and experiences. These laws and policies can determine the differential access that men and women have to a country of immigration, as well as their legal status, right to citizenship, and political subjectivity. Sociologists Cecilia Menjívar and Olivia Salcido (2013: 2) argue that in general immigration policies "assume dependencies that privilege male applicants over females and that often make women an after-thought in the implementation of immigration laws." Laws and policies are built on ingrained gender-specific ideologies that position men as breadwinners and women as family dependants.

Similarly, contemporary refugee and asylum law is also rife with gender biases (Calavita 2006). Certainly these laws have developed and changed over time from their initial formulation as part of the 1951 United Nations Convention Relating to the Status of Refugees. In the period following World War II, the typical asylum seeker was a male claiming persecution for his political beliefs or actions. "Women, on the other hand, [were] not considered to engage in 'real' politics that would make them the object of persecution" (Calavita 2006: 111). It was only after 1980 that private sphere persecutions began to be considered and in 1996 a political asylum appeal based on gender (the potential for genital mutilation, were the female asylum seeker to return to her home country in Africa) resulted in the granting of asylum. And yet, Calavita argues, there remains a contradiction between a gendered perspective and a human rights perspective. The human rights perspective that undergirds asylum and refugee law "has all too often been a subterfuge for, or has led to, stereotyping in which domestic violence, genital cutting and other such gendered behaviors are ascribed to 'barbaric' Islamic cultures" (Calavita 2006: 112).

Such philosophical conflicts are equally present in the differences between immigration laws that define women as dependent on their husbands for both legal status and economic support on the one hand and domestic violence laws (such as the 1994 Violence Against Women Act in the United States (VAWA) that was reauthorized in 2000, 2005, and 2015) that make it possible for immigrant women to take action against their abusers (Das Gupta 2006: 91). VAWA sets aside green cards for undocumented immigrant women who have been physically abused by a citizen or lawful permanent resident spouse. It permits them to petition for permanent residency without the knowledge or support of a spouse. But to secure legalization under this Act, it is necessary to produce documentation of joint residency. Very often a woman's name is not included in this documentation – that is, on household bills, bank accounts, tax returns, insurance policies etc. This contradiction in legislation, as sociologists Menjívar and Salcido (2013: 7–8) argue, offers further evidence of the subtle gender biases in immigration and other social legislation.

The gender-bias in immigration laws is also present in debates about citizenship which, as feminist scholars have observed, pay little attention to the distinct and different ways in which citizenship is experienced by men and women, let alone how it is accorded (Yuval-Davis 1997; Lister 1997a, b; 2001; Friedman 2005; Tastsaglou and Dobrowolsky 2006). As philosopher Alison Jaggar (2005: 92) has argued, citizenship in Western societies has been "gendered masculine . . . the activities regarded as characteristics of citizens – fighting, governing, buying and selling property, and eventually working for wages – have all been viewed as masculine, as have been the social locations where these activities are undertaken." Criticism of the gendered and exclusionary language of citizenship has been part of feminist discourse since the writings of Mary Wollstonecraft (1792) in the later eighteenth century. The citizen in a liberal democracy generally referred to a white male property-holding individual who had access to certain rights and assumed certain responsibilities. This construction endured through much of the nineteenth century and only began to change once women were accorded the right to vote, something that occurred in the US with the Nineteenth Amendment to the Constitution that was passed by Congress in 1919 and ratified in 1920. By the end of the twentieth century, sociologist Nira Yuval-Davis (1997: 22) was advocating for an approach to citizenship that dismantles "the identification of the family with the private domain and the political with the public domain" and instead constructs "citizenship as a multi-tier concept" that severs it "from an exclusive relation to the state." This conception of citizenship would encompass the state, civil society, and the family, thus bringing gender fully into the discussion.

This chapter explores the gendered dimensions and gender biases in US immigration policy and citizenship laws from the late nineteenth century through until the present. Where relevant, comparisons will be made within a global context. Among the questions addressed are: When and how were women defined solely as dependants – that is, classified in relation to men? How do such policies place women in a family role rather than a market or economic role? How have men's and women's citizenship rights been defined and changed? And how do gendered policies in relation to migrants differ, if they do, from those related to refugees and other legal statuses? This chapter also considers the gendered implications of legal status, exploring, for example, the case of mixed status families where often the husband and some of the children are legal while a wife and older children are undocumented. It also explores the contested dimensions of immigrant women's reproduction, as related in particular to debates regarding birthright citizenship and so-called "anchor babies" as a path to citizenship. Finally, it turns do a discussion of the gendered dimensions of political activity for those who are able to secure citizenship. Theoretically, therefore, the chapter draws on an intersectional understanding of the gender/race/class system as a set power relations that produces inequalities in the way in which migrants are socially constructed by the state and hence differences in how they experience processes of mobility, settlement, politics, and belonging.

Gendered Immigration and Citizenship Policies during the Third Wave of Immigration

From their inception immigration laws in the US have been shaped by gender ideologies and have in turn generated gendered patterns of mobility.[1] In accordance with the middle-class social ideals and morals of the Victorian period, women have been constructed as powerless, deferential, and dependent on men who were correspondingly constructed as the heads of household and breadwinners. Single women with no relationship to a male head of household to assume responsibility for them were often barred from entry for fear that as independent and unattached persons they might fall into prostitution.

In the US, the first restrictive federal immigration law, the Page Act of 1875, fully revealed both gender bias and these moral concerns. This law, which particularly impacted the immigration of Chinese women, was designed to ensure that they were entering the US of their own free will rather than as indentured prostitutes (Hirata 1979). The law contained five sections. The second section stipulated a fine and jail time for anyone who tried to transport any individual from an Asian country into the US against her/his will – a clear response to the anathema that slavery had itself become. The third section stated that bringing any woman into the country for the purpose of prostitution ("for lewd and immoral purposes") was against the law and subject to fine and jail time. The fourth section forbade the illegal supply of coolie labor and the first section stated that a foreign person convicted of a crime and any woman transported to work as a prostitute in the US would be denied entry. Historians have observed that this law shaped Chinese migration patterns by preventing the entry of most Chinese women. Chinese immigrants, mostly men who outnumbered women by twenty to one during the 1880s, were thus constructed as sojourners and became a "bachelor society." Men's efforts to bring their wives to the US were generally met with hostility. Historians have also noted that this law served to "protect" white men – to prevent them for contracting the diseases spread through prostitution and to control their immoral behavior in an American west where prostitution was by no means rare. The law ultimately sustained the institution of monogamous marriage itself (Abrams 2005), controlled Chinese reproduction in the US, and upheld "white values, lives and futures" (Luibheid 2002: 37).

Between 1875 and 1882, as a result of the Page Act, several hundred women were returned to China. And in the year 1882, just prior to the passage of the Chinese Exclusion Act,[2] only 136 of the close to 40,000 Chinese who were admitted to the US were women (Abrams 2005). Ironically, by creating such a gender imbalance in the Chinese immigrant community, the Page Act promulgated "the very vice it purported to be fighting: prostitution" (Abrams 2005: 701, 702). Only after World War II was gender balance restored. Indeed, in the six years following the end of this war close to 90 percent of all Chinese immigrants were women (Abrams 2005).

The gendered moral concerns reflected in the Page Act were equally present in the assessment of entrants at Ellis Island, which opened in 1892. Men and women travelling alone were treated differently upon their arrival. Married women who were travelling on pre-paid tickets were seen as dependants and hence were routinely detained until a husband or other close relative arrived to meet them (Gabaccia 1994: 37). Single women were also detained until a relative appeared to escort them. By contrast, a man on his own and without language skills was processed through to find his own way in the city. Unlike a woman travelling alone, he was not considered likely to become a public charge.

There was always concern about prostitution. If an unmarried woman was pregnant or someone reported that a single woman was sexually active on the ship crossing the ocean, Ellis Island inspectors became concerned. In 1909, 573 immigrants at Ellis Island were detained as prostitutes and 273 were returned to their homelands (Bayor 2014). These actions were reinforced by the 1907 Immigration Act which, while largely directed toward imposing limitations of entry upon those with disabilities or disease or likely to become a public charge for any other reason, had also given further ballast in section two to the exclusion of women and girls who entered the US for purposes of prostitution.[3] Women continued to be viewed at this time as dependants of men and hence laws that limited the immigration of individuals who could not support themselves often resulted in greater restrictions on female immigrants, especially those who were single or unaccompanied.

The Immigration Act (or Expatriation Act) of 1907 had other gendered dimensions. In particular it took the principle of *coverture*, whereby a husband and wife shared a legal identity in marriage, in new directions. As historian Martha Gardner (2005: 14) has written, beginning in 1855 with the Naturalization Act, "any alien woman who wed an American citizen became a citizen by virtue of her marriage, and until the 1920s and 1930s a woman's citizenship was derivative, through her father as a child and through her husband as a married woman." In fact this law, which identified foreign wives as the first and sole group of adults to be accorded derivative citizenship, applied only to white women. Further, no reference was made to American women who had married alien men until the 1907 Act which specified that an American-born woman lost her citizenship if she married an alien man. In many ways this was a patriarchal law with a subtext of trying to control whom women married by penalizing them for marrying foreign men, and particularly foreign men (i.e. Asians) who were not eligible for American citizenship (Bredbenner 1998; Cott 1998). Race and gender were complexly intertwined in these citizenship laws. "By law, American women who married foreigners after the 1907 act assumed their husbands' racial identity as well as his political identity. If he was not a citizen, neither was she. If he was ineligible for naturalization, so was she" (Nicolosi 2001: 2–3).

It was as a result of the 1907 act that the notion of "derivative citizenship" for women was fully codified. Derivative citizenship,

> deprived American women of their political birthright: membership in the American polity . . . Derivative citizenship also provided the state with a means to manipulate women's citizenship in order to obtain the objectives of foreign and domestic policy and of prevailing racial attitudes . . . It reveals an anxiety concerned with guarding both the white American female and the concept of American citizenship. Legally, the American female citizen was any female born in or naturalized by the United States, but ideologically, she was a woman of Anglo descent who embodied the racial and cultural ideals of American identity
> (Nicolosi 2001: 1–2)

Derivative citizenship was certainly not unique to the US and as such it suggests the extent to which citizenship itself was gendered as a male attribute.[4] Historian Ann Nicolosi goes so far as to argue that this was another form of trafficking in women – that is, trafficking in women's civic rights! And she observes that there was no consideration of the fact that women might become stateless if they married a man whose own country did not extend citizenship to the foreign wives of its male citizens.

The Expatriation Act remained in place until 1922 when the Cable Act (or Married Women's Independent Nationality Act) was passed and began to poke holes in some of its elements. The Cable Act, which terminated the loss of citizenship for women (white or black) upon marriage to a foreigner, clearly followed on the heels of extending the right to vote to American women in 1920. It separated marriage and citizenship. While positive for many women, for immigrant women it made the process by which they could enter the US, as the wives of immigrants or as foreign-born wives of the native-born, more challenging. "Immigration and naturalization laws now required that women have independent status as admissible aliens or as permissible citizens" (Gardner 2005: 125). Further, the racial dimensions of limiting rights to citizenship contained in the 1907 act remained in place for several more years. Thus, some immigrant women were excluded based on their race, as were women who were married to men who could not naturalize because of their race. Only in 1931 was this latter provision dropped.[5]

Japanese immigrants on the west coast were subject to a different set of immigration laws from those that impacted Chinese immigrants. Japanese immigration, primarily of men, began in the late 1880s. Women started to arrive in greater numbers only after 1900. Married men sent for their wives, while single men returned to Japan to find a bride or, quite commonly, arranged a marriage long distance. A tradition of "picture brides" (or marriage by proxy) was established. One such woman comments on the process: "I had but remote ties with him. Yet because of the talks between our close parents and my parents' approval and encouragement, I decided upon our picture-bride marriage" (quoted in Seller 1981: 54). Another describes the efforts by Japanese husbands to look western and make them look western so as to distinguish themselves from the Chinese who remained in traditional Chinese clothing.

> I was immediately outfitted with Western Clothing at Hara's Clothing Store . . . Because I had to wear a tight corset around my chest, I could not bend forward. I had to have my husband tie my shoe laces. There were some women who fainted because it was too tight . . . In my case, I wore a large hat, a high-necked blouse, a long skirt, a buckled belt around my waist, high-laced shoes, and, of course, for the first time in my life, a brassiere and hip pads.
>
> (quoted in Seller 1981: 56)

Eventually, the Japanese, like the Chinese, became subject to more restrictive immigration policy. The Gentlemen's Agreement of 1907 to 1908 banned further immigration of Japanese laborers but did permit men who were already in the US to continue to bring over their wives. The picture bride practice continued but remained disconcerting to anti-immigrant white activists concerned that these women would produce US citizen offspring (Sinke 2006b: 298). This concern, emerging from worries about racial purity, and compounded by new charges of the possible immorality of these women, ultimately resulted in further restrictions on immigration from Japan.[6] By 1920, the Japanese Government ceased to issue passports to Japanese picture brides in accordance with the "Ladies' Agreement" with the United States.

Other laws and policies of this period of increasing restrictionism also shaped gendered and racial immigration and citizenship patterns. The Mann Act (or White Slave Traffic Act) of 1910 prohibited the importation or interstate transportation of women for immoral purposes while the Immigration Act of 1910 revised a three-years-after-US-entry limit on the ability to deport any immigrant woman who was found to be practicing prostitution (written into the 1907 Act). In the 1910 Act there was no time limit on deportation if the woman had not become a citizen. Historian Martha Gardner (2005: 79) points out the extent to which moral dictates were given the force of law and caught women in a kind of Catch 22.

> Without access to citizenship women, especially those women classed as racial outsiders, were left without legal recourse. Immigrant women accused or suspected of prostitution could not become citizens

through marriage to a citizen. Nor in the years after women achieved independent citizenship could women charged with immoral behavior demonstrate the "good moral character" necessary for citizenship. The result was a class of permanent noncitizens.

Once World War I had begun, immigrant men, but not Asians, were offered a path to citizenship through military service. The Immigration Act of 1917 identified "homosexual" as an excluded category, virtually banned all future Asian immigration except for the Japanese and Filipinos, increased the tax paid by new immigrant arrivals, gave immigration officials more discretion in decisions on who might be excluded, and introduced a literacy test for immigrants that stipulated that all immigrants over the age of sixteen had to demonstrate a basic reading comprehension in any language. The literacy requirements impacted women more harshly than men because their literacy rates were often lower than those of men. However, women entering as wives, under coverture policies that defined a woman's legal, political, and economic status in relation to her husband and that favored family reunification, were exempted from deportation. Thus, it was marriage that gave immigrant women access to the United States (Gardner 2005: 29).

In 1924, the Johnson-Reed Act, otherwise known as the National Origins Quota Act, was passed. Influenced by the growing eugenics movement in the US and rising xenophobia, this act put in place a system of quotas based on national origins. It stipulated that only 2 percent of the total number of people of each nationality who were resident in the country according to the 1890 census would be admitted. It also barred from admission all those individuals who were prohibited from becoming US citizens, specifically Asians. Finally the annual quota for all immigrants was lowered from 358,000 to 164,000. The National Origins Quota Act was formulated to preserve the racial and ethnic profile of the United States by placing limits on the immigration of individuals who were not of northern European origins and by totally excluding Asians.

During the 1940s and 1950s there were several additional

pieces of US immigration legislation, some of which had gendered and racial dimensions that produced inequalities in treatment and access. The Nationality Act of 1940, which stipulated that natural-born American citizens would lose their citizenship if convicted of military desertion during time of war, clearly impacted men more than women and was struck down by the Supreme Court as a violation of the Eighth Amendment. The Chinese Exclusion Act was repealed in 1943 but China's quota was set at only 105 admissions annually. The War Brides Act of 1948 made it possible for US citizen male veterans to sponsor foreign-born fiancées, spouses, and children for entry, laying the foundation for family reunification principles that were to characterize much of post- World War II immigration policy. The 1948 Displaced Persons Act allowed for the admission of 205,000 refugees over two years as quota immigrants. This Act included some technical conditions that were exclusionary toward Catholics and Jews. By 1953 these provisions were dropped and 205,000 refugees were admissible as non-quota immigrants. The McCarren-Walter Act of 1952 lifted the total ban on Asian immigrants but replaced this with very small quotas – 185 for Japan, 105 for China, and 100 for other Asians. There were strict limits on those who could enter from former British colonies – something that helped to contain those who wanted to come to the US from the West Indies. This Act also specified that "subversives", gays, and lesbians were excludable and deportable – thus retaining sexual orientation as an overt dimension of immigration policy. And finally, in this Act the husbands of American women could be admitted as non-quota immigrants. Thus, while some overt discriminatory measures related to gender, race, and even religion remained in immigration policy, others were removed.

Law, Policy, and Gender in Late Twentieth-Century Immigration

If pre-World War II US immigration laws and policies were hardly gender neutral, the same can be said for those formulated during the latter half of the twentieth century. However, what is different is that while the gender (and racial) biases in immigration and citizenship laws developed between 1850 and 1924 were explicit and overt, the gender biases and inequalities of more recent laws are more subtle. These inequalities impact both legal and undocumented immigrants as well as those seeking political asylum. For example, sociologists Olivia Salcido and Cecilia Menjívar (2012) argue that employment visas (H1B specialized skill visas, H2A temporary agricultural worker visas, or L1 corporate transfer visas) are the most skewed in relation to gender because they are most commonly extended to men. By contrast with employment visas, entry based on family reunification is the most important avenue by which immigrant women legally enter the US. This section treats each of these categories of immigration in turn, occasionally drawing comparisons with policies in other parts of the developed world that manifest similar gender biases.

Gender Biases in Family Reunification and Skills-Based Immigration Policy

The US Immigration Act of 1965 (Hart-Cellar Act) replaced the 1924 National Origins Quota Act. The 1965 Act constructed an immigration policy based on principles of family reunification and workplace skills.[7] Seven categories of preference for relatives of US citizens and permanent resident aliens were established. Two categories of immigrants not subject to numerical restrictions were identified: immediate relatives (spouses, children, parents) of US citizens; and special immigrants such as certain former employees of the US government abroad and certain individuals who had lost citizenship (by marriage or by serving in a foreign armed service). The Act retained numerical restrictions, limiting Eastern hemisphere entrants to 170,000 and capping Western hemisphere entrants to 120,000. But neither preference categories nor the 20,000/country limit applied to the Western hemisphere figure.

Sociologist Pierrette Hondagneu-Sotelo (2011: 224) has astutely observed that while we generally consider the 1965 Immigration

46

Act to be a liberal piece of immigration legislation because it definitively ended Asian racial exclusion and placed legal family immigration at the center, it can also be considered exclusionary "because it reifies a narrow heterosexual definition of family". It also continued to construct women primarily as dependants upon male breadwinner migrants. They enter as wives of the primary migrant. Some scholars have observed that this law, formulated with an American understanding of marriage, discriminates against women who come from countries where common law unions are widespread (Menjívar and Salcido 2013). Women in such unions find it hard to offer proof of the longevity of their relationships. Further, family reunification policies often require extended waiting periods; rather than wait in the country of origin, some women (and children) have entered the US without papers, and thus become even more dependent on a sponsoring husband. In addition, even women who have joined their husbands legally must often refrain from working until a work permit is issued. This also increases dependence, can cause family hardship, or opens the possibility for exploitation on the part of employers who know that a woman does not have papers and hence has little recourse to complain about low wages or poor working conditions.

An example at the other end of the class spectrum that explicitly demonstrates the vulnerability of women who enter the US in a dependent status associated with family reunification policies is offered by legal scholar Jacqueline Bhabha (2009: 187–188). She discusses the case of a British widow of a trader killed on September 11, 2001. This woman left her country to follow a husband who had taken a job in the United States. Her visa was dependent on that of her British husband. After his death, the US Immigration and Naturalization Service took steps to deport her despite the fact that she had two children who were born in the United States. She had no rights of her own as caretaker to these two young American citizens. Her right to be in the US was dependent on that of her husband who was now dead. Only after the personal interventions of prominent individuals, including Tony Blair and Hillary Clinton, was she granted a green card in accordance with a special provision of the USA Patriot Act that permitted foreign-born spouses of 9/11 victims to apply for residency. As Bhabha writes (2009: 188), "high-profile leverage, British heritage, and the sympathy surrounding the events of September 11 resulted in these two American children being spared the trauma of being uprooted from their country or being separated from their mother." Such privileges might not be extended to persons of color or lower social class, indicating the racial and classist dimensions of these special exceptions. However, more broadly the case illustrates powerfully the problems with dependent visas and with regulations that often prohibit women from securing jobs and their own independent visa status.

These same subtle gendered biases are present in the policies of other major western receiving nations. For example, geographer Margaret Walton-Roberts (2004) writes about the Canadian system and its discriminatory effect on immigrant women who are sponsored by their husbands. This system "exacerbates their unequal status within the marriage, diminishes their dignity and degree of independence, aggravates existing socio-economic disadvantages and violates their most basic human rights" (p. 270). Walton-Roberts describes a reformulation of these policies that occurred in the first decade of the twenty-first century to address the gendered inequities in the law, particularly as they related to marriage. In essence, the Canadian government has implemented a gender-based analysis to evaluate the differential impact of policies on men and women and to identify any inequities in their formulation and implementation. However, it is often the case that gender discrepancies are only amended when there is public pressure to do so and when the changes are acceptable economically (p. 274). This pressure has often come from immigrant women "actively exercising their citizenship rights and benefiting from state-based political rights" (Walton-Roberts 2004: 279).

A second dimension of Canadian immigration policy that appears to have a differential gendered impact is the point system.[8] Several authors have noted that this system often results in a deskilling process that impacts immigrant women in particular because they often enter the country as dependants on their husbands who are the primary immigration applicants. Sociologist Guida Man (2004; see also Iredale 2005) illustrates this impact among highly educated Chinese women who have migrated to Canada since the late 1980s. As a result of employer requirements for "Canadian experience", as well as professional accreditation systems, and other gendered and racialized state policies and practices, these Chinese women find themselves channeled into menial or part-time employment or remain unemployed. This situation is then exacerbated by other factors – the absence of a support network to help with childcare and other domestic responsibilities; a diminished earning power which makes it more difficult to pay for daycare; and the lack of English-language skills, which diminishes the professional qualifications they have. Man argues that state policies need to be changed to halt this brain-drain/deskilling process.

In the European Union marriage and family reunification are now the primary basis for legal entry for women, although prior to 1973 countries such as Germany and France were recruiting women to work in particular industries – the electronics industry, for example (Lutz 1997: 103). The policies for reunification are however quite stringent in many European countries, requiring, for example, proof of uninterrupted residence for five to eight years, having a minimum income level, and a minimum contract for future employment of a year or more. In addition, couples sometimes have to prove the quality of their relationship, and demonstrate that they have access to adequate housing for the family. If a spouse dies, a wife being sponsored is often left in a precarious position. Sociologist Helen Lutz (1997: 104) points out that family unification regulations in host societies often use a nuclear family definition of the family.

For some immigrant groups this has led to the isolation of women from their family networks. Social parenthood (custody and care for children by the extended family, including nephews and nieces) or the active involvement of grandmothers in childcare, which are features of many immigrant groups' cultures, are not accepted by the current regulations.

In general, then, these European policies of immigration, like their American counterparts, are built on an assumption of a male breadwinner and place women in vulnerable positions as non-working dependants responsible for the domestic sphere and child-rearing.

The emphasis on family reunification in post-1965 immigration has made marriage a focus of controversy. Are individuals using marriage as a way to secure permanent residence status (a green card); that is, paying someone to participate in a marriage of convenience and act as the sponsor for the individual interested in immigration? The marriage then terminates after a successful entry with legal papers in place. This "fraudulent marriage" scenario was the theme of the popular 1990s film "Green Card" starring Andie McDowell and Gerard Depardieu, the former playing the role of the US citizen wife, the latter that of the would-be immigrant. The United States Citizenship and Immigration Services (USCIS) has estimated that between one-fifth and one-third of marriages between US citizens and immigrants are fraudulent, although there is often no way of knowing for sure and no way of knowing how many involve American citizen wives versus American citizen husbands. It is important to emphasize that there are barriers in place to make such marriages as a path to legal immigration difficult. In 1986 the United States passed the marriage fraud amendments to the Immigration Act. Penalties for those who were involved in "sham marriages" were increased and a two-year provisional green card was created for immigrant spouses of citizens and permanent residents.[9]

This questioning of the legitimacy of marriages is also prevalent in other national contexts. For example, in the early 1990s Asian men were refused entrance into Britain at a high rate (86 percent in 1991 and 84 percent in 1992) because they were suspected of arranging marriages of convenience in order to enter the country (Lutz 1997: 103). Eventually, the interrogation system that yielded this result was abolished on the grounds of gender discrimination. Other countries placed minimum lengths of time on marriages before an application for family reunification could be filed. Thus, as in the US, suspicion of fraudulent marriages often guides evaluations of family reunification petitions, particularly when men are applying to join a wife already in the country of immigration. There is an inherent gendered bias in which marriages are more subject to suspicion of fraud and hence more scrutiny, again rooted in an idea that men should be the primary immigrants.

Gender and the Undocumented

Some scholars have examined the effects of the legalization process on immigrant families as well as the gendered dimensions of mixed-status families. Both of these are important aspects of late twentieth-century immigration to the US where the number of undocumented immigrants has risen to approximately eleven million.

Within Mexican families it is often wives who push for family reunification, frequently leaving home villages of their own accord (with or without their children and generally without documents) to join husbands living in the US. However, once they arrive they find themselves dependent on husbands who may already have legal residence or citizenship and who are therefore the ones who must file all the paper work to legalize a wife's status (Hagan 1994). This was a common scenario after the passage of the Immigration Reform and Control Act of 1986 (IRCA) – an act that extended amnesty and a path to legalization for all immigrants in the US who could prove they had been living and working in the country for five years prior to the implementation of this law.

IRCA legalized close to three million undocumented immigrants, most of them from Mexico and Central America. Many husbands began to sponsor their wives and families once they had obtained a green card (legal permanent residency) for themselves. Others brought their families but failed to proceed with the paper work, leaving their wives and children in legal limbo and vulnerable. Prior to IRCA about one quarter of all migrants were undocumented women; during the period of transition when IRCA was being implemented that proportion increased to one third (Massey et al. 2002). Several scholars have documented cases of abuse among women who entered the country illegally and whose spouses then failed to pursue legal status for them. A husband may threaten his wife with deportation (i.e. informing "la migra" that she is in the country illegally) if she does anything contrary to his wishes, including reporting physical violence. Salcido and Menjívar (2012: 349) observe that women "whose presence is not formally recognized even when they contribute monetarily (including through paying taxes), who are not 'attached' to a family member who has LPR [legal permanent residence] or is a US citizen . . . , or who are 'attached' but the LPR or US citizen is unwilling to petition for them, have little if any chance of regularizing their status."

IRCA was supposed to halt the entry and hiring of illegal immigrants to the US. But, during the 1990s, with the US economy booming and no further opportunities for amnesty, millions more Mexicans and Central Americans, many of them single and married men, entered the country without papers. After 2001, the border between Mexico and the US was tightened, breaking the pattern of easy back and forth movement that had been characteristic of the 1990s. Men, the primary migrants, stopped returning to Mexico to visit their wives and children and began instead to smuggle their families into the US. As a result, numerous families of mixed legal status were created.

Sociologists Michael Fix and Wendy Zimmerman (2001) found that one in ten US families were mixed-status families (that is, a family where at least one immigrant parent is unauthorized and at least one child is a US citizen) at the end of the 1990s[10] and that 75 percent of children in immigrant families are citizens. By the end of the next decade, demographers Jeffrey Passel and Paul Taylor (2010) were reporting that 79 percent of the 5.1 million children of unauthorized immigrants who were younger than eighteen were born in the US and hence US citizens. Further, 37 percent of all adult unauthorized immigrants were parents of children who are US citizens. The number of US-born children in mixed-status families expanded from 2.7 million in 2003 to 4 million in 2008, while the number of children who are unauthorized themselves (1.5 million in 2008) hardly changed in five years.

These families face any number of challenges, many of them exacerbated by changing immigration policies. As Fix and Zimmerman observe (2001: 398), laws that have made it increasingly difficult to adjust from an illegal to legal status have fixed individuals in a particular status, thereby perpetuating these legally unstable families as well as the categorization of one or both parents as forever "outsiders" who do not belong. This creates serious inequities. Citizen children in mixed-status families may not have the same opportunities and access to resources that are accorded to those in families where everyone is a citizen. Mixed-status families comprised 40 percent of low-income families in California at the end of the 1990s and 20 percent of low-income families in New York. Twenty-one percent of all uninsured children nationwide in the late 1990s lived in mixed-status families (Fix and Zimmerman 2001: 402). Fix and Zimmerman suggest that welfare reforms and immigration laws have in effect created two classes of citizens – those eligible for benefits and those ineligible. Within one family some children may be eligible and others not, a situation that generates inequality and divisiveness (Pine and Drachman 2005; Glick 2010). Further, undocumented parents may simply be afraid to apply for benefits for their children, even those who are eligible, because they are afraid of being detected and deported.

Certainly, as the twenty-first century has unfolded, unauthorized parents have faced the increasing risk of deportation. Between 1990 and 1995, deportations averaged approximately 40,000 per year; from 1996 to 2005 the figure rose to an average of more than 180,000 per year (Hagan et al. 2008: 66). In 2005, more than 200,000 were deported, the majority of them citizens of Mexico but also including significant numbers of Central Americans. Recent reports have estimated that approximately 600,000 children have been separated from one or both parents as a result of deportation policies that have been implemented aggressively under the Obama administration.[11] The majority of these children are US citizens. Deportation destabilizes families and impacts parents' emotional well-being, their relationships with their children, and overall household finances (Thronson 2008; Brabeck and Xu 2010).

Legal scholar Jacqueline Bhabha (2009: 188) describes the case of a Guatemalan woman who was arrested and handcuffed in front of her US citizen husband and eight-year-old daughter. She was deported to Guatemala, having missed a hearing to regularize her status in immigration court because the notification that she received listed the date incorrectly. She was in Guatemala staying with a friend. The family had little recourse. Bhabha observes, in relation to this case, and that of the British widow discussed above, that "from the perspective of international human rights, both mothers and children experienced a radical rights deficit. In one case, government discretion was exercised in favor of family unity, in the other case it was not – a bonus for the privileged white family but a casualty for the working-class Hispanic one. In both cases, the parent's legal and social credentials rather than the child's nationality were the deciding factor" (Bhabha 2009: 188–189).

Sociologists Jacqueline Hagan, Karl Eschbach, and Nestor Rodrigues (2008) have explored the implications of deportations on Salvadoran families, some of whom were long-time settlers in the US. They found that the majority of deportees were young and male, demonstrating that deportations are gendered. Women are at less risk of removal because "migrants are generally apprehended at locations where males dominate in number and are more visible to the official eye, such as ports of entry, prisons, labor pools, public streets and job sites" (Hagan et al. 2008: 71). But they do observe that Mexican women are more likely to be apprehended and deported because they are more likely to enter the US without documentation. And in a follow-up study (Hagan et al. 2011: 1383) of Latinos in North Carolina a particularly poignant case of the impact of a female deportation is presented:

In summer 2008, a Latina business owner in Johnston County, Veronica, was approached by a sister of one of her customers with an unusual request.

The sister had a 9–year-old boy and a baby with her. The mother of the children, Veronica's customer, had been arrested for driving without a license and deported. The deported woman was a single mother and her children were left with her sister who was unable to care for them, since she was unemployed and living with a friend. Veronica ... decided to take in the 9–year-old boy but not the 6–month-old baby. As she explained, "I can't keep an infant in the restaurant and there is no one at home to care for it. The boy still lives with me but he is sad, shy, and regularly cries for his mother and baby brother." His mother has not been able to get back to the States.

Deportations have not only disrupted stable families in the US, they have also impacted families in the home country by rupturing the flow of remittances sent back to support those left behind, including elderly parents.[12] In the research sample of 300 Salvadorans studied by Jacqueline Hagan and her colleagues (Hagan et al. 2008), 31 percent were living with a spouse and child in the US prior to being deported to El Salvador. Further, 73 percent of deportees with children in the research sample reported having a child under the age of eighteen living in the US (90 percent of these children were American-born). Thus, if it is the breadwinner who is deported, he leaves the family, which may include US citizen children, in a precarious situation and potentially more dependent on government services. On the other hand, if the individual deported left his family in El Salvador, he is reunited with them after deportation but this family too may face hardship if they were dependent on the remittances that the breadwinner father had been sending back from the US.

Those who have left families behind in the US express an intention to return as soon as they can, generally illegally. Hagan and her co-authors thus observe that the practice of deportation has in fact created a circular migration pattern. It does not stop illegal immigration, it just raises the costs for migrants and for their families; it "undermine[s] long-standing family reunification principles of US immigration policies" (p. 85) and disrupts communities. Deportation policies are hence full of irony and have gendered impacts.

The Immigration Reform and Control Act of 1986 also introduced employer sanctions as a mechanism for supposedly halting future undocumented immigration. As a result of this Act, all employers are now required to ask for proof of the right to work (and by extension legal status in the US) from employees and are subject to fines if they knowingly hire undocumented immigrants. They are required to fill out an Employment Eligibility Verification Form. Few employers have been fined and there is always the possibility that they can claim they saw documents and that it was reasonable evidence. This aspect of IRCA has also had some gendered impacts. For example, sociologists Edna Bonacich and Richard Appelbaum (2000) have demonstrated that male immigrant workers, after the implementation of employer sanctions, have gravitated to the garment industry. Prior to this legislation these undocumented and mostly male workers were able to find work in manufacturing jobs that paid better. But after sanctions the larger manufacturing plants as well as some non-immigrant industries tended to enforce the legal documents requirement and hence male immigrants were driven into the underground and informal economy.

The gendered dimensions of undocumented immigrants are present in other national contexts. The best example are the so-called *"sans papiers"* (without papers) of France. As feminist scholar Catherine Raissiguier (2010: 2) has argued, increasingly restrictive immigrant policies have transformed large numbers of immigrants into *clandestins* – illegal immigrants. As a result of the repressive Pasqua laws of 1993, several categories of immigrants (for example, asylum seekers who had had their files rejected, spouses or children of legal immigrants, parents of children born in France) could not regularize their status. Family reunification policies that had long been in place in France became more restrictive.

Immigrants who file a family reunification request on behalf of family members now need to document at least two years (instead of one) of legal sojourn in France and their ability to meet appropriate personal housing resource requirements. The 1993 immigration law demands that family reunification happen in one unique step. No longer can immigrants bring family members incrementally over time as their social standing improves and they are better able to meet the necessary housing and income requirements. The Pasqua laws of 1993 also prohibited the entry of polygamous families into France through the process of family reunification ... It also prohibited the renewal of residency permits of foreigners in polygamous situations.

(Raissiguier (2010: 62–63)

These laws increased the legal vulnerability of immigrant women in particular. Not only was legal reunification harder to attain, but papers could be rescinded in cases of divorce or estrangement. If an individual became illegal, they were deportable. Mothers of French children are protected from deportation but they are nevertheless undocumented and hence unable to work and unable to claim health and other social benefits. The undocumented population in France, as a result, became increasingly feminized. They comprised a large portion of the *sans papiers*. Many of the women in this situation were African women, some of whom had no economic resources of their own and others of whom worked illegally for low wages in difficult conditions in sweatshops, as domestic workers, in the informal small-business economy, or as sex workers.

Raissiguier's research focuses largely on the political activism of the *sans-papiers* – men and women – to protest the repressive immigration laws, their undocumented status, and their potential deportation. Her discussion is framed within a broader analysis of the construction of the immigrant woman as a threat to the nation – a discussion that also includes reference to the "head-scarf debate" (*l'affaire du foulard*) that erupted in 1989 and that has continued. "The wearing of Islamic scarves in French schools, polygamy, arranged marriages, and female genital cutting are important threads within anti-immigrant discourse that present North and sub-Saharan Africans as undesirable immigrants who are unwilling or unable to assimilate into French culture" (Raissiguier 2010: 33).[13] Thus, like scholars who have worked on the US context of immigration and citizenship laws, Raissiguier also sees the powerful gender (and also racial) biases contained in immigration laws (in this case of France) that are presumed to be gender neutral, biases that disproportionately impact women, frequently locking them into domestic roles within a traditional sphere, and enhancing their precarious economic and social status.[14] Similar biases characterize refugee and political asylum laws.

Gender, Refugees, and Political Asylum

The United Nations Convention of 1951 defines a refugee as any person who "owing to a well-founded fear of being persecuted for reasons of race, religion, nationality, membership of a particular social group or political opinion, is outside the country of his nationality and unable or, owing to such fear, is unwilling to avail himself of the protection of that country; or who, not having a nationality and being outside the country of his former habitual residence . . . is unable or, owing to such fear, is unwilling to return to it" [Geneva Convention 1951 (Refugee Status), Art 1A (2)].

The language of this convention is masculinist, written with a male asylee subject in mind. As sociologist Jane Freedman (2012: 48) has observed, the UN Convention was first formulated at a time when gender equality and women's rights "were far from the center stage of politics, and particularly international politics. More seriously, the high commissioner's observation that he could not envisage persecution on the grounds of sex seems to have endured in many interpretations of the Convention, and the male model of rights on which it was based has in many cases not been challenged in its implementation." More recently, a number of scholars have begun to critique the UN Convention for not focusing sufficiently on gender-specific and gender-based forms of persecution and violence and for not considering women a particular social group (Inlender 2009; Freedman 2012).[15]

Many of the gendered claims for asylum are legally invisible, deemed the result of private sphere rather than public sphere persecution. Private sphere persecution is not considered relevant to refugee and asylum law (Freedman 2012: 50). Legal scholar Talia Inlender (2009) engages the pros and cons of this status quo position, arguing that gender-specific claims can be dealt with under the current five categories for granting asylum (race, nationality, religion, political opinion, membership of a particular social group), but that gender-based claims might call for an additional or sixth ground for political asylum. But the fact of the matter is that it is only recently that gender-specific asylum claims have been recognized, and, even so, this recognition is rare. Further, scholars have noted that while women and children outnumber adult males as refugees in developing countries that neighbor their country of origin, male asylum seekers outnumber females in developed countries. "Women historically have had less access than men have had to the formal and informal structures that facilitate migration . . . and this lack of access along with their dependent family status, personal history, and social positioning" (Kerber 2009: 88–89) is a barrier to individual flight and hence the possibility of asking for asylum in a western democracy.

These issues are very much the subject of current debate, and social scientists have only recently begun to focus their attention on the gendered dimensions of asylum-seeking as it is experienced by those who have fled their countries. Few Central Americans seeking asylum in the United States are successful with their applications but it appears that the law has been more on the side of men's experiences with political persecution as a result of their direct involvement in conflict than with the often more indirect experiences with political violence to which women were subjected (Salcido and Menjívar 2012: 342). Not only was recognition of the level of persecution and fear that women have suffered an obstacle, so too were recognition of the precise forms of persecution specific to information and access to information about them, since women do not always appear on registration lists in their own right but rather as members of family groups. "As the United Nations admits and scholars of gender and refugee law indicate . . . the problem is not only that the lack of the use of the terms *sex* and *gender* in the UN Convention of 1951 (on which the 1980 US Refugee Act is based) creates the exclusion of gender-specific needs, but also once again that the perspective and interpretation of a framework based on male experiences reproduce gendered hierarchies and serve to maintain a heteropatriarchal state" (Salcido and Menjívar 2012: 363–364).

The gendered biases in political asylum law pertain as well to refugee laws. Nahla Valji and her colleagues (Valji et al. 2003: 61) observe that refugee women "have not been afforded anything like the protection offered refugee men in refugee-receiving countries throughout the globe, particularly in the developed world." They emphasize that until recently refugees were considered male almost by default, while women and children were part of a "family package" with a derivative status which makes them vulnerable. These authors point to media reports in refugee-receiving countries of the North of a rise in domestic abuse on the part of husbands who are aware of the power they have over their wives as a result of the refugee determination process. Wives may lose this status if they leave their husbands or they may lose access to public funds. Only recently have agencies and other gatekeepers come to recognize that women may be at special risk and should be addressed in their own right.

The issues of asylum law that are addressed in the context of the United States are also of concern elsewhere around the world. Thus, writing about South Africa, Middleton (2010) observes that this is one of the few countries that brought gender into prominence as a seventh ground for asylum as a result of its 2008 Refugee Act. However, distinctions between the political and the personal often remain part of decisions about who is granted asylum – gendered claims, as mentioned above, are frequently deemed personal and generally dismissed. Further, gendered harm is often only viewed as persecution "when it occurs during the time of an officially recognized conflict, or where it can be associated with a foreign culture, or cultural backwardness" (p. 68). As a result, female genital mutilation is often viewed as persecution and a basis for asylum, while rape, forced marriage, and domestic violence are not. The United Kingdom has recently tightened some of the grounds for asylum claims despite the fact that the UN Convention has been opened up to more gender-based claims, allowing that sexual violence that is the result of civil war and conflict, even when perpetrated by non-state actors, can be potential grounds for asylum, while ordinary domestic or sexual violence (i.e. "harmful cultural practices") is not (Chantler 2010).

What has happened in the United Kingdom is also occurring in the European Union and has created particular challenges for women seeking asylum on the basis of gender-related persecution (Freedman 2012). Asylum seekers are very often constructed as a threat to the states of the global north that increasingly see themselves as being overrun by those seeking refuge whether for political or economic reasons. The securitization of borders has taken precedence over the security protection sought by those leaving their homelands because of war and conflict. While the European Parliament adopted a resolution in 1984 urging member states to consider women a particular social group and hence to consider gender-specific persecutions, in general European states have shown resistance. As a result, the voices of women asylum seekers in particular fall on deaf ears. Where they are heard, women have often been forced to "present themselves as idealized 'victims' of 'barbaric' other cultures in order to have any chance of receiving protection under refugee regimes" (Freedman 2012: 45). This, sociologist Jane Freedman argues, deprives them of any political agency and essentializes gender differences. "It fixes an opposition between 'them' and 'us', between 'Western women' and 'Other women', which might obscure the real structures of gender inequalities in different societies and the reasons for the persecutions that women suffer as a result" (Freedman 2012: 56).

In the European Union women comprise about one third of total asylum claimants. They face more difficulties leaving their countries because they have fewer financial resources and the primary responsibility for children. They are more susceptible to the violence of smugglers, including sexual violence. They may be persecuted for political activities, but they may also be persecuted, Freedman (2012: 50) argues, for less overt political activities "such as sheltering people, providing food or medical care" or for "not conforming to religious and social norms". They may even fear persecution and violence for simply being the spouse of or related to a male who is considered a political dissident. These forms of persecution are rarely considered by countries of the European Union even though refusing female circumcision or forced sterilization can be constructed as highly political acts. Thus, "rape and violence are often effectively normalized, and considered as part of the universal relations between men and women. This normalization or relegation of rape to a private affair between individuals means that it might not be taken seriously when women make claims for asylum" (Freedman 2012: 51). In other words, sexual violence often goes unrecognized as a tool of war and political oppression. Few European states have responded to the range of gender guidelines formulated by the UN High Commissioner for Refugees in recent years to accommodate gendered persecutions in their determinations for granting asylum and if they have been adopted their implementation is rarely consistent.

In summary, the feminist critiques of asylum and refugee policies are broadly rooted in concerns about both the masculinist and universalistic dimensions of the UN Convention. Female forms of persecution are evaluated according to masculine forms of dissidence and universalism fails to accommodate the cultural diversity in gender norms and ideologies. Further, a western model of rights is held up as the standard. The result is that many women are denied access to international protection.

Women's Bodies:
Birthright Citizenship, Anchor Babies, and Trafficking

The Fourteenth Amendment to the US constitution, ratified on July 9, 1868, extended citizenship to all persons born or naturalized in the US. This amendment firmly established what is referred to as "birthright citizenship" or *jus soli* citizenship. Other nations have had a principle of *jus sanguinis* citizenship – that is citizenship by blood relationship or ethnic heritage.[16] In relationship to immigration, this principle of citizenship has occasionally caused controversy, particularly in relation to women's fertility and so-called anchor babies. Specifically, the argument is that women, and particularly pregnant women, enter the US, often without documents, in order to have their child in the territory of the United States. These children are then automatically American citizens and can "anchor" the family. That is, when they reach adulthood, as natural-born citizens, they can help their parents to acquire legal citizenship. Conversely, if undocumented parents are deported, by extension one is also deporting American citizens – that is, children who have been born in and have grown-up in the United States and who have no necessary relationship to the country of their parents' birth. There is a not insubstantial segment of the US population that, given the thorniness of these scenarios, wishes to deny the privilege of birthright citizenship to those born of individuals who enter the country illegally – women, and their bodies, are hence at the center of a critical debate regarding immigration and citizenship.[17]

Women migrants, from this perspective, are constructed not as workers but as reproducing mothers (Gutierrez 2008). As part of what anthropologist Leo Chavez (2008) dubs the "Latino Threat narrative" these women, most of them from Mexico, are identified as individuals who cross the border between Mexico and the US and bear large numbers of children. They, and their families, so the narrative goes, are a burden on our institutions and our welfare system, including the public hospitals where they give birth.

Anthropologist Phyllis Chock (1995) quotes Congressional Testimony of the mid 1980s – leading up to the passage of the Immigration Reform and Control Act of 1986 – on precisely these issues, thereby illustrating the extent to which anti-immigrant sentiments at this time were rooted in concerns about the reproductive capacities of Mexican immigrant and Mexican-origin women:

> The district I represent . . . is but a few hours away from the porous United States–Mexico border . . . Approximately 70 percent . . . of the babies born in country [sic] hospitals are to undocumented alien women. These babies are automatically American citizens, and are therefore eligible for all the welfare benefits available to any US citizen.
> (William E. Dannemeyer, R, CA, Congressional Record, 1986: p. H9729; quoted in Chock 1995: 173)

> I am told 80 percent of all children born in Los Angeles County public hospitals are born to illegal alien mothers – 80 percent!
> (Harry Reid, D, NV [added remarks], Congressional Record, 1986: p. H9775; quoted in Chock 1995:173)

As Chock emphasizes, these testimonies clearly indicate the idea that the fertility of women is considered by many of these Congressmen as a threat to the nation. "Women and children figured here as signs of social disorder. In the talk about fertility, women (women of color, in particular Caribbean, Mexican, Central American) were also silent tokens for speakers' fears – to be confirmed or allayed – about population growth and its effects on quality of life and national unity" (p. 174). Chock rather astutely observes that the preference for many of these speakers would be to keep this uncontrollable reproduction of labor power ("female, natural instinctual") outside the United States, while maintaining an immigration policy that was rational, administrative, and market-driven (masculine?) and that brought adult, and primarily male laborers to the United States to work (p. 174).

These fears of massive births and overpopulation were not allayed even by demographers called in to testify who tried to assure the members of Congress that the fertility of immigrants soon comes to resemble that of the general American population. While IRCA was passed, the Latino Threat Narrative did not disappear, making it necessary for anthropologist Leo Chavez to take it on again two decades later and to demonstrate once more that apocalyptic assumptions about out-of-control Latina reproduction has no basis in fact (Chavez 2007; Chavez 2008). He notes that fertility rates in Mexico have been declining, "from 7 to 8 children before 1970, to 4.4 by 1980 . . . to 3.4 in 1990 . . . to 2.4 children per Mexican woman in 2000" (Chavez 2007: 71). Similarly, the average number of children born to Mexican-origin women living in the United States also declined such that by the final years of the twentieth century they were averaging 1.81 children per woman between eighteen and forty-four years of age. Within the Hispanic population, however, the foreign-born do tend to have higher rates of fertility than the native-born (3.1 versus 2.3 in 2008) (Passel and Taylor 2010).

In his own research, on Latinos in Orange County, California, Chavez shows that (1) Latina immigrants were more likely to report having had two or fewer sexual partners compared with Anglo women who reported having five or more; (2) Anglos were

64

more likely than Latinas to have their first child after age twenty-five but for Latinas the mean age for having a first child was 21.6; and (3) Both Latinas and Anglo women in prime childbearing years (eighteen to forty-four) had fewer than 2.0 children per woman and those who are of Mexican origin who migrated as adults have slightly more children on average than do those who migrated as children (Chavez 2007: 81–85). Clearly, he concludes, the evidence does not support rampant and out-of-control reproduction. "The politics of Latina fertility have obscured a rather dramatic story of reproduction over the last thirty years. Latinas and Anglos both have fewer children today than they did three decades ago" (p. 88). Chavez ends by calling for an alternative discussion about the relationship between immigration and fertility – one that focuses on the value of children to reproduce the population of a nation. Many immigration scholars have suggested that the United States does not share a critical problem faced by other western democracies, the aging of their populations, precisely because of immigration.

In general, the fears about anchor babies and out-of-control Latina reproduction are unfounded. As legal scholar Jacqueline Bhabha (2009: 197) asserts, it is hard to prove that having an anchor baby is the sole motive for immigration. Further, she argues, the birthright citizenship repeal argument "seems to ignore the economic roles that migrant women play, casting them essentially as breeders" when they are anything but. And yet this argument endures, in the US and elsewhere. Perhaps the most vocal recent debate outside the US has occurred in Ireland, resulting in a shift away from birthright citizenship with the passage of the Irish Nationality Law of 2004 (Smith 2008). Much of the debate in Ireland emerged from discussion of the motives of childbearing female asylum seekers, most of them from Africa. Eithne Luibhéid (2004) argues that the discourses and practices that targeted these women provided the opportunity for the Irish government to set itself up as the legitimate defender of "the sovereign Irish nation while at the same time reconfiguring racial and ethnic hierarchies" (p. 335).

Ireland has always been a country of emigration, but the economic boom that it began to experience in the 1990s began to attract immigrants and after that those seeking political asylum. The number of asylum seekers in the country rose above 1000 in 1996 and just eight years later it reached over 11,000. Nigerians were the largest group seeking asylum, followed by Romanians. Policies about how to handle them eventually resulted in a Direct Provision Program which is characterized by a strict set of rules and regulations. Individuals are provided with a bed, three meals/day, and health care. They cannot look for alternative accommodation, they cannot work, and adults cannot attend full-time education or training. They receive a weekly allowance calculated at a different rate for adults and children. They cannot travel outside Ireland without permission. Asylum seekers are, in essence, "largely excluded from meaningful participation in Irish life" (Luibheid 2004: 337). Faced with these restrictions, childbearing became a more reliable path to legalization. Irish law, until it was changed in 2004, made it possible to apply for residency based on the birth of a child who was automatically an Irish citizen and had a "right to the company, care, and nurture of her or his parents" (p. 338). One could move into different accommodations and have access to certain benefits once pregnant.

The debates surrounding this right began to emerge in the 1990s. Childbearing on the part of asylum seekers was portrayed as being out of control and with the potential to erode Irish sovereignty. The maternity residency clause associated with birthright citizenship was portrayed as a "mechanism for invasion and colonization" (p. 338), with women gaining entry so that they could have a child and enjoy the benefits of the Irish state. This discourse, Luibheid (2004: 340) argues, conveyed "beliefs and concerns about crime, welfare abuse, cynical exploitation, cultural dilution, economic difficulties, and a crisis of national sovereignty. What was so striking was that all these themes become linked through non-national asylum seeker women's bodies, which were reduced to their sex organs and reproductive capacities." Many viewed government action against them as a legitimate defense. The result, in this case, was the revoking of birthright citizenship with the enactment of the Irish Nationality Law of 2004.[18] What is important here is how similar the debates are in the US and Ireland

and that they perpetuate ideas that have long been present – to use immigration and citizenship laws as a way to control women's bodies, and by extension to control, overtly or more indirectly, the racial boundaries and hierarchies of the nation.

A second issue revolving around women's bodies that raises a question of how much attitudes have really changed in the US since the formulation of immigration laws at the beginning of the twentieth century relates to anti-trafficking legislation. In 2000, during the waning months of the Clinton presidency, the US Congress passed HR 3244 – the Trafficking Victims' Protection Act. As sociologist Wendy Chapkis (2003) points out, this law was a welcome relief from the series of anti-immigrant legislation that had been passed prior to it, including the 1996 Illegal Immigration Reform and Immigrant Responsibility Act (IIRIRA), the 1996 Personal Responsibility and Work Opportunity Reconciliation Act (PRWORA), and the USA Patriot Act of 2001.[19] However, close examination reveals that the Trafficking Victims' Protection Act was not as charitable as a first glance might suggest. This Act, while exempting a small number of severely abused and exploited immigrants who had been trafficked from the punitive immigration and welfare reform measures of the late 1990s (by providing visas, work permits, welfare support ,and other special protections, and even the possibility of a green card for qualified victims and their families), it in fact mobilized

> anxieties surrounding sexuality and gender in the service of immigration control ... Language within and surrounding the [Trafficking Victims' Protection Act] works to neatly divide "violated innocents" from "illegal immigrants" along the lines of sex and gender. Trafficking victims, described as vulnerable women and children forced from the safety of their home/homelands into gross sexual exploitation are distinguished from economic migrants who are understood to be men who have willfully violated national borders for individual gain. The law justifies offering protection to the former and punishment to the latter.
> (Chapkis 2003: 924)

It does this by stirring up "a moral panic about 'sexual slavery' created through slippery statistics and sliding definitions", by differentiating between "innocent" and "guilty" prostitutes, and by requiring that victims would receive aid only if they helped in the prosecution of traffickers (p. 924–925). It is intriguing to reflect on this legislation in relation to the legislation of the early twentieth-century US which was also focused on the question of women's bodies and women's agency in relation to prostitution.

It is impossible to leave this discussion of gender and racial biases in immigration and citizenship laws without a comment on the highly gendered policy (the National Security-Entry-Exit Registration System) that emerged in the United States after 9/11. It was announced and implemented in June of 2002. This policy required Arab and Muslim men aged 16 and older to register their presence in the country with the authorities. Those who failed to comply faced criminal and immigration penalties – they could be deemed to have violated their visas making them subject to removal, barring them from receiving future visas and prohibiting them from adjusting their status to permanent residency. Further, failure to notify the Department of Justice of a change in address was classified as a misdemeanor offense (Chishti and Bergeron 2011).

This program was an overt example of racial, religious, and gender profiling, targeting male non-citizens of a particular age and from predesignated countries. While the Department of Homeland Security scaled back the program in 2003 (for example, no longer requiring "check-ins" with immigration officials and filing information about changes of address), it was not fully terminated until the spring of 2011. During that time it came under criticism from any number of civil and human rights group, politicians, law enforcement experts, and the media. Between 2002 and 2003, of the approximately 85,000 individuals who were interviewed and registered, only 11 were found to have ties to terrorism and just under 14,000 were placed in removal proceedings. A number of lawsuits were filed challenging the constitutionality of the policy but in general federal district courts across the US ruled in its favor, as did the Second US Circuit Court of Appeals in 2008 (Chishti and Bergeron 2011).

Although this registration policy has been discontinued, while it was in place it made the lives of many Arab and Muslim men difficult and for some the legacy of the policy remains. Several years ago *The New York Times* (Dolnick 2011) reported the case of Mohammed G. Azam, a 26–year-old Bangladeshi who came to the US when he was 9 years old. When he registered in Manhattan in 2003 officials began deportation proceedings because he was in the country illegally. His father had applied for permanent resident status in 2001 (Azam was 16) through a program that permitted immigrants to pay a fine of $1000 and clear their records of any visa-related violations. Because of the backlog, his father's approval did not come through until 2007 and by this time Mr. Azam was an adult. His father was able to sponsor his wife and daughter but not his son because he was now too old.

As of 2011, Mr. Azam was still caught in this net after numerous hearings. A small business owner with a college degree, Azam reported "big plans" which he was fearful of executing because the prospect of deportation still hung over his head. Judges have ruled in his favor but the immigration agency stands firm. In 2011, Mr. Azam commented to the *New York Times* reporter: "One-third of my life has gone to this immigration process. I grew up here. This is my country."

Gendered Political Practice and Political Socialization

In response to a broader literature on gendered differences in political engagement, scholars of immigration have begun to examine this issue for the most recent migrants to the United States. The broader literature tends to find that women are less politically engaged than are men. Is this also the case among immigrant populations? Jamal (2005: 53) notes that there are any number of obstacles that confront immigrants, both men and women, but particularly women, in their access to mainstream society. It is challenging to learn about the politics of the new environment and to surmount the language barriers. It is also challenging to reconcile their attachments with their homelands with their developing

American identities. Living a daily life largely among co-ethnics may have a different impact than living detached from members of their own groups.

Political scientist Carol Hardy-Fanta (1993) discovered in her field research that Latino men and Latina women understand and talk about politics differently. This difference is encapsulated in two statements: one from a Latina woman named Silvia who "adores" politics which for her means "reaching out to other women and improving their living conditions"; the other a Cuban–American activist named Jesús for whom politics is about "creating political organizations and increasing Latino electoral representation" (p. 1). Her work challenges the idea that Latina women are passive in the political sphere by documenting their activities of running for office, promoting voter registration, providing political education, and forging links between city officials and the Boston area Latino community where she conducted her research. At many political events that she attended during the course of her research, Hardy-Fanta discovered that women were in the majority as participants and activists. Their vision of politics is more participatory than that of men, for whom politics is about elections and access to government positions (p. 3); that is, about power. For Latina women politics is about making connections, "connections between people, connections between private troubles and public issues, and connections that lead to political awareness and political action" (p. 3). It is about "taking a stand". It is about achieving change by linking people together. This understanding of politics "is more effective in part because it is more in tune with cultural expectations and it overcomes many of the structural constraints of Latino political participation in [the United States]" (Hardy Fanta 1993: 2).

Building on the work of Carol Hardy-Fanta (1993), political scientist Michael Jones Correa (1998) quickly called for a gendered understanding of immigrant politics and immigrant political socialization. Based on his own research among Latino immigrant activists in Queens, he argues that men, who often experience downward mobility, are politically mobilized through their own ethnic organizations where they regain, as mentioned above, some social status in their respective immigrant communities. These organizations are dominated by men; for example, the Hermanos Unidos club in Corona, to which Dominicans belong, had 350 male dues-paying members at the time of Jones-Correa's research and 15 female dues-paying members (p. 341). The organizations of various South American immigrants were more balanced in terms of the sex ratio of members but men monopolized the leadership positions. Male dominant organizations tend to appeal to the political life of home countries. Women, by contrast, through their work and childcare responsibilities, come into more contact with the public institutions of the host society and are mobilized in different ways as a result. Within their organizations they tend to focus more on issues of political life in the new environment. They become activists in the interface between immigrants and American laws and institutions. They serve as intermediaries. The differences between male and female political engagement for these Latinos in Queens, New York, is perhaps best summed up by an Ecuadoran woman who commented as follows to Michael Jones-Correa:

> It was natural that people who came over in large numbers would want to get together, so they formed civic organizations. And men were always the leaders, because in Latin America men were always the leaders. Women in politics were seen as strange. When I was growing up as a girl in Ecuador, it was not the thing for women to do. Men here are more interested in politics there. They do good things, raise money, but they are not interested in what goes on here. They have status in the community; they are *caciques* [leaders]. But they aren't interested in starting over – to begin with, to have to learn English. If they got involved in politics here they wouldn't be *caciques* anymore. They would only play a small part. So women and Puerto Ricans tend to dominate local politics in Queens – Puerto Ricans because of their experience in politics, women because they are willing to work with others.
>
> (Jones-Correa 1998: 343)

Jones-Correa leaves open the question of whether men will move more rapidly into electoral politics than will women, deeming it more appropriate for them given culturally based ideas about leadership. On the other hand, he documents the cases of several Puerto Rican women from the Queens area who won elections to various positions. At the time that he was writing these issues were relatively new but from the perspective of the middle of the second decade of the twenty-first century and across various immigrant populations it appears that both men and women have moved in this direction, although more commonly among the second-generation than the immigrant generation. Other recent research (Pantoja and Gershon 2006) shows that Latina immigrants have higher rates of naturalization than do Latinos, that there is variation from one national origin group to another (Cubans have the highest rates of naturalization, Salvadorans the lowest, and Mexicans are in between), and that men and women are motivated differently in their pursuit of naturalization. These authors explain the higher rate of Latina naturalization to women's stronger desire to settle permanently in the US. Their decisions to naturalize are more strongly related to family issues than are those of men. Further, while being interested in politics is positively related to naturalization for men, political interests "has no effect on women's decision to naturalize." For Latinas, a "positive orientation toward voting is tied to naturalization, [while] among men the presence or absence of this orientation is unrelated to naturalization". Finally, it is not a difference in the attitude toward voting – more positive or more negative – that matters but that for men and women "this orientation leads to different outcomes" (Pantoja and Gershon 2006: 1182).

What is quite apparent as a lesson derived from this research on Latino politics is how important it is to view processes of immigrant political incorporation through the lenses of gender and culture (Piper 2006) and to broaden our understanding of political incorporation beyond documenting voting patterns to include forms of civic engagement and participatory citizenship (Brettell and Reed-Danahay 2012). These differences also need to be framed, as Carol Hardy-Fanta (1993: 30–31) argued more than twenty years ago, in relation to gendered concepts of power. Male concepts derive, she suggested, from the ability to use one's own influence, authority or force to control and impact the behavior of others – "to exercise dominion or dominate". Female concepts have more to do with processes of empowerment – the ability to collaborate with others to do together what one cannot do alone to effect change.

The issue of empowerment through the development of political consciousness in the public sphere is taken up by anthropologist Patricia Pessar (2001) in her study of Guatemalan refugee women who developed a feminist consciousness and became transnational subjects claiming citizenship in multiple contexts and as members of global communities. Reflecting on how these refugee women reacted to the acts of terror and violence to which they had been subjected, Pessar writes: "The process of feminist conscientization, initiated in exile, helped to convert [their experiences], and the accompanying emotions of helplessness and shame, into powerful structures of meaning and action" (p. 471). In the camps they became involved in rights-based initiatives promoted by the UNHCR. They were exposed to "alternative ways of leading gendered lives" (p. 477) and opportunities to expand their social relations. While some men in the camps resisted this empowerment of women, others recognized that the women were drawing attention to the common goals that they had to end the conflict in Guatemala and hence worked alongside the women. However, when they were resettled and after they returned to their local communities, these refugee women were essentially abandoned by the international organizations that had previously encouraged and facilitated their empowerment. Promises about co-ownership of land were broken, even by the men who had supported the idea in the camp. "In a few of the original return communities, women who pressed for their rights to land were threatened by male cooperative leaders with rape, and expulsion from their communities" (p. 481).

Pessar's study was an effort to situate women's political consciousness and practices of citizenship more centrally in the study of gender and migration. There have been some, although by no means enough, additional efforts to explore dimensions of gendered citizenship and political engagement among immigrant populations. For example, in a study of Arab-Americans in Detroit, Amaney Jamal (2005) found that political engagement is mediated by civic engagement. By contrast with several other immigrant populations, Arab women in the US are more likely than their spouses to be involved in the life of the Mosque and other ethnic organizations. This contrasts with patterns of behavior in sending societies. While 37 percent of Arab Muslim women in the Detroit level reported attending a mosque at least once a week, the comparable figures for Jordan and Morocco were 10 percent and 20 percent respectively (p. 56). As a result of this involvement, Jamal argues that Arab-American women have developed a greater sense of group consciousness than have men. "Women see their location in the US as one linked to the broader communal Arab and Muslim interests while men tend to situate themselves *vis-à-vis* their personal economic success" (p. 54). This makes them more likely to use their political voice when they see the community targeted than do men. They do this in particular to counter discrimination and stereotyping in the media and elsewhere, making the mosque a center of advocacy for the community in addition to a place of worship. Thus, the mosque and other ethnic institutions not only serve as vehicles for the preservation of cultural identity but also as vehicles for increased political participation. Women in particular develop discourses of individual rights and responsibilities as they serve as communal guardians (p. 74).

Another body of research on gendered immigrant political activism is offered by Hinda Seif (2008), who focused on gendered circuits of political power among Mexican undocumented women farm workers. These women are linked to Latino/a politicians through their participation in United Farm Worker electoral mobilization events. Seif (2008: 79) observes that power flows from politicians to the undocumented women and vice versa. She acknowledges that this involvement, if only indirect, of the undocumented in the electoral politics of the US might be considered controversial. But, she argues, it is also "essential for the democracy and well-being of the agricultural communities in which they constitute a significant proportion of the adult population." Her research revealed that innovative approaches to mobilization that blur the boundaries between political and maternal roles, that include activities that are sex segregated and involve children, and that provide food, are particularly successful, despite the limitations of language barriers, transportation difficulties, undocumented status, and the vagaries of farm labor (p. 94). And "while undocumented women participate in visits to the offices of elected officials and group demonstrations mediated by documented organizers, they may be excluded from or fearful of engaging in door-to-door organizing in non-immigrant neighborhoods" (p. 95). The women she studied felt most comfortable when they were wearing union T-shirts because it linked them to other groups and drew attention "away from their legal status and toward their economic contributions, their linkages with Chicano and other US citizen activists and voters, and a national labor movement that, though weakened, still wields substantial legislative and electoral power" (p. 95).

The political activism on the part of immigrant women in particular that is described by Seif has also been documented by anthropologist Lynn Stephen (2003) in her research on female Mexican migrant farm workers in Oregon. These wives of *campesinos* created their own political forum, *Mujeres Luchadores Progresistas*, as an offshoot of labor union in the region. Through this forum they developed the leadership and public speaking skills that helped them to operate in the male-dominated public square. Stephen invokes the concept of cultural citizenship to describe a form of activism and claims-making on the part of immigrants who are not legal citizens.[20] This organization illustrates one form of cultural citizenship, providing women who rarely attended public meetings or expressed opinions outside the extended family in Mexico with opportunities "to foster a sense of satisfaction, pride, [and] mutual support" (Stephen 2003: 34).

Yet another example of research that also draws on the process and practice-oriented approach encompassed by the concept of cultural citizenship is provided by anthropologist Kathleen Coll's (2010) research on a grassroots social justice organization among immigrant women in San Francisco. Coll argues that the women with whom she worked "challenged their political marginalization as low-income, non-English-speaking women and the dehumanization of terms such as *illegal* and *alien*. In doing so, they embodied claims against the legitimacy of cultural, administrative, and legal obstacles that prevent full social and political participation of immigrants in US life" (p. 8). The women involved in *Mujeres Unidas y Activas* based their political actions on a principle of *convivencia* (spending time together). They developed *autoestima* but linked it, not to an American sense of self-esteem, but to their collaborative work with their peers and the process of learning how to speak up and articulate their claims and rights in relation to the various public institutions and entities (schools, public assistance, health care, subsidized housing) with which they had to interact on behalf of their families. Their narratives, told to Coll the ethnographer, described a process of personal and political transformation. The book she writes about them, she claims, is a story of "how a group of immigrant women worked together in a contentious time to write themselves into American history as neither victims nor heroes, but rather as mothers, workers, Latina, and human beings bearing rights regardless of their gender, class, nationality or location" (Coll 2010: 154).[21]

At the other end of the human capital spectrum represented by these studies of Latinos and Latinas in the US, one has the case of professional and educated Chinese immigrant women in Canada (Man 2004), who are channeled into menial work or unemployment as a result of gendered and racialized policies and practices, as well as employer requirements for "Canadian experience" and professional accreditation systems that do not recognize their foreign training. Some of these women are voicing their criticism of the Canadian system and have refused to take on jobs for which they are underpaid. They have formed their own professional organizations such as the Chinese Professional Women of Canada, the Chinese Professional Association of Canada and Immigrant Women in Science (Man 2004: 146). They have collaborated with other groups to lobby the Canadian government regarding issues of accreditation, retraining, and job-related language courses.

Despite this important work on practices of the civic engagement and grass-roots organizing dimensions of political incorporation described above, much research remains focused on gendered differences in voting patterns among immigrant populations, thereby continuing to frame politics almost exclusively as electoral politics. Thus, in a fairly recent comprehensive study of Asian American politics, political scientists Pei-te Lien, M. Margaret Conway, and Janelle Wong (2004) begin with the broader generalization that women are less interested in politics, have less of a sense of political efficacy, and are generally discouraged from running for office. They are socialized to think about politics as men's business. Among Asian Americans, they find that both men and women are members of ethnic organizations which can provide the basis for political engagement. They found that more Asian American men are interested in politics than are women but that the more educated women are, and the more family income they have, the greater the interest in politics. They also found that citizenship mattered in the level of political activity for both men and women, but citizen men were more active than citizen women. They found that men were more likely to perceive local public officials as responsive to their complaints than were women and generally Asian American men have a higher level of political knowledge than do their female counterparts.

Asian American women are more likely to vote democratic and they hold more compassionate positions on issues by comparison with men but this varies with ethnic origin, nativity, degree of cultural and social adaptation, perhaps more so than with gender (p. 205). In the end these authors conclude that while there is gender variation, gender itself is a relatively insignificant predictor of Asian American political attitudes and behavior with the exception of explaining patterns of ethnic self-identification and the chance of being contacted by individuals for political mobilizations. Such a conclusion lacks the more nuanced approach to gendered understandings of politics put forward by Carol Hardy-Fanta and Michael Jones-Correa.

77

However, there is recent research on Asian immigrants in the United States that does emphasize the more participatory approach framed to include patterns of broad civic engagement. For example, in her book *Unruly Immigrants*, Monisha Das Gupta (2006) describes the "emancipatory politics" (place-taking and place-making) of feminist, queer, and labor organizations that have emerged within South Asian communities in the United States. She emphasizes that immigrants in these organizations claim rights as immigrants not as citizens. "They mobilize survivors of domestic violence, lesbians and gays, domestic workers, and taxi drivers who live and work in spaces where they do not enjoy the protections of citizenship because of their gender, sexuality, economic standing, race, and nationality" (p. 5). She traces the lines of division as well as the arenas of collaboration between first and second-generation, between working-class women and middle-class women, between lesbians and straight women and gay men, and between workers from different national origins who operate in the same employment sector. These organizations, in their range of activities, provide spaces where South Asian immigrants, male and female, working class and middle class, can "become politicized, act on their politics, and envision a full life for themselves and their families, communities, and political comrades" (Das Gupta 2006: 153).

Conclusion

The critical theoretical question in this chapter has been to explore the intersectional dimensions of migrant engagement with the state and how these have changed over time.[22] The chapter has addressed the multiple inequalities that have and continue to characterize not only the formulation of immigration and citizenship laws in receiving countries but also how they are put into practice. These laws and policies are the foundations for determining who can and who cannot cross borders, who comes first and who follows, and who is considered deserving or undeserving of being granted a right to stay, and a path toward citizenship. This chapter has also explored outcomes in relation to gendered and ethnic differences in participation in the civic sphere through voting and other forms of political activism.

Immigration and citizenship laws are shaped by ideas about gender, sexuality, class, race, ethnicity, and nation; sometimes they are also influenced by gendered conceptions of the nations whence people have come. On occasion, these laws respond to constructions of women as breeders and men as terrorist threats. More commonly, they position men as breadwinners and women as dependants, thus perpetuating gendered inequities and often depriving women in particular of their own agency. There are a number of scholars who call for immigration reform that would not only resolve the problem of the undocumented but also of gender inequalities. Immigration laws, in their view, should make access to legal entry for women "less dependent on a principal visa holder who petitions on her behalf as well as [provide for] more expedited access to work permits in order to shorten their dependency status" (Menjívar and Salcido 2013: 3).

It is worth mentioning that, while the focus here has been on immigration and citizenship laws in host societies, those of sending societies may be equally gendered and directly impact who leaves and why they leave. Writing about Mexican state policies that impact perceptions and experiences of migration, social scientists Michael Peter Smith and Matt Bakker (2008: 201) observe the structural biases against women "such as the taken-for-granted assumption of migration as an exclusively male phenomenon, [that] became ideologized in state policy documents and discourses that made heroes out of male migrants, while ignoring female migration altogether as a social phenomenon." They note that the term "el migrante" is used exclusively in documents and the male-headed household is the unit with which state policies interact. "Nowhere in these state-policy formulations is any space created for female migrants as potential agents in the reproduction or transformation of their home communities. Female agency is absent from official discourse, except in the form of the wives and mothers left behind who are represented, both in the language of state policy and in statues that glorify the male migrant, as simple

79

appendages of adventurous transnational male breadwinners" (p. 201).

As should be apparent in the discussion here, immigration laws and policies are not only shaped by broader ideas about gender, race, nation, and citizenship, but also by labor market needs and structures. Thus it is to the gendered dimensions of the immigrant labor force that we now turn.

3

Gendered Labor Markets

New York City is a magnet for immigrants from the Dominican Republic. By 1990, the United States Census reported 332,713 Dominicans living there, comprising two-thirds of all Dominicans in the US. By 2000, the number of Dominicans living in the city rose to 554,638. While early arrivals settled in the traditional receiving area of New York, the Lower East Side, eventually Dominicans began to settle in other parts of the city. Soon the upper Manhattan neighborhood of Washington Heights, stretching from 145th Street to 190th Street on the west side, came to be home to roughly a third of all Dominicans in the city. Some of these residents pursued economic opportunity as small-business owners, resulting in a localized ethnic economy comprised of *bodegas* (neighborhood markets), restaurants, travel agencies, beauty salons, clothing stores, and other shops catering to the needs of the burgeoning Dominican population.

Many Dominicans found employment within this ethnic economy but others found work in the manufacturing industries of the city. Forty-nine percent of Dominicans were employed in this sector in 1980; a decade later this had declined to 26 percent and by 2000 to 12 percent (Hernández and Rivera-Batiz 2003). In the early years of Dominican settlement in New York, the garment industry provided work for many Dominican women: some were good and well-paid jobs, others were precarious and low-paying. The retail and wholesale trades also have provided employment opportunities for Dominicans, as has the urban service sector. Anthropologist

81

Patricia Pessar (1995: 39) describes a couple, Gloria and Iván Espinal, who with only eighth-grade educations found employment beginning in 1973 as orderlies for a large nursing home. "With their accumulated savings, they have purchased homes in New York and in the Dominican Republic, and they have sent their three children to college. By contrast, Gloria's newly arrived sister earns less than the minimum wage in her job as a live-in caretaker for an elderly Puerto Rican woman." Reflecting the observations of her own research participants, Pessar emphasizes that there was more opportunity for those who came early by comparison with those who came later. The decline in the manufacturing sector during the final decades of the twentieth century hit the Dominican immigrant population very hard.

According to Hernández and Rivera-Batiz (2003: 34–49), the labor force participation rate for Dominicans nationwide was 64 percent for men and 53.1 percent for women, in both cases lower than that of the rest of the US population. In New York City in particular, the labor force participation rate for Dominican men declined from 76 percent in 1980 to 61 percent in 2000; while that for Dominican women rose slightly from 47 percent in 1990 to 49 percent in 2000. The average per capita income for Dominicans in New York City was below the average for the United States in 2000 and the poverty rate (32 percent) was the highest of the major racial and ethnic groups in New York. Many of these poor Dominican households are female-headed. Male Dominicans in New York had an unemployment rate of 9 percent in 2000; the rate for Dominican women was 13 percent and yet by 2012 immigrant women from the Dominican Republic had a higher proportion engaged in the civilian labor force compared with all immigrant women – 62 percent versus 56 percent (Nwosu and Batalova 2014). By 2012, nationwide, 35 percent of Dominicans were in service occupations; 21 percent in sales and office occupations, and 22 percent in production, transportation, and material moving occupations.

In an informative and exceedingly useful article reviewing theories of international migration, sociologist Douglas Massey and his colleagues (Massey et al. 1993) outline a host of models that have been formulated to explain why international migration begins and how it is perpetuated.[1] Many of these theoretical models focus on labor markets. This includes neoclassical economic approaches that emphasize the wage differentials as well as differences in conditions of employment between sending and receiving societies. Migration from this perspective is about individuals who are seeking income maximization. By contrast, the "new economics of migration" emphasizes migration as a household decision pursued to alleviate capital constraints and minimize risks to family income. The household here is formulated as a unit of production and consumption that engages in a cost-benefit analysis of migration. In contrast with these micro-level explanatory models that focus on small-scale interactions among individuals, macro-level models that focus on large-scale social structures and processes (for example, dual labor market theory and world systems theory) either "link immigration to the structural requirements of modern industrial economies [or] see immigration as a natural consequence of economic globalization and market penetration across national boundaries" (Massey et al. 1993: 432).

These models generally consider a generic migrant or a generic migrant worker. Gender is rarely mentioned, although admittedly there is some reference to women and children in the discussion of dual labor market theory and of a feminized labor force in the discussion of world systems theory. Similarly, in the review of the factors that perpetuate migration once it has begun – migrant networks, the institutional context that emerges to facilitate and support migration, the culture of migration – little reference is made to how these factors might differ in terms of their impact on or meaning for men versus women. In short, some of the most powerful explanatory models of population mobility do not take gender seriously into account. This is particularly surprising given the extent to which labor markets across the globe are segmented, not only by gender, but also by race/ethnicity, and/ or class. The example of Dominicans that opens this chapter illustrates this segmentation and, in particular, the gendered dimensions of waged work among immigrant populations. This chapter examines the segmented labor market and its impact on migratory populations. While the theoretical emphasis is on gender segmentation, attention is also given to ethnic and class differences when these are relevant.

Class differentiations are important because by comparison with migration streams of the past, what is notable about those of the present is the participation of skilled professionals. The migration of male IT workers from China and India to the United States is a significant characteristic of late twentieth- and early twenty-first-century global population mobility. So too is the migration of health care workers, among them nurses from countries like the Philippines, India, and the islands of the Caribbean. Women with these skills are responding to global labor market shortages and are often better able than those without skills to minimize the impact of traditional gender hierarchies. But such work also comes with challenges of licensing and with racialized working contexts that constrain opportunities for rising to managerial positions. On the other hand, some medical professionals (men and women) find that their credentials are not valued in the immigrant context and hence they experience a form of downward mobility. They are channeled into an immigrant labor market, placing all their hopes on the ability of their children as the ones to be able to participate in the skilled labor force of the host society.

This chapter begins with an examination of gendered differences in labor force participation rates in the US over time, comparing native-born men and women with foreign-born men and women. It then explores the sectors of the US economy and occupational niches that have been differentially filled by foreign-born men and women in the past and at present. This allows for a consideration of gendered labor recruitment strategies as well as of the role of social networks in the structure of gendered labor markets. The chapter also addresses more specific topics such as global care work, sex trafficking, and immigrant entrepreneurship (the role of immigrants, men and women, in small business). Global care work in particular points to further dimensions of inequality whereby immigrant women from less developed countries are now doing the reproductive domestic work of women of the wealthier developed countries. National contexts other than the United States are occasionally introduced largely to demonstrate that segmented labor markets and their impacts on migrants are a worldwide phenomenon.

Labor Force Participation: The Native-Born and the Foreign-Born, 1900 to the Present

In 1850, the US economy was primarily based on agriculture but by the end of the nineteenth century it had become an industrial economy. Cities grew as the native-born left the countryside to pursue urban work opportunities but also as increasing numbers of the foreign-born began to settle in New York, Boston, Philadelphia, Chicago, and the myriad cities of the so-called "rust belt." By the end of the twentieth century, as industrial jobs were increasingly exported overseas, the US economy had become a largely service and knowledge-based economy. These major shifts have caused changes in the extent and nature of male and female participation in the US labor force. Women comprised only 18 percent of the total waged labor force in 1900 but by 1950 they were 29 percent, and by 2000 47 percent. While the labor force participation rate for men (that is, the number of men in the labor force divided by the total number of men in the population over 16 and eligible to work) in 1900 was 80 percent, the rate for women was 19 percent. By the end of the twentieth century, the labor force participation rate for men was 75 percent and that for women 60 percent.

According to the Bureau of Labor Statistics of the US Department of Labor, in 2013, of the 127.1 million working-age women in the United States, 57.2 percent were in the labor force. The rate for men in 2013 was 69.7 percent. No doubt the decline in labor force participation for both men and women during the first decade of the twenty-first century is in part a reflection of an aging population and were it not for immigrants, both men and women, the decline might be even more rapid in the years to come. By 2022, the Bureau of Labor Statistics predicts a labor force participation rate of 56 percent for women and 68 percent for men. In 2013, 74.2 percent of single mothers with children under eighteen years of age were in the US labor force, as were 67.8 percent of married mothers (spouses present) with children under eighteen. Rates varied depending on the age of children, with the lowest rate, not unexpectedly, for mothers with infants.[2] The life cycle is particularly important for female labor force participation rates.

What about the foreign-born population? Those women who entered the US during the so-called "third wave of immigration" (between 1880 and 1924) were, in general, more economically active than their native-born counterparts. While only 21 percent of "single white women" participated in the labor force in 1900, the comparable rates for single women with parents born abroad and for women who were themselves foreign-born were 34 and 61 percent respectively (Blackwelder 1997: 14–15). However, over the course of the twentieth century, as the total number of women in the US seeking waged employment outside the home has increased, the difference between native-born and foreign-born labor force participation rates has diminished.

By contrast with foreign-born women, foreign-born men were employed at a very high rate. But for both sexes, employment rates varied with age. According to demographer Katharine Donato (2012b), 85 percent of immigrant men were in the labor force at age eighteen in 1900; 95 percent by age twenty-five. The figure declined to 80 percent by age sixty-four. At that same period 60 percent of foreign-born women were working by age eighteen but the rate dropped to 20 percent by age twenty-six and to 10 percent by age thirty-four and remained at that level for women at older ages. Marriage clearly deterred work outside the home for immigrant women.

Over the course of the twentieth century the labor force participation rate for younger men declined such that by 1940 only 55 percent of foreign-born men were in the labor force at age eighteen; but by age twenty-four the proportion rose to 90 percent. The pursuit of education most likely kept these young men out of waged work for a little longer. The comparable figures for women were 45 percent at age eighteen, 60 percent at age twenty; but by age sixty only 10 percent of foreign-born women were working. Donato (2012b) observes that by 1980 the entry of immigrant men into the labor force was more graduated such that the labor force participation rate only reached 90 percent at age thirty, rising from 55 percent at age fifteen through 80 percent at age twenty-four. For women the proportion rose from 50 percent to 60 percent between ages eighteen and twenty-two and remained at 60 percent for the remainder of the female working life course. To summarize, the most significant change over the course of the twentieth century was that while immigrant women in 1900 tended to work for a few years and then stop at marriage, by the end of the century many remained working after marriage. Further, immigrant women have always been less likely than immigrant men to participate in the waged labor force but the proportion has increased between 1900 and 2000.

There are, of course, important differences in labor force partic-ipation according to national origins. At the end of the twentieth century, the highest levels of foreign-born female employment were among Filipina and West Indian women; Pakistani, Bangladeshi, and Mexican women had the lowest levels. It is significant that the groups with low female labor force participation rates include Muslims and women who face issues of unauthorized status (i.e. Mexicans). As discussed in the previous chapter and as devel-oped further in a subsequent chapter, law and gender ideologies are both powerful influences on the lives of immigrant men and women.

What is the picture in the early part of the second decade of the twenty-first century? In 2013, according to American Community Survey data, the foreign-born, at 25.3 million, comprised 16.3 percent of the total US labor force.[3] Of these, 47.8 percent were Hispanic and 24.3 percent were Asian (compared with 9.7 percent Hispanic in the native-born labor force and 1.7 percent Asian). Men comprised 57.7 percent of the foreign-born labor force and 52.3 percent of the native-born labor force and while just under 75 percent of foreign-born male workers were between twenty-five and fifty-four years old, the proportion of the native-born in this age group was 63 percent. Native-born women participated in the labor force at a slightly higher rate (57.7 percent) than did foreign-born women (54.6 percent). Further, foreign-born mothers who had children under eighteen were less likely to participate in the labor force than native-born mothers (59.7 percent compared with 72.7 percent) and younger children decreased their likelihood of employment outside the home especially by comparison with native-born women. Thus foreign-born women with children under age three had a labor participation rate of 46.7 percent compared with 64.9 percent for native-born women. Conversely, while the labor participation rate of native-born men was 68 percent, that of foreign-born men was 78.8 percent. Native-born and foreign-born fathers with children under eighteen had similar labor force participation rates, 92.6 and 93.6 percent respectively.

During the first decade of the twenty-first century, immigrant workers in the US were overrepresented in some of the fastest-growing sectors of the economy, among them home health, childcare, and personal care aides; nursing, health aides, and orderlies; post-secondary teachers; food preparation and services; sales and cashiers; heavy tractor trailer and truck drivers; movers and other hand laborers; office clerks (Singer 2012). More specifically, in 2013 the Bureau of Labor Statistics reported greater numbers of foreign-born workers than native-born workers in the United States could be found in service occupations (24.8 percent) and of these about a third were employed in building and grounds maintenance and cleaning, the former characteristic of foreign-born men, the latter of both men and women. Production, transportation and material moving also attracted more foreign-born (15.4 percent) than native-born, as did natural resources, construction, and maintenance (12.9 percent). These were mostly occupations filled by foreign-born men. Conversely the native-born could be found more than the foreign-born in management, professional and related occupations (39.5 percent compared with 30.3 percent foreign-born) and in sales and office occupations (24.4 percent compared with 16.5 percent). Foreign-born women were more likely to work in service occupations (32.9 percent in

2013) as compared with only 19.8 percent of native-born women whereas 31.8 percent of native-born women could be found in sales and office occupations, compared with 22.4 foreign-born women.

In summary, there are important differences between the native-born and the foreign-born and between men and women, not only in rates of labor force participation but also in particular sectors of the US economy in which they are engaged. These differences have been sustained into the present, although across the twentieth century and into the twenty-first century there have been some fluctuations and variations in labor force participation rates that have not only been influenced by the composition of the foreign-born population, but also by changing gender ideologies and a changing economy that has created different labor demands. As the twentieth century drew to a close it became apparent that while more immigrant women in the past were classified as dependants who moved in the context of family reunification, more recently they have been migrating to pursue economic opportunities, responding to an international division of labor that offers positions for women not only on the global assembly line but also in global care work (Ehrenreich and Hochschild 2002). It is imperative to examine more closely the occupations that immigrant men and women have pursued over time in what was and remains a gendered and segmented labor market, and a labor market that reveals inequalities between the native-born and the foreign-born.

The Gendered Immigrant Labor Market During the Third Wave of US Immigration

Male and female immigrants in the United States more often than not fill different occupational niches, reflecting not only the labor demands of the society of immigration, but also gender ideologies (those of both the sending and the host societies) that define what is considered acceptable work for men and women. Very generally, labor markets are often divided, just like household economies, into productive and reproductive tasks; the former predominated by men and the latter by women. Thus, the late nineteenth century industrial economy drew Polish and Slovak immigrant men to work in Pittsburg's steel mills and Chicago's slaughter and meat-packing houses. It drew Chinese and Irish men to work in agriculture and railroad construction, and those of other national origins to the logging, milling and mining industries. It drew immigrant women from a variety of ethnic backgrounds into the garment industry, "perhaps one of the most transparent examples of capitalism's use of patriarchal schemas to link women's reproductive functions to their productive ones" (Green 1996: 414).

This labor segmentation does not obviate situations where immigrant men and women have worked alongside one another in the productive sector of the economy, as on the farms of the American Midwest or some of the canneries of the American West during the nineteenth century, or in some of the chicken processing plants in more recent times. Writing about Norwegian immigrants in the upper Midwest of the United States during the nineteenth century, historian Jon Gjerde (1985: 194) claims that the participation of women in farming distinguished the Norwegians from their American-born neighbors. From the perspective of the Norwegian settlers, using the labor of women on the farm saved the expense of paying hired hands. It was wheat farming and increasing mechanization that ultimately brought the division of labor into greater disequilibrium, making farming largely a male domain. The role of female labor in farm production was on the decline by the end of the nineteenth century.

The primary occupational niches for single immigrant women during the late nineteenth- and early twentieth centuries were in garment factories, as mentioned above, and in domestic service. Textile towns drew a more balanced sex ratio of immigrants, suggesting, as historian Ardis Cameron (1993: 78) observes, the significance of "female employment opportunities in determining immigrant destinations." It was employment in the mills of New England that drew, for example, French-Canadians to towns such as Lowell and Holyoke, Massachusetts, and Manchester,

New Hampshire (Hareven 1982; Hartford 1990). In 1900, the percentage of the French-Canadian labor force working in the textile industry in Lowell, Massachusetts, was 80.5 of females and 40.6 percent of males; in Fall River it was 52.8 percent of males and 83.9 percent of females; and in New Bedford, Massachusetts, it was 87.9 percent females and 61 percent males. Mothers did not work outside the home but rather cooked, cleaned, did the sewing and the washing, cared for the children and sometimes took in boarders (Brault 1986: 61). This mill work was debilitating, requiring operatives to be on their feet for twelve hours each day. It was hot and it was noisy. Cotton dust invaded the lungs of women and many also developed eye problems. Young immigrant women no doubt looked forward to marriage and homemaking as a welcome alternative.

As mentioned in Chapter 1, single Irish women, pushed out of their homeland by poverty, limited opportunities for waged-work, and few prospects for marriage, found a livelihood in the domestic servant sector of late nineteenth-century American society. As live-in maids, their work was healthier and safer than that of factory girls and they earned enough to remit money back to Ireland to pay for the passage of other family members. Further, unlike other sectors of the American economy, domestic service was not subject to the volatility of depressions that often impacted male immigrant employment. Domestic service gave these Irish girls access to the American way of life in a way that enhanced the "Americanization" process. And finally, as noted by historian Suzanne Sinke (2006b: 294), the Irish domestic "who did the dirty worked helped make possible the ideal woman of the Victorian middle class."

The Irish were not the only group attracted to domestic service. In Chicago, at the turn of the twentieth century, a quarter of all domestic servants were Swedish (Matovic 1997). While native-born servants were preferred (Katzman 1978), those from Scandinavia were highly valued: "as live-in servants they had a reputation for being honest, diligent, hardworking, willing to learn, and unlikely to complain" (Matavic 1997: 288). Like their Irish counterparts, Swedish immigrant women found the conditions better than those of other working opportunities, and the pay better than they had received in Sweden as servants. They found the work of a domestic servant as a path to acquiring important skills (including learning English) and a solid means of earning a livelihood that sometimes included promotion within a domestic hierarchy of service.

However, Swedish immigrant women were not exclusively employed in domestic service. Some found, or even preferred, work in factories as garment workers or shoe-stitchers. For some this work provided financial security; for others it did not.

Writing about the German immigrant population in Chicago in the nineteenth century, historian Christiane Harzig (1997) describes a gendered division of labor that took on new meaning for both immigrant men and immigrant women. For men, most of whom where unskilled laborers, it meant back-breaking work in brick and lumber yards, in grain-processing, or on the truck farms at the outskirts of the city. It also meant working in an industrial context according to a time clock and with the potential for unemployment as well as the burden of providing greater support for the family. For women, she writes "it became running a household under the constraints of the amount of cash at hand and the availability (or unavailability) of urban services" (pp. 185–186). German-born women also became successful entrepreneurs or founded small shops catering to their own communities and offering employment to others among their female compatriots. So too did some Irish women. Historian Hasia Diner (1983: 96) observes that some of the boarding houses that these women ran expanded into hotels and restaurants. In addition Irish women established millinery and dressmaking shops, grocery and liquor stores, and bookshops.

Although shop-keeping was an avenue to self-employment outside the home for some late nineteenth and early twentieth-century immigrant women, more often married immigrant women who may have been employed in their homeland in small enterprises or in agriculture were relegated to the domestic sphere upon arrival in the United States. In New York City in 1905 in only one percent of Jewish households were wives working for wages outside the home; the comparable figure for Italian households was

6 percent (Friedman-Kasaba 1996). Elaborating further on these differences between Italian and Jewish women, historian Nancy Green observes that Jewish women performed more skilled work by comparison with Italian women who were in less skilled work. "Jewish girls in one out of three Jewish families worked; Italian girls, in one out of five. Furthermore, married Italian women most often took in home work, whereas Jewish women, once married, took in boarders instead" (Green 1996: 428). The piece work done at home by immigrant women as part of a decentralized garment industry, has been powerfully captured in photographs by Jacob Riis. Other immigrant women took in laundry or applied their needlework skills to the manufacture of artificial flowers (Kessner and Caroli 1978). Their economic contributions were essential to supplement the low earning capacity of their husbands. Women also helped their husbands in the small shops and pushcarts that proliferated in the Lower East Side of New York City and other urban immigrant neighborhoods in cities such as Chicago, San Francisco, and Philadelphia.

While married immigrant women were working at home, many husbands, particularly in the Jewish community, worked as tailors – in 1890, 91.5 percent of male tailors were foreign born (Friedman-Kasaba 1996). Historian Nancy Green has argued that as ready-to-wear clothing manufacture expanded, men were drawn back into the garment trade, often in the higher skilled positions. "In New York City, some 41.5 percent of the women's ready-wear operatives and pieceworkers were male in 1890. In 1910, men comprised 46 percent of the garment industry factory operatives there, increasing to 50 percent in 1920. . . Men constituted 77.7 percent of the higher-skilled women's cloak-and-suit workforce in New York City in 1919, while women were moving into the less-skilled but expanding shirtwaist and dress factories" (Green 1996: 419–442).

Among the Chinese, the gender ratio of migration, as noted in Chapter 2, was one of the most imbalanced of all immigrant populations at the time and resulted in an unusual gendered labor market. As discussed in Chapter 2, the few Chinese women who were in the United States came to be associated with prostitution, resulting in the passage of the Page Law of 1875 outlawing the immigration of prostitutes. Further, the small numbers of Chinese women made the service sector (working in domestic service and in laundries) an occupational niche for Chinese men, resulting in their feminized image. As historian Suzanne Sinke (2006b: 295) has written, "the stereotypical physical image of Chinese migrant men – long queues and baggy clothing – set them off from dominant 'manly' ideals". Sinke goes on to observe that the high number of young Chinese men was also responsible for the development of other images associated with late nineteenth-century Chinatowns – disease, gambling, opium, organized crime and prostitution. The Chinese pattern of migration to nineteenth-century America resulted in one of the first examples (but by no means the last) of a transnational division of labor – wives were left in China to handle childcare and agricultural tasks while their husbands earned cash as migrant wage earners.

The Bracero Program: Gendered Labor Recruitment in the United States during the Middle Years of the Twentieth Century

During the late nineteenth century, small numbers of Mexicans crossed a largely unpatrolled US border. These numbers increased after the start of the Mexican Revolution in 1910, reaching to as many as 1.5 million people but during this period accounting for less than 2 percent of the overall immigrant population in the US (Camarillo 2007). Settling primarily in the states of the southwest, Mexican immigrant men worked in the agricultural and transportation industries. Gradually, they began to settle in cities and after the Immigration Act of 1924, which restricted European and Asian immigration, Mexicans accounted for 16 percent of the total immigrants entering the US between 1925 and 1929. Mexicans faced discrimination and segregation and by the early 1930s the US, in the depths of the depression, initiated programs of repatriation and deportation. Immigration from Mexico was virtually halted.

However, once the US entered World War II and began to experience a labor shortage, particularly in agriculture, it looked south again for manpower, launching the Bracero Program in 1942, a regulated and engendered guest worker program of male labor recruitment. According to the terms of the bilateral agreement with the Mexican government, the US guaranteed transportation, housing and other resources while the Mexican government recruited the workers. Mexican men, the majority of them single, but some married and leaving their families behind, arrived as temporary seasonal workers and cheap labor for agribusiness. In the initial five-year period of the program (1942–1947), 219,000 Mexican agricultural laborers entered the US. In need of railroad workers, the US government signed an additional agreement with Mexico that resulted in the importation of close to 150,000 additional Mexicans between 1943 and 1945 (Melnick 2007). It is estimated that between 4 and 5 million Bracero contracts for temporary work in the US were issued between 1942 and 1964 when the program was terminated.

The Bracero Program was not without its abuses. The unlimited labor supply south of the border allowed the agribusinesses to maintain low wages for all workers, to refuse to pay wages, to ignore labor laws specifying hours and conditions of work, and to violate regulations calling for transportation and decent housing. Poor economic conditions in Mexico meant that workers kept signing up despite these abuses. Further, this program matched a culture of migration or work mobility in Mexico whereby men were expected to travel in search of work, leaving wives behind in their villages of origin. Over its duration, the governments of Mexico and the US often came into conflict over the parameters of the program (FitzGerald 2009).

The Bracero Program is just one of a number of so-called guest worker programs that are designed to add temporary, and mostly unskilled workers to the labor force and that direct them toward jobs that are "dirty, dangerous and difficult" (Martin et al. 2006:83). The other prime example can be found in the German *Gastarbeiter* program launched in the post-World War II period. It began in the mid 1950s when German farmers, under a labor recruitment agreement, hired Italian workers to harvest their crops (Martin et al. 2006: 88). As the need for labor in construction, factories, and mines increased, Germany formulated a series of bilateral agreements for temporary guestworkers with Italy (1955), Greece and Spain (1960), Turkey (1960), Portugal (1964) and Yugoslavia (1968). In 1960 the number of foreign workers in Germany was 329,000. Both men and women were recruited, although the proportion of women among foreign workers only rose to approximately 30 percent by 1973 when the total number of foreign workers in the country had reached 2.6 million. In the early years women came from Italy, Spain, and Greece; in later years from Turkey and Yugoslavia. Women were particularly needed in sectors of the German labor market such as hotels, restaurants, hospitals, and the textile industry. Until the recession of the latter 1960s, the recruitment of women workers was a challenge, not only because it was in the interests of southern European countries to send young and unskilled men abroad in order to alleviate the challenges of unemployment in their own countries, but also because of gender ideologies in these sending countries. This began to change by the late 1960s and early 1970s and more and more women from these sending countries began to emigrate, not only to Germany, but also to France and Switzerland. Some of the early anthropological work on immigrants in Europe (Buechler and Buechler 1981; Brettell 1983/1995; Phizlackea 1983) in fact focused on the role of women in these migration streams.

After 1961, the largest source for guestworkers in Germany was Turkey (Erdem and Mattes 2003). While the majority of these Turkish workers were men, there were also women who participated in these programs and sometimes Germany recruited Turkish married couples together – the women to work in the clothing and textile industries, as well as in the electronics industry. Other sectors in which these women could be found were in food processing, cleaning services, and in hotels and restaurants. These were jobs that most native-born German women refused to do and they were jobs for which wages were particularly low.

Once the *Gastarbeiter* program was shut down in 1973, family reunification remained as the only legal avenue by which immigrants could enter Germany. Women became more dependent on male breadwinners or they entered the country without documentation. As a result of the latter, more women were directed toward work in private households (the informal sector of the economy) as nannies and maids simultaneously with the increasing employment of married German women outside the home. By 2010 there were four million people of Turkish descent in Germany – a figure that supports the often quoted observation that there are few temporary guestworker programs that do not result in permanent immigration. As economist Philip Martin and his colleagues (2006: 93) have put it, "rotation and return rules are difficult to implement while protecting the human rights of migrants, a fact underscored by the Swiss writer Max Frisch in 1965: 'We asked for workers and people came.'"

Gendered Occupational Niches in the Late Twentieth and Early Twenty-first Centuries

In 1983, the anthropologists June Nash and María Patricia Fernández-Kelly published an edited volume titled *Women, Men and the International Division of Labor*. The international division of labor emerged as a result of the globalization and the relocation of manufacturing industries from the developed and advanced capitalist countries of the world to the developing countries. As those who write about this international division of labor point out, prior to about 1970, the underdeveloped world primarily acted as the supplier of raw materials (agricultural products and minerals) for the developed world. However, by the late twentieth century the countries of the developing world have become centers of production (something referred to as the global industrial shift) because they are the places where wages are lower and where rules and regulations that impact manufacturing (labor and safety laws) are more lax.

It is, of course, important to note that despite the demise of manufacturing in the US, the garment industry has remained an important sector of the immigrant workplace in the American economy, often for young single women within specific immigrant populations. In Los Angeles at the close of the twentieth century there were 140,000 garment workers employed in apparel manu-facturing, many of them Latinas. Even the Asian-owned garment factories employ primarily Latinos, largely women but also some men. In the early 1990s in San Francisco, there were more than 25,000 workers in the garment industry, 90 percent of whom were women. Of these women, 80 percent were Chinese. A similar concentration of Chinese immigrant women could be found in New York City where approximately 60 percent were employed in small garment sweatshops in Chinatown.[4] As in the sweat-shops of the early twentieth century, home-based piecework in the US-based sweatshops of the late twentieth century is critical to remaining competitive (Zentgraff 2001: 60-61). As in overseas sweatshops, those in the US offer workers very little in the way of benefits (health insurance, paid vacations, maternity leave, overtime pay). And from time to time egregious cases of abuse are revealed – for example, the seventy-one Thai garment workers in El Monte, California, who were held in slavery during the 1990s (Su and Martorell 2001).

But, by the final decades of the twentieth century, the produc-tion of clothing and other items for American consumers had largely been relocated overseas. This process has attracted inter-nal migrants who leave their agricultural villages to work on the *maquiladoras* located close to the US–Mexico border (Bustamante 1983; Fernandez-Kelly 1983; Wright 1997), in the export pro-cessing zones of Sri Lanka (Gunewardena 2007), the Philippines (Chant and McIlwaine 1995), and Malaysia (Ong 1987) among others, and in the growing urban areas of Morocco (Cairoli 1998) and China (best portrayed by the documentaries *China Blue* (2005) and *Red Dust* (2010)).[5] A study carried out by the International Labor Organization in the 1990s (ILO 1998) revealed that in the export processing zones around the world, 99 percent of the workers were women. Scholars who have written about this new class of mobile female factory workers draw attention not only to how they are subjected to "numerous practices of moral and labor disciplining that reinforce their social subordination along the contours of gender and class, [but also] to women's responses in resistance to the constraints of such practices" (Gundarwena 2007: 36).

The emergence of this international division of labor, or in other terms the penetration of capitalism into remote areas of the globe, has also generated gendered international population flows. Of particular significance is the impact on reproductive labor which has created a new surge of migration of domestic workers, many of them female who now participate in what has been described as the "global transfer of services associated with a wife's traditional role – childcare, homemaking, and sex – from poor countries to rich ones" (Ehrenreich and Hochschild 2002: 4).

Nannies and Domestic Servants

Many researchers have described a global care chain comprised of nannies, domestic servants, and eldercare workers that has emerged during the latter twentieth century.[6] Those who work as nannies are often being paid to care for the children of native-born female employers who themselves hold professional positions outside the home; and they in turn use the money they earn to support others in their home country to take care of their own children – creating gendered and racialized hierarchies that link the women of the developed world with those of the developing world.

In the US, many of the women who find themselves in domestic service, whether as live-in/live-out nannies/housekeepers working for a single employer or housecleaners working on an hourly basis for multiple employers, are from Mexico and Central America (Hondagneu-Sotelo 2001; Ibarra 2007). Writing about Mayans in Houston, sociologist Jacqueline Hagan (1994) demonstrates that while 84 percent of the men in her sample worked as maintenance and stockworkers (largely for a large retail chain), 97 percent of the women worked as domestics, the majority live-in domestics. In a study of Central Americans in Washington, DC, Terry Repak (1995) found that 61 percent of the men in her survey sample worked in construction, 18 percent in food service, and 7 percent in landscaping; 65 percent of the women in her survey sample worked in domestic service, 9 percent in food service, and

5 percent in the retail sector. Often, domestic service is the only kind of work that Mexican and Central American (Guatemalan and Salvadoran primarily) women can find because they are undocumented. This legal status puts them in especially vulnerable situations. Those seeking domestic work frequently find employment through social networks; similarly, employers also tend to rely on social networks (friends, neighbors, co-workers) to locate a housekeeper or a nanny. Hagan argues that the male networks for the Mayan population she studied are more extensive and hence provide them with almost immediate access to jobs. For women, who usually live at their place of work, there is "less time and opportunity to interact with newcomers and to assist them in finding work. Moreover, employment is based on a small workplace in an unpredictable industry" (p. 65).[7]

Sociologist Pierrette Hondagneu-Sotelo (2001), based on interviews with both domestic workers and their employers in the Los Angeles area, describes the structural conditions that have created the demand for such workers, the differences in working conditions depending on whether one is live-in or live-out, and the changing relationships between worker and employer over time. She also discusses situations where domestic workers, once they have been employed for a while, begin to take more charge of their own working conditions and the balance between work and family. They gain more agency and demand recognition of their personhood. In her conclusion she calls for more formalization of the employment standards for immigrant domestic workers that would benefit both employee and employer.

One dimension of the scholarship on immigrant women in domestic service explores the potential for abuse, particularly when these women are undocumented or on special work visas that tie them to a particular employer. A recent report of the National Domestic Worker Alliance (2012) indicated that wages are often below the minimum wage, rarely are there employment benefits or employment contracts, and for live-in workers the hourly work week is often longer than stipulated by law. Domestic workers enjoy little economic mobility or financial security. And there are few outlets to report abuse. This report notes in particular that 85 percent of the undocumented immigrants who were surveyed in the study who encountered problems with their working conditions did not complain because they were afraid that their immigration status would be used against them.

A specific example of the abuse tied to special work visas is the "kafala system," a sponsorship system used in parts of the Middle East (Jordan, Lebanon, Saudi Arabia, and certain countries in the Persian Gulf) to monitor and control migrant laborers in domestic service and in construction.[8] It is a form of "indentured servitude" that is ripe for exploitation and abuse. Very often, when cases of abuse arise, the "madams" who employ domestic workers are blamed. Indeed, such cases are sometimes reported in the media (for example, Barker 2014, Hewson 2014). But sociologist Amrita Pande (2013: 430), writing about kafala in Lebanon, argues that the system itself creates the conditions of abuse.

> By making the worker dependent on the employer for everyday existence and renewal of legal papers, [the system] not only creates the bases for much of the violations, it also allows the violations to go unpunished. Migrant domestic workers have limited options of getting out of an abusive contract. They cannot change employers unless the employer agrees to sign a release waiver.

Pande notes that those who run away from their employers immediately become illegal and this too makes them subject to abuse and exploitation. She also cites a Human Rights Watch report of 2008 claiming that in Lebanon one migrant domestic worker each week commits suicide by jumping from a balcony of a high-rise building. "A high level of abuse, isolation, and a feeling of helplessness were cited as the reasons that drive these women to plunge to their deaths" (Pande 2012: 383).[9] This system offers an excellent example of intersectional inequality within like-gender social relations – that is, between the "madam" and her servant.

Research has demonstrated the myriad forms of resistance that emerge among domestic workers who are conceptualized in certain ways by their employers, sometimes in relation to their sexuality (Chang 2000; Ford and Piper 2007). For example, anthropologist

Nicole Constable (1997: 553) describes how Filipina domestic workers in Hong Kong "contest, resist and appropriate specific sexual images", especially through their use of fashion and dress. They do this in relation to the control that their Chinese female employers try to exert upon them in the efforts to make them into "docile social bodies . . . and to craft for them a less morally ambivalent – but sufficiently subordinate – position within the household" (pp. 553).

Some forms of resistance are akin to the "weapons of the weak" described by James Scott (1985) – mockery, foot dragging, chicanery (Gamburd 2000; Lan 2003; Parreñas 2001b) – while others involve declaring a presence in public space. African-origin immigrant women working in Lebanon deploy several strategies to claim spaces that are generally denied to them (Pande 2012). One such space is the balconies of the buildings from which one woman can hold conversations with others who are similarly confined to the domestic space by their employers. Others who are less confined use ethnic spaces, such as churches. Especially for undocumented workers, churches become protected spaces where they can develop a sense of belonging (Raijman et al. 2003).

Nurses and Eldercare Workers

The kafala system is a labor recruitment process that channels immigrant women into a particular sector of the immigrant economy – domestic service. Another labor recruitment program, but of skilled immigrant workers, is that which recruits nurses from countries like the Philippines, India, the Caribbean, and more recently some African countries, to work in the health sector of the developed world (Choy 2003; Rodriguez 2008). Some scholars have argued that the increasing demand for nurses in the global labor market is changing gender norms regarding migration in sending societies but in complicated ways. In Ghana, for example, some women stated that seeking work abroad was just too complicated and too costly, given their domestic and family responsibilities; these barriers were not expressed by male nurses (Nowak 2009). However, other women are beginning to view themselves as breadwinners and hence have seized the opportunities offered by work abroad. They further acknowledge that men's ideas about gender norms are changing and that they are increasingly "letting" women migrate. The migration of women is not just in pursuit of better pay, but also as a way to expand their professional skills. Nowak (2009: 275) quotes one middle-aged female nurse:

> I don't wish to stay outside Ghana for a long time, like be there permanent. I would love the experience. That is what it would take for me to leave – get to experience different atmospheres, get to experience different aspects of the nursing. I have the zeal to know more about the things I am reading in books. I want to show them, experience them, and see how they are.

If African women like the Ghanian woman quoted above are among the most recent participants in the global mobility of nurses, Filipina women are among the earliest. By the first decade of the twenty-first century estimates were that 250,000 Filipino nurses were working outside their country; that 30 percent of nurses employed in Switzerland and close to two-thirds of those in Ireland were foreign educated; and that in the United States and the United Kingdom 60 to 70 percent of the nurses in a given health facility were recruited internationally (Kingma 2006: 2–3). In the US, only 7 percent of foreign nurses in 1960 were from Asia but by 1972 this number had risen to 63 percent. In 1989, in response to a shortage of nurses, the US Immigration Nursing Relief Act allowed the immigration of roughly 16,000 nurses. Mireille Kingma, a trained nurse herself, has observed that the competition for nurses, "both within and among countries, is generating unregulated international recruitment practices on a scale without precedent" (Kingma 2006: 4). She also emphasizes that while many nurses may freely choose to migrate, a deeper investigation reveals that social and economic conditions in the sending societies often oblige them to leave to seek employment abroad.

The international mobility of nurses offers business opportunities to intermediaries who train them for foreign labor markets as well as to travel agencies that assist with flows. Banks are involved in assisting with the remittances that nurses invariably send back to their families. Sometimes these nurses migrate on their own on three or five-year contracts and then return to their country of origin and to the families left behind. This is the case for many nurses recruited to the Middle East. Others, especially those who come to the US, receive a green card and can then sponsor the rest of their family to join them.

Indian nurses began arriving in the US after the Immigration Act of 1965. In the period between 1975 and 1979, close to 12 percent of nurses who were admitted to the US with a green card (as permanent residents) were from India, compared with 28 percent from the Philippines and 11 percent from Korea. Sociologist Sheba George (2005) describes how the nurses from Kerala develop a sense of professional pride which they do not experience in their home state in India – a place where the nursing profession is looked down upon.[10] Clearly, the migrant medical labor force of skilled workers challenges the assumptions of women as tied migrants and demonstrates that "skilled migrant women may be better able than unskilled women to utilize their privileged position within labor market hierarchies to mute gender hierarchies, particularly when there are global shortages within these labor markets" (Raghuram 2004a: 316). However, George shows us that what goes on regarding gender hierarchies is much more complicated and that these hierarchies intersect with class (and caste) hierarchies. In her work on nurses from Kerala, geographer Margaret Walton-Roberts discusses the impact of international nursing on marriage, suggesting that the dowries assembled abroad sometimes perpetuate patriarchal customs. She also describes at length the stigma that remains associated with the nursing profession and nurses who work abroad.

In Kerala, when compared with the male migrant, female migrant identities can be devalued because of their mobility, but this process of devaluation is mediated and subject to transformation over time. Even as the nursing profession has transformed, the residue of impurity remains, and the economic benefits of migration are socially devalued through the moniker of sexual impropriety. The independence of female nurses, working with men, sometimes at night, and the mobility nurses experience has challenged the gender norms of south Indian society. In response to these transgressions, the idea of the nurse as a 'suspicious' figure gains salience, and is used to challenge the class mobility female nurses may experience through the migration process.

(Walton-Roberts 2012: 189)

Walton-Roberts concludes by wondering how male nurses will be constructed and suggesting that the interpretations of female migration and mobility in Kerala offer a lens on changing gender relations and gender empowerment, not only locally and regionally but also nationally.

One dimension of this discussion of the global care chain focuses on the particular needs of the developed world, given their aging populations, for eldercare workers. This is a subject that has captured the attention of the news media (Newman 2006; Hampton 2010). By the middle of the first decade of the twenty-first century, the American Health Care Association (representing for-profit nursing homes) and the National Association for Home Care were lobbying the US Congress for a special visa that would admit low-skilled workers for their industry. The initiative did not succeed but the need was made apparent. Long-term direct care of the elderly, one of the fastest growing service occupations in the US, has become increasingly reliant on minority and immigrant women, particularly in the in-home eldercares sector (Browne and Braun 2008; Lowell et al. 2010). Eldercare work is often part-time, wages are low, and turnover is high. One study of Filipina migrant women in this sector of the US economy revealed that most were not properly trained, that they were paid "under the table," that they generally carried no health insurance, and that most planned to return home and hence remitted a large portion of their income to their families in the Philippines (Tung 2000). In short, these eldercare workers are often subject to exploitation, necessitating more work on social justice policies that regulate the industry, particularly in the face of a growing aging population across the globe in both the developed and developing world.

Scholarly research on this sector has begun to appear. For example, Maria Ibarra (2002, 2003) has studied Mexicana eldercare workers in private homes in Southern California. She explores the power-laden work relationship between employer and employee, some of which leads to abuse of the paid elder-care worker. But she also describes the active agency with which Mexican women in these positions make decisions about the ethical model of care to be applied. They do it in a Mexican way and consequently often fall into a "tender trap" characterized by a long work day with multiple chores. They earn low wages and they stay on the job because of the emotional relationship that they develop with the individual for whom they are caring. Some see their work as an act of charity; others comment on the skills they are learning and the pride they feel in helping an elderly person to hold on to his or her humanity (Ibarra 2003: 105–106).

The US is not alone in its need for eldercare workers and in its focus on immigrant workers. In Singapore, migrant domestic workers are channeled into private domicile care while foreign workers are channeled into work in nursing homes. These care workers are "othered" according to gender, nationality, and ideas about eldercare work as being demanding, demeaning, and dirty (Huang et al. 2012). In the Italian context, the growing demand for home eldercare workers has been linked to shorter hospital stays and the increasing number of Italian women who have entered the paid labor force and hence do not have the time to take care of elderly parents as women did in the past. Based on narratives with 35 of these eldercare workers living in Italy, Francesca Degiuli (2007) describes the varying circumstances of work (live-in or live-out), the varying demands (depending on the level of infirmity of an elderly person), the range of responsibilities (often including house-cleaning), the long hours, and the overall vulnerability of the positions (some of these workers are undocumented, others are on special work visas). The work is labor-intensive, both physically and emotionally.

Not all this private health care work is in the hands of immigrant women. Sociologist Cinzia Solari (2007) offers a very original analysis of the differences in attitudes between Russian men and women involved in this employment sector in San Francisco. Although one might expect, she suggests, that women would develop a more personal and familial relationship with those for whom they are providing care, while men would adopt a more professional stance, in fact the major differences were rooted in religion rather than gender. Russian Jews "deployed profession-alizing discursive practices while Russian Orthodox Christians deployed discursive practices of sainthood" (p. 186). Some of the Christian men in her study "actively renegotiated dominant notions of masculinity, arguing that paid care work is a Christian calling" (p. 187). Given that this care work represented down-ward mobility for men, adopting a professional stance would not have been compatible with their ideas of masculinity. "Russian Orthodox discursive practices allowed men to reinterpret hegem-onic notions of masculinity and see homecare work as manual work that follows in Jesus's footsteps" (Solari 2007: 208).

The Gendered Labor Market of Male Immigrants

So far the discussion in this chapter has focused on the gendered labor market from the perspective of female immigrants, with only minimal references to their male counterparts. But there are equally labor recruitment programs as well as sectors of both the formal and informal economy that largely attract men. One arena is in landscape maintenance and grounds-keeping. Sociologists Ramirez and Hondagneu-Sotelo (2009: 72), based on research in Los Angeles, observe that while in 1980 there were 8,000 Mexican foreign-born men who were working as gardeners in the Los Angeles-Long Beach metropolitan area, by 1990 there were almost 20,000 and by 2000 there were over 30,000. These authors pose the question of whether the teams of Mexican men whom one sees in US suburban neighborhoods every day, mowing lawns and blowing leaves, are workers in low-wage, dead-end, and dirty occupations or small and autonomous entrepreneurs who are building a business. They are both; some of them, these researchers note, following in the footsteps of Japanese-American gardeners during an earlier phase of immigration who made land-scape gardening into a legitimate occupational niche because they were racially excluded from other forms of employment. As with women's domestic work, social networks are important to this masculinized labor sector and these immigrant men are now doing the work that once used to be performed by fathers and sons in a household.

Those working in this industry can be broken down into three occupational categories – waged employers (*ayudantes/* helpers); independent, self-employed route owners who own their own trucks and equipment and who have a roster of residential customers for whom they provide landscape services; and licensed landscape contractors (Ramirez and Hondagneu-Sotelo 2009: 77). There is occupational mobility within the sector depending on the development of social and financial capital as well as legal status.

> By strategically managing their routes, and by working long hours and six and seven day workweeks, some Mexican immigrant gardeners earn six figure incomes. Few occupations in the contemporary, post-industrial service economy offer Mexican men with less than a primary school education and limited English fluency this opportunity.
>
> (Ramirez and Hondagneu-Sotelo 2009: 85)

Of course, the work is not without its physical and emotional costs and, unlike domestic workers, there is little intimacy with those whose property these men are tending to. Subjugation coexists with entrepreneurship.

Many Mexican and Central American immigrant men, largely because of their undocumented status, also work as day labor-ers, often on dangerous farming and construction projects which expose them to high risk for workplace injuries that is equivalent to the exposure to risk that nineteenth-century male immigrants faced not only in construction but also in the steel mills of Pittsburgh. Researcher Nicholas Walter and his colleagues (2004) explore how day laboring impacts not only health and suffering, but also ideas of patriarchal masculinity, particularly when these immigrant workers are disabled and cannot continue to provide for their families who often remain in Mexico. These scholars describe the "competition, insecurity and public embarrassment of tenuous survival on the streets" that generates "anxiety and a sense that their identity as men is under assault" (p. 1162). A common response to help maintain self-esteem is to manifest a hyper-male identity – as hard-working men of honor who are tough, stoical, and courageous. "They have sacrificed, they have courage, and despite all the indignities and the precariousness of employment and their illegal status when they send money back they are fulfilling their role and their images of themselves as the 'arms' of the family" (p. 1163). But, as these men provide for their families materially they still worry about their inability to remain emotionally engaged with their children – much like some of the transnational mothers who will be discussed in Chapter 4. And those who are injured on the job often suffer from depression or substance abuse and are at risk of more serious psychiatric illness.

Not all immigrant men are working in high-risk occupations. In some host countries they find work, as women do, in the hospitality sector. Batnitzky et al. (2008) describe a gendered and economically selective recruitment process that draws middle-class Indian men into the hospitality sector in London, a sector where 60 percent of all workers are migrants. Among the critical questions driving this research were why this employment sector was so attractive to young middle-class men from India and what the gendered process of recruitment to this kind of work reveals about ideas and experiences related to Indian middle-class masculinity. Among the factors that result in a higher representation of male middle-class migrants from India in the hospitality sector are the cost of finding a position through an agency, the geographical displacement that is required within India to attend a job interview, and the anti-social hours of hospitality that obviate childbearing/rearing. For many of these men, work in this sector was glamorous and a potential resumé-builder for their return to India, which most of them planned to do; it both challenged and reinforced their class and gender identity. They became more financially independent, but the work they did in London (such as cleaning rooms) was not work they would do in India.

Another sector of the UK gendered immigrant labor market that draws men, particularly Polish men, is domestic work as handymen. Majella Kilkey and her colleagues (2013) describe this as a good example of migrant niche formation. These handymen often hold other jobs (in the construction and building sector) and carry out their handyman work during the evenings and on weekends to supplement their income. While working as a handyman restricts time with family, the pay is much better than many other daily or hourly rate positions working in a restaurant, an office, or as a bank teller. Further, this sector lends itself to self-employment and interaction with the private sector. Kilkey et al. (2013: 86–88) describe three working models for these handymen. The first model includes those who are formally self-employed by subcontracting their services to other English or Polish small-business owners. These individuals tend to have limited language skills, few tools, no driver's license, and no vehicle. They are on the lowest rung of the hierarchy. The second model includes handymen who operate independently and work alone (although a wife may be included as a partner). Their working conditions are better and they earn more. The third model includes handymen who take on larger maintenance contracts with rental agencies or landlords or larger renovation projects for private households. These men tend to have more initial capital as well as better language skills. But no matter at what level they operate, these men view themselves as hard-working and reliable and they see their work as masculine despite its association with the domestic sector. This is partially because the work is associated with male gendered attributes of strength, the use of machinery, and with formal male skilled trades. By comparison with feminized domestic work, the pay is better. But similar to feminized domestic work performed by immigrant women, these male handymen also do work that native-born homeowners, in this case men, do not want to do themselves – whether because they do not possess the skills or because they want to spend more time with their families and hence outsource household maintenance.

An additional dimension of gendered labor market migration that "tilts male" is that of Information Technology (IT) workers

(Iredale 2005). Globally, the IT sector is the twenty-first century's most extensive temporary labor migration program, but of skilled workers (Boyd 2013). The majority of these skilled workers are men. In the US, for example, in the early part of the first decade of the twenty-first century just 27 percent of computer/mathematical scientists as well as computer/information scientists were women (Raghuram 2004b: 165). Many of these IT workers are immigrants who have entered the US on H1B visas. These visas, issued for three years, allow a worker to enter and work in the US for a maximum of six years. Very often these workers are paid lower wages and do not have opportunities to advance. As other scholars have noted, "US companies favor IT workers from India because they offer a unique set of technical skills, [are] well-versed in English, do not demand higher wages, are willing to relocate, [are] not very demanding, and help companies to build or strengthen their business in India. Many body shopper recruiting agencies have emerged in India to facilitate the migration of skilled workers on H1B visas" (Varma and Rogers 2004: 5647).

Why is there gender disparity in the IT sector? Some of it reflects differences that already exist in sending countries where IT work is socially constructed as masculine. However, based on research in the UK, Raghuram (2004b) points to additional factors such as the frequent mobility of IT workers who often work on short-term contracts. The expectations on women to perform unpaid reproductive labor (their household duties) are often seen as incompatible with the more flexible requirements of the IT sector. Men do not face these conflicts and hence find it easier to meet the hypermobility expectations of the IT profession. But skilled IT workers in the US, particularly if they move into a legal status (their company has applied for a green card for them) often face a glass ceiling in this sector, leading some of them to strike out on their own, founding their own companies (Varma and Rogers 2004).

Family Businesses: The Immigrant Entrepreneur

The literature on immigrant entrepreneurship is by now extensive, beginning with pioneering theoretical work by Ivan Light and Edna Bonacich (Light 1972; Bonacich 1973; Light and Bonacich 1988) and eventually extending into case studies of specific populations in the United States and elsewhere.[11] There are a few key theoretical debates that characterize this literature, one having to do with group differences. For example, scholars have asked why Asian immigrants in the United States start small business enterprises at a greater rate than Latinos. Explanations have emphasized on the one hand distinct cultural traits that predispose certain groups to entrepreneurship and on the other variations in human capital and other class resources or social capital/ethnic resources that facilitate self-employment (Bun and Hui 1995; Volery 2007). A second debate centers on the question of why the rates of self-employment are higher among the foreign-born by comparison with the native-born. Here explanations point to the structural/opportunity factors that advantage or disadvantage immigrants. It is hard for immigrants to find employment in the mainstream economy because they lack the linguistic skills, because they cannot be accredited for employment in the field they worked in prior to migration, or because of discrimination. Min and Bozorgmehr (2003) formulate this as the "disadvantage hypothesis." Self-employment offers an avenue for labor market assimilation when other avenues are blocked. A third debate focuses on outcomes: does self-employment increase earnings and is employment in an ethnic enclave economy a cost or a benefit in relation to longer-term social and economic mobility?

Curiously, in the by now extensive corpus of scholarship on contemporary immigrant entrepreneurship, systematic attention to the gendered dimension of self-employment is minimal.[12] Among the earliest scholars to study the more contemporary role of women in family-operated businesses among post-1965 immigrants to the US was Alice Chai (1987a, b), based on research among Korean families in Hawaii. These families owned grocery stores, restaurants, and gift shops in which both husband and wife worked long hours alongside one another. The work was preferred over factory and other service sector jobs for its flexibility and freedom from the more racist and sexist dimensions of the broader immigrant labor market. A decade later, based on research conducted among Koreans in New York City, sociologist Pyong Gap Min (1998) found that 38 percent of the women in the labor force were working with their husbands in the same business; 12 percent ran their own businesses independent of their husbands; and 36 percent were employed in co-ethnic businesses. When husband and wife work together, a division of labor emerges: "The wife is usually in charge of the cash register and the husband takes care of the total management of the store. The wife's control of the cash register is one of the central factors that make Korean retail businesses, such as produce, grocery and liquor retail businesses, successful" (Min 1998: 40). Min and others have been interested in the impact of these family enterprises on gender roles and the division of labor in the immigrant household. Often work in a family operated business is viewed as an extension of women's domestic roles and hence does not challenge extant gender ideologies (Bhachu 1988; Dhaliwal 1995; Espiritu 1999). On the other hand, research has also shown that immigrant women who are employed in small businesses within enclave economies do not achieve the same level of success as their male counterparts. Indeed they are often highly exploited (Gilbertson 1995).

What about women who set up their own business independent of a spouse? Can it be a site of empowerment for immigrant women? Sociologist Arlene Dallalfar (1994) describes Iranian women in Los Angeles who are sole owners and operators of their businesses and often the primary breadwinners. These women are found in both family run and home-operated businesses. Those who launch home-operated businesses, generally characterized by minimal start-up costs, draw on personal savings as well as ethnic and class resources. They cater to a largely co-ethnic clientele, use word of mouth as the primary mechanism for attracting their customers, and operate primarily through cash-based exchange. In the family run businesses, women work longer hours but are coequal partners. This co-equality is equally evident among Greek Cypriot immigrant women in England who "perceive themselves as building up a family business with their husbands rather than working for them." These women are "tenacious entrepreneurs" who are "constantly looking for openings in the market" (Josephides 1988: 48).

Family run businesses are often found in particular economic niches into which immigrants of specific national origins have entered. For example, among Indian motel owners from the state of Gujarat, women work either in partnership with their husbands or they assume full responsibilities while their spouses work elsewhere (Dhingra 2012). According to anthropologist Karen Leonard (1997: 86), this is a pattern at variance with how work and the division of labor operate in India where family businesses "rarely employ women as managers and clerks . . . It seems . . . that the management of ethnic businesses by wives is a new strategy to maximize economic security and family income." Leonard goes on to describe the impact on the family. "Women make more decisions about spending than do their mothers-in-law back home, and they make more decisions than do their visiting or even co-residing mothers-in-law in the United States . . . The contribution of women to business efforts is publicly recognized in the ethnic press."

In the US, another occupational niche into which immigrant women of any number of national origins, but particularly the Vietnamese, have entered is the nail salon business. This business requires very little overhead to get set up and a minimal amount of training. Miliann Kang (2003) describes the gendered work of body labor that takes place in Korean immigrant women-owned nail salons in New York, placing her emphasis in particular on how racial and class inequalities between Korean provider and customer shape particular patterns of body labor: high service, expressive and routinized. These variations were identified in salons in three different neighborhoods in New York City: one white middle and upper class, one largely black, and the third in a mixed neighborhood.

My own research on this issue (Brettell 2007) emphasizes the agency of immigrant women entrepreneurs, including the decisions they make to become entrepreneurs and how they operate their businesses. Across a range of different immigrant populations, I found women working in family grocery businesses catering to an ethnic market, in restaurants catering to a broader clientele, in personal care businesses such as nail salons, and in other enterprises that are perhaps less typically described in the immigrant entrepreneur literature. In general my research supported previous findings that female immigrant entrepreneurs start up their business with small amounts of personal or family capital and sometimes pursue the necessary short-term training to do so. Like men, they are motivated to be their own boss and self-employment for many offers a different path from domestic service, factory work, or home piecework. Self-employment also provides them with more flexibility in balancing home and work life, although many work longer hours than they imagined. Most of the women interviewed demonstrated business acumen in assessing market and locational niches for their enterprise and some can be described as innovators who introduce new products and services into both the ethnic and the mainstream economies.

Outside the US context different occupational niches emerge as attractive to migrant entrepreneurs. In South Africa, Ghanaian migrant women predominate in hairdressing and fabric retailing (Ojong 2007). In New Zealand, Indian immigrant women can be found in the beauty business, in food and catering, in hairstyling, and in childcare and retail food stores – all these enterprises largely catering to their own ethnic community and, if employing others, largely co-ethnics (Pio 2007). In Sweden, eldercare has offered some opportunities for immigrant women entrepreneurs (Hedberg and Peterson 2012). In this case it is the knowledge and competence in care, as well as an interest in improving the quality of health care more generally that motivates them. Hedberg and Peterson (2012) found that many of their research participants fell into this sector by accident, while others experienced ethnic exclusion and gender segregation in the labor market and hence pursued the opportunities in eldercare as a way to get ahead and to be one's own boss.

One other dimension of entrepreneurship worth mentioning

is the participation of many immigrant women, particularly those who are undocumented, in the informal economy of street-vending, not only around the world, but also on the streets of cities like Los Angeles (Bhimji 2010). These women operate in a contested terrain, working in defiance of specific city regulations, facing constant police harassment, and subjecting themselves on a daily basis to the risk of deportation. As they do so, anthropologist Fazila Bhimji argues, they engage in claims-making and demonstrate a sense of belonging. She describes a time in 1993 when more than 100 street vendors showed up at a Los Angeles city council meeting to ask for a hearing on an ordinance that would legalize street vending. In 1994 a pilot program was approved but it did not improve the situation and by the end of the first decade of the twenty-first century, with additional federal immigration laws in place, undocumented street vendors had become even more vulnerable and were facing increased competition as a result of the economic downturns in the country at large. They cannot pay all the fees that are required to operate legal food carts. And yet they persist because even what little they earn helps to support their families. As Bhimji (2010: 481) emphasizes, they do not see their work as illegal; what is illegal is selling without a permit and that is not a crime. Thus, they distinguish "between criminal activities and their rights to work" as microentrepreneurs.

Migrant Sex Workers and Sex Trafficking

Across the globe, people, and especially women, are on the move to work in the sex industry. By the early 2000s, sex trafficking had become an eight billion dollars/year business, with 4 million women, girls, and boys prostituted daily (Agathangalou and Ling 2003: 134).

Many link the increase in the volume of sex trafficking with the neo-liberal policies of the global economy.

The existence of a supply of women to be trafficked for sex work is associated with the feminization of survival which derives from the disruptive and unstable economic conditions associated with development, and linked to international neoliberal monetary policies.

(Boyd and Pikkov 2008: 36)

Sociologists Monica Boyd and Deanna Pikkov (2008: 36) describe the epicenter of trafficking women for sex work as within Asia, and then fanning out to the former Soviet Union countries and to Europe. Estimates of the number of sex trafficked women in Canada range from 8,000 to 16, 000 annually and in the United States from 18,000 to 20,000.

Social scientist Rutvika Andrijasevic (2007: 31–32) observes that after domestic/care work, the most common job venue for undocumented migrant women in the European Union is sex work, although she cautions that not all this work is prostitution. Migrant sex workers comprise anywhere from 40 percent to 90 percent of the sex worker population in a given country. Some move voluntarily while others are moved forcibly, or trafficked. The debate about choice or coercion permeates the literature on the global sex trade (Agustin 2006; Parreñas 2011). Those who always see it as coercion "base their arguments on the principle that women's bodies are the site of women's oppression, and that the male use of female bodies for sex is about power, and not about sex. Consequently, all prostitution is unequivocally defined as sexual exploitation" (Gulcur and Ilkkaracan 2002: 412). Conversely, other scholars acknowledge that there are women who choose to engage in sex work and hence sex work should be "viewed as a labor practice based on women's autonomous use of their own bodies as a source of income" (Gulcur and Ilkkaracan 2002: 412). Researcher Chandré Gould (2010: 35) further observes that paying attention to the agency and intentions of those who are trafficked may reveal that they have no desire to be rescued and returned home – the foundation of many anti-trafficking policies and programs. These programs are criticized for being patriarchal and for being rooted in ideas of "infantalized femininity" (Palmary 2010).

This debate may never be settled but certainly there are significant variations in the reasons why female migrants enter the sex work industry.[13] Indeed, public health specialist Joanna Busza (2004), who has worked with Vietnamese sex workers in Cambodia, urges us to recognize the complex dynamics that undergird why women enter the sex industry. In some instances it is viewed as more lucrative than employment in domestic service or manufacturing. In other instances it is an occupation that women turn to when other alternatives have failed. In still others, women are tricked about what kind of job they are migrating for, or they are obligated to pay off the cost of their migration and are coerced into sex work to do so. These latter instances are most character-istic of the global "trafficking in persons." But Busza (2004: 232) also notes that "individual sex workers may go through different phases; for example, a woman who was originally tricked into selling sex might then independently choose to continue doing so. Initial pathways into sex work, therefore, do not necessarily define sex workers' current perceptions, motivations, or priorities." Busza found that the Vietnamese women she studied who were engaged in sex work in Cambodia often juxtaposed a sense of shame about the work (it is "bad work") with an appreciation for its earning potential (they can make important contributions to sustain their families) (p. 241). Similarly, Rutvica Andrijasevic (2003: 262), writing about Eastern European women in Italy who work in prostitution, argues that these women view their work as a path out of poverty and unemployment and away from family abuse, low self-esteem, and a perception of a life in stagnation. She further observes that borders, visa regimes, and other restrictive mecha-nisms on immigration that are meant to control trafficking may in fact "work in favour of the third parties who organize trafficking, whether individuals or agencies, because they become a kind of supplementary migration system." Women make use of trafficking networks because it is one of the few options available to them. Andrijasevic (2003: 265) concludes by arguing that the discourse on trafficking is itself gendered, reproducing "stereotypical narra-tives of femininity and masculinity. The narratives of victimization and criminality are a form of contemporary/fiction that discloses the dissymmetry of power relations in the new Europe", that is between West and East.

In addition to the example of the sex workers of Eastern Europe working in Western Europe that is well represented in the literature (Malarek 2003), there is also that of West African women, particularly from Nigeria, who are brought to Europe. Carling (2005) observes that one in three women in Benin City in the early 2000s was receiving an offer to go to Europe. In this same period there were approximately 10,000 Nigerian prostitutes in Italy alone. After an initial contact, according to Carling (2005: 3)

> the victim is put in contact with a madam . . . In many cases, the madam also has the role of sponsor, the person who finances the journey . . . the victim and her sponsor make a 'pact' that obliges repayment in exchange for safe passage to Europe. The pact is usually religiously sealed by an *ohen*, a priest of the indigenous religious traditions . . . Emigration pacts are frequently also sanctioned with prayer rituals in the Pentecostal churches to which most of the victims belong, further broadening the pact's legitimacy . . . In Europe, the women live and work under the control of a Nigerian madam, a counterpart of the madam in Nigeria . . . In Italy Nigerian sex workers are usually street prostitutes and constitute the low-wage end of the prostitution market.

They work sometimes as long as three years to pay off their debt. But as Carling notes, once the debt is paid off it is not uncommon for the victim to continue to work for a madam as a supervisor of other prostitutes or to become a madam herself.

Leyla Gulcur and Pinkar Ilkkaracan (2002) describe the experiences of sex workers, most of them from the former Soviet Union and Eastern Europe, in Turkey. Turkey allows sex work as long as the individual is registered. However, sex workers must be Turkish citizens and sex workers are barred from emigration or immigration. Thus, foreign and migrant women in this industry in Turkey are illegal and hence subjected to discrimination and state-sanctioned harassment. Nevertheless, they have entered the country, particularly after the economic collapse of the former Soviet Union – hence the construction as "Natashas" – blond bombshells from the east. One woman, called Lena by these authors, reports that she "came from Kazakhstan from a small city near Alma-Ata. After the fall of communism I lost my job.

I looked for a job and couldn't find any. I got a loan from my neighbor and came to Istanbul. At the beginning I looked for a job and I stared working for 5 US dollars a day. This money wasn't enough for food, accommodation, clothes. So I started work as a sex worker" (Gulcur and Ilkkaracan 2002: 415). Most of these women described experiences of violence and abuse, as well as lack of access to services, including national health care and banking. These authors conclude that rather than focus on the forced or voluntary nature of sex work, it is more important to document the working and living conditions, to identify rights violations, and to work to improve all of these. These strategies need to be built, they argue, on the recognition of sex work as labor and "liberalizing immigration policies in order to prevent abuse by third parties, including organized criminal networks . . . And local operational arms of the state (e.g. police and other officials). Decriminalization of sex work, accompanied by labor standards applied to migrant sex workers that promote and protect their human rights, will enable migrant workers to access social services and systems without penalty" (p. 419).

While much of the attention in the literature on sex trafficking has focused on Europe, the United States is in fact the second largest destination country (after Germany and before Italy, the Netherlands, and Japan) for individuals trafficked to work in the sex industry, with estimates of approximately 18,000 persons per year. Ninety percent of these persons are female and almost half are children of both sexes (Schauer and Wheaton 2006: 146). The major sources for trafficked women and girls are Mexico, Asia, and the countries of the former Soviet Union. These women are brought into the US by means of the illegal use of legal documents, the production of fake documents, or without inspection in the company of men (often US military men) who are "recruited to act as escorts or false marriage partners for trafficked women" (Schauer and Wheaton 2006: 154).

In the US, in recognition of the problem of sex trafficking, the Trafficking Victims' Protection Act was passed in 2000 (Gozdziak and Collett 2005). The aim of this legislation was to combat the abuse and exploitation of undocumented workers, particularly those forced into prostitution. Whether it has had that result is debatable. Chapkis (2003: 924–925) reveals the gendered dimensions of the legislation:

> Trafficking victims, described as vulnerable women and children forced from the safety of their home/homelands into gross sexual exploitation, are distinguished from economic migrants who are understood to be men who have willfully violated national borders for individual gain. The law justifies offering protection to the former and punishment to the latter through the use of three sleights of hand. First it relies on a repressive moral panic about "sexual slavery" . . . second, despite offering symbolic support to the notion that all prostitution is sexual slavery, the law carefully differentiates between "innocent" and "guilty" prostitutes and provides support only to the innocent. And third, by making assistance to even "deserving" victims contingent on their willingness to assist authorities in the prosecution of traffickers, the legislation further seals US borders against penetration by "undeserving" economic migrations.

Sociologists Elzbieta Gozdziak and Elizabeth Collett (2005: 117) observe that the majority of studies of trafficking in the US focus on women such that we understand very little about the trafficking of men and boys, whether for sex work or for some other form of bonded labor. But overall, these authors argue, there are large gaps in our knowledge about the problem. "Research on trafficking has not moved beyond estimating the scale of the problem; mapping routes and relationships between countries of origin, transit, and destinations; and reviewing legal frameworks and policy responses" (p. 121–122). We know little, they suggest, of the characteristics of the traffickers and the trafficked and of the lives of those who live through and survive the experience – what anthropologist Denise Brennan (2005) calls "ex-captives."

In her study of Filipina hostesses working in Japan, sociologist Rhacel Parreñas (2011) problematizes whether or not the women themselves identify as being trafficked. She prefers to label it a form of "indentured mobility." Many of these hostesses, however, describe their own agency in following the profession – that it was a path out of poverty. They have gained self-reliance, financial independence, personal autonomy and sexual freedom. They view themselves as breadwinners who have acquired decision-making power, earned respect from their families, and challenged patriarchal boundaries. And yet these women face serious structural constraints in relation to their migration and their work, including the absence of workplace regulations, the stronghold of middlemen brokers, and the criminalization of those who become undocumented. These issues are what should be addressed, Parreñas argues, not the elimination of the hostess occupation itself which has been liberating and empowering for many who have pursued it.

Conclusion

A critical theoretical argument in this chapter is that the immigrant labor market is segmented and must be viewed through an intersectional lens that examines the relationships among gender, race, and class. Employer demand, whether for nannies or nurses, for agricultural laborers or gardeners, for sex workers or computer programmers, shapes migration streams and particularly gendered and class-based migration flows. Such demand can induce movements that might not otherwise have occurred (Mahler and Pessar 2006) and once a migration stream has been launched the flow of information as well as the links of social networks (both kin and non-kin) perpetuate it, and perpetuate as well the gendered labor markets into which male and female migrants enter. Women migrants are often found in temporary and precarious jobs in the private sector, doing the reproductive care work of their wealthier employers. But they can also be found in positions on the global assembly line, working for low wages and hence making it possible for their employers to produce less expensive products for sale in the global marketplace. Men tend to find work as manual laborers in agriculture or in the construction sector. The work of immigrant men can be equally unstable and precarious and more so if their legal status in the country of immigration is an issue. These are the characteristics of the majority of immigrants who move around the globe in search of employment and better incomes.

Of course, there are immigrants, both male and female, who demonstrate agency in the context of structural constraints by becoming small-business owners; and there are others with high human capital – higher education and linguistic skills – who find more professional and more stable employment. However, no matter what the class status and income level, migrant couples must develop strategies for balancing home and work life. The gendered labor markets that shape the migration process thus impact households and families in significant ways. This topic and others related to the immigrant family are addressed in the next chapter.

4

Gender and the Immigrant Family

While the United States is more traditionally considered as a destination for migrants from Latin America, beginning in the latter decades of the twentieth century and continuing into the twenty-first century various European countries have also become destinations. There are Peruvians and Ecuadorans living in Spain; Bolivians, Colombians, and Ecuadorans living in England. In these countries, as in the US, immigrant families are confronted with different gender ideologies and they experience transformations in domestic gender relations. Geographer Cathy McIlwaine (2008: 11–12) offers an analysis of these transformations from the perspective of the immigrants themselves. Catalina, a migrant from Santa Cruz, Bolivia, living in England, told her: "I think that here women have equality, they can do the same things as men without any problems. This is very different from where we are, from where women are for the home and there they must stay." Another migrant, Elizabet, who arrived in London from Quito, Ecuador, stated: "Here, men and women are both in charge, both work, earn, spend, and go out equally." Carla, from Ecuador, reported that "there's hardly any machismo [here]; men have to do the same things as women, they have to help each other out." And finally, Sebastian, from Palmira, Colombia observed that in his home country he would "burn water ... first my mother did everything for me and then my wife and I just went along with it. But not now, when I went to work in the coffee shop I learnt a lot. Now I cook, I make some really good dishes, I look after the

children, sometimes I wash the dirty clothes, I mow the lawn . . .
and I like doing these things, I like to keep the house in good order.
In Colombia, I did nothing."

Across the Atlantic, within a community that has grown up in
the city of Philadelphia, Vietnamese refugees have made similar
observations about the impact of immigration on family life
(Kibria 1993: 4–6). Binh, a man who left Vietnam in 1981 with
his three sons, while his wife remained behind to look after their
aged parents, found a job as a janitor soon after his arrival in the
United States. But an injury kept him out of work and relying
sometimes on public assistance. He also found himself doing the
laundry and the cooking and fending off his sons' complaints
about the food he prepared. He felt sad and expressed the most
regret about his sons and how they had changed. They had
become Americanized and no longer respected him or listened to
him. Lien, a young woman who left Vietnam under the guardian-
ship of an aunt, first arrived in Hawaii, but eventually joined her
brother who was living in Philadelphia. Her brother was living
in a one-room apartment and working in a restaurant. Lien went
to school. Her brother began to beat her every day when she
came home from school and eventually she left him to live with
some friends and their parents. After a few months, however, she
dropped out of school to marry a Vietnamese-American man she
had met and the young couple moved into an apartment shared
with three of her husband's brothers.

The Latin American migrants and Vietnamese refugees described
above provide insight into how family and gender relations are
impacted by geographical mobility and by living and working in a
country culturally and socially distinct from one's own. Immigrant
women in particular, through their participation in the labor force,
make important economic contributions to the household and this
in turn may give them a greater sense of power and autonomy
within the family, thereby altering traditional gendered domestic
hierarchies. But the kinds of jobs that immigrant women do are
often poorly paid and lack benefits and hence in some cases may in
fact yield little in the way of equality and independence. In many

immigrant families women bear a larger burden of childcare and housework and therefore juggle these responsibilities with waged work – experiencing what feminist scholars have long referred to as the "double-day." But in other immigrant families, men begin to engage in household tasks that they would never have done in their home countries. Thus, it is important to explore how immigration transforms masculine identity and status, not only within the family but also in relation to gender ideologies and specific class, racial, and legal hierarchies in the country of immigration. This chapter focuses a gendered lens on the immigrant family. It is guided by broader theoretical questions such as: is migration disempowering or empowering to men and/or women within their families; are gender roles and gender ideologies (ideas about masculinity and femininity) changed in the immigrant context and, if so, how; what impact does migration have on social and intimate relationships within households, including relationships of conflict and violence?

The chapter also focuses on the immigrant family in a transnational context, and particularly on forms of transnational parenting that have often redefined ideas about the meanings of motherhood and fatherhood.[1] Anthropologist Steven Vertovec (2010: 3) has argued that "transnationalism has become one of the fundamental theoretical ways of understanding contemporary migrant practices across the multi-disciplinary field of migration studies."[2] Transnationalism highlights the fundamental social, economic, political, and cultural connections between sending and receiving societies. It situates global population movements in relationship to the broader circulation of commodities, technology, and capital. And perhaps most importantly, it captures the social process whereby migrants and their families operate in interconnected social fields that transgress geographic, political, and cultural borders (Glick Schiller, Basch, and Szanton Blanc 1992: ix).

Recently, scholars have called for the "engendering of transnationalism" – that is, exploring how gender (and the hierarchies and inequalities associated with it) is constructed and reconstructed in transnational social space and analyzing similarities and differences in how men and women participate in transnational social fields. Men and women may, for example, experience different impacts on their social status as a result of migration, leading them to develop divergent attitudes toward their homeland and the country of immigration. To capture the complexity of an engendered transnationalism, Mahler and Pessar (2001) have developed a theoretical framework which they label "gendered geographies of power." By this phrasing they intend to emphasize the nature of "gendered identities and relations when conducted and negotiated across international borders [according to] multiple axes of difference [and] across many sociospatial scales – from the body to the globe" (Mahler and Pessar 2006: 42). Important to their analysis is the question of agency – what kind of power and control do men and women, respectively, have over their own movements and activities in transnational space and what agency accrues to those who are left behind who are equally part of the families constructed by means of transnational practices, including the transmission of social and economic remittances.

Immigrant Families Then: The Third Wave of Immigration

For many immigrant women of the past, especially those who entered as wives and mothers, immigration was disempowering. Uprooted from their village communities and from extensive kinship networks that these afforded, these women found themselves living in small tenement apartments and often unable or forbidden to leave their households or the few local streets in their neighborhoods. They were confronted with American social reformers who contributed to the process of "institutionalizing social inequality between women, especially by nationality/race/ethnicity and class and between women and men in households and families" (Friedman-Kasaba 1996: 186). And yet as immigration historian Donna Gabaccia (1994: 68) has pointed out, immigrant children in turn-of-the-twentieth-century families viewed their mothers as powerful.

Children described immigrant mothers as collectors of wages, as organizers of expenditures and everyday life, as engagers of their help in domestic chores and industrial production, as dispensers of discipline and punishment, and as women who rewarded children with food, affection, small gifts and personal services. Immigrant mothers spent little "quality time" with their children, yet fostered emotionally close ties to them.

These immigrant mothers controlled domestic earnings, doling out an allowance to men rather than men providing a household allowance to their wives. Working daughters generally handed over weekly wages to mothers and retained little for themselves. By contrast, sons were accorded more freedom including the freedom to keep much of what they earned.

All of these contradictions reflect a deeper contrast between the private sphere and the public face of the family. Thus, writing about Chinese families in San Francisco in the late nineteenth and early twentieth centuries, historian Judy Yung has argued that immigrant women offered a submissive image in public but ruled at home. "As homemakers, wage earners, and culture bearers, [Chinese women were] indispensable partners of their husbands" (Yung 1995: 77). Most of these women, upon coming to America, were liberated from the traditional joint families of China where they were dominated by their parents-in-law. Any number of theoretical questions about the relationship between gender and power and between domestic space and public space can be informed by an examination of the gender relations within immigrant families who entered the US in the late nineteenth and early twentieth centuries.

During the third wave of immigration, as indicated in the previous chapter, more single than married women worked for wages outside the home and overall the rate of female waged work was low (20 percent in 1900) by comparison with the end of the twentieth century (60 percent) (Foner 1999: 96). Married women, particularly within the Italian and Jewish immigrant communities, took in piece work or boarders and hence were able to earn money and care for their children within a single social space. A report from 1911 indicates that more than half of Jewish households had boarders (cited in Foner 1999: 99). There is little evidence that husbands contributed much to the management of the household and childcare. This remained the woman's sphere. But historian Donna Gabaccia also suggests that because immigrant men often earned so little, it is likely that few of them defined their masculinity exclusively in relation to their breadwinner role (p. 65) especially by comparison with the American middle-class men, many of whom experienced the shattering of self-esteem during the Great Depression.

Gender ideologies impacted immigrant family life in the US in myriad ways. Historian Virginia Yans-McLaughlin (1973) argues, based on research on Italian immigrant families in Buffalo, that women preferred occupations that did not strain traditional family relations so that Old World family values could continue to function.

> The mother's roles as arbiter of household organization and tasks and as disciplinarian and child-rearer were reinforced by her economic position as manager of the domestic undertaking, be it artificial flower-making, basting, or sewing. Because she still had not become, in the strict sense of the term, a wage-earner, she presented no clear threat to her husband's authority and power.
>
> (Yans-McLaughlin 1973: 143)

Further, the behavior of immigrant women, especially in Italian families but among some other immigrant groups as well, was closely scrutinized and the comings and goings of unmarried daughters was monitored. Parents in many immigrant communities kept close watch not only on their daughters' places of employment but also on their courtships, in an effort to prevent premarital pregnancy. Even daughters who earned enough to be able to live independently generally remained at home until marriage (Gabaccia 1994: 69, 70).

Historian Robert Orsi (1985), writing about the Italians of Harlem during the early part of the twentieth century, describes a *domus*-centered society focused on home and family. Marriage was viewed as a union of two *domuses*. The father ritually presided over the *domus* and particularly at Sunday dinner when everyone gathered. And members of the *domus* surrounded it "with a dense screen of privacy, refusing to allow any public expression of its inner life" (Orsi 1985: 102). Oldest sons had a lot of authority, sometimes more so than fathers. This often stemmed from the close relationship they had with their mothers who were powerful figures in the household and responsible for upholding the traditional mores. "Mothers were the disciplinarians of the family, either meting out punishment themselves or instructing their husbands or older sons to administer it. They controlled the family finances, and the various members of the household were expected to hand their paychecks over to them" (Orsi 1985: 133).

The Italian immigrant *domus* was also a place of conflict, particularly across generations. Italian immigrant parents demanded respect and deference from their children and they were most concerned that their children were losing their culture. They worried about what their children were exposed to in the public schools, on the city streets, and even in the workplace (Ewen 1985). And they worried about how the state might intrude on domestic life. Broadly speaking, Americans of the time considered immigrant childrearing practices to be particularly strict; but they also were capable of charging immigrant mothers with neglect of their children who often played outside unattended (Gabaccia 1994: 66). Italians feared too much Americanization and the lax morality of American society and hence subjected their children to "relentless, demanding pressure" to maintain the traditions and values of the *domus* (Orsi 1985: 109). This pressure was particularly intense for daughters within a community that staked its reputation on the morality of its women (p. 135). "A woman who dated more than one man was considered frivolous and irresponsible, if not worse; likewise, if a couple dated four or five times and did not get engaged . . . both the man and the woman – but especially the woman – were in danger of doing permanent harm to their reputations" (Orsi 1985: 116).

Some of these gendered dimensions of the late nineteenth- and early twentieth-century Italian immigrant family were equally present in other immigrant families of the time. For example, within French Canadian families that settled in Central Falls, Rhode Island, fathers, daughters and sons worked outside the home, largely in the textile mills, while widows, wives, and mothers worked at home. Daughters handed over their earnings to their mothers, who used it to help run the household. Rose Forcier, whose story was recorded as part of a University of Rhode Island Oral History project, explained that her mother never worked. "In them days very few mothers worked. They stayed home and did their cooking and laundry and all that stuff. We used to help at home too, when we'd come back and at night we used to help with the ironing but then we used to wear so many aprons and petticoats at that time" (Lamphere 1987: 141). This gendered division of labor was equally characteristic of English, Scottish, Irish, and Polish families in the area, although there was some variation from one group to another regarding the extent to which housewives also took in boarders to help supplement the household income. The presence of working daughters in these households did not appear to undermine male authority. "Daughters developed their own autonomous sphere at work and many participated in strikes and other types of workplace militancy as the twentieth century unfolded . . . Only with the advent of the wage-earning wife and mother have substantial domestic transformations emerged" (Lamphere 1987: 257). The wage-earning wife was more characteristic of the families that immigrated as part of the post-1965 so-called "fourth wave" of immigration initiated by the Immigration and Nationality Act.

Immigrant Families Now: The Fourth Wave of Immigration

The fourth wave of immigration is characterized by dramatic changes in the composition of the immigrant population entering the US. No longer are they predominantly from eastern and southern Europe; rather, they are economic migrants and refugees coming from Latin America, Asia, and most recently Africa. Negotiations and conflicts surrounding gender roles and relations within the immigrant family have been heightened for these fourth-wave immigrants, by comparison with their counterparts of the third wave, largely because married immigrant women have increasingly entered the labor force. Some immigrant women, as indicated in the previous chapter, were recruited for professional positions; others easily found work in the growing service economy. The need to work outside the home has often altered the scripts for who does what and when and how husbands and wives, and sons and daughters, interact within the family context.

Grasmuck and Pessar (1991), based on research among Dominicans in New York City, were among the first to draw attention to changing gender relations within the late twentieth-century immigrant family and what these changes might mean for the empowerment of immigrant women in particular. Families in the Dominican Republic are most commonly nuclear and formal authority rests with the senior male head of household. The male patriarch is the primary, if often the sole breadwinner in the family and represents the family to the outside world. By contrast, a woman's place is in the home. Men have more freedom in appropriating household income for their own use and women are taught to accept these expenditures, and sometimes the extramarital affairs that accompany them, with resignation in order to avoid marital discord.

In the immigrant context, more equitable household arrangements – in relation to household authority, the allocation of housework tasks, and budgetary decisions – are often necessary. This is generally linked to the enhanced breadwinning roles of Dominican immigrant women. In the Collado household, for example, Tomás prepares dinner, claiming

> that he would never be found in the kitchen, let alone cooking, in the Dominican Republic. But, he added, there his wife would not be working outside the house; he would be the breadwinner. Tomás explained that since he made his living in the United States as a chef, it seemed natural that his contribution to running the household should include cooking at home. He joked that if he wore out more pairs of socks running around in the kitchen it was all right because his wife

worked in the garment trade and she could apply her skills at home by darning his socks. Tomás and his wife said that soon after they were both working they realized that "if both worked outside the home, both should work inside, as well. Now that we are in the United States we should adopt American's ways."

(Grasmuck and Pessar 1991: 152)

In Dominican immigrant households, income is pooled and decisions about how to spend household resources are shared. There appears to be a correlation between the amount of money a woman earns for the household and the extent to which a husband involves himself in household tasks. However, these changes may be more in the social practices within the domestic sphere than in actual gender ideology and norms. Dominicans talk about men "helping" at home and women "helping" to earn money outside the home. Ultimately, ideas about primary responsibilities may not have changed. As Pessar (1995: 53) has noted, none of her research participants "went so far as to suggest that men could or should act as women's equals in the domestic sphere." One woman in her study put it this way: "I know of cases where the man assumes the housekeeping and childcare responsibilities. But I don't believe a man can be as good as a woman; she is made for the home and the man is made to work" (Pessar 1995: 53).

While gender parity exists in many of these Dominican immigrant households, and while many women enjoy the independence that earning their own wages yields, some of these families experience tensions and conflicts that in some cases have resulted in disbanded unions. Fourteen of the fifty-five women interviewed by Pessar (1995: 56) indicated that conflicts over domestic authority and social practices were major factors disrupting their marriages. In some cases, women find that men are using their salary for personal expenditures and yet expect their wives to contribute disproportionately to large household expenses. In other cases, Dominican women precede their husbands as migrants and the long separation leads to suspicions of marital infidelity. In still other cases, the challenges that men sometimes face in finding employment results in arguments. Pessar (1995: 59–60) concludes that immigrant life in the US may provide Dominican women with new economic, social, and cultural resources that are empowering, allowing them to place more demands on their spouses and giving them the freedom to walk out of a union when a husband refuses to be more supportive. However, this empowerment comes with a cost. "When household bonds are severed, the goal of the migration project – social advancement for the family – often falters, because the individual resources of single members, especially women, are insufficient to sustain it. The newfound autonomy of many immigrant women may, in the end, lead to poverty."

In addition to the challenge to gender values and norms between husbands and wives, there are also conflicts that emerge inter-generationally as Dominican youth contest dimensions of parental authority and Dominican parents, just like Italian parents of a previous period of immigration, bemoan the excessive "Americanization" of their children. The male household head's role as the voice of and representative for the family *vis-à-vis* the outside world is often undermined by migration. Children often assume this role because they have a better command of the English language. They interpret and sometimes even negotiate for their parents. They help them fill out forms or arrange for benefits. Parents also sometimes feel that American institutions – schools, the police, child welfare agencies – undermine their parental authority. Ideas about discipline vary from one country to another and hence what might be appropriate in one context is considered child abuse in another.[3] One Dominican man expressed his frustration in the following way: "There is no respect for the father in this country. Back home, just let my son pick up the phone and call the police. Let them come. It wouldn't matter. There they know it is the father who has the ultimate authority" (Pessar 1995: 65).

The issues that confront Dominican families also confront other post-1965 newcomers to the United States. In their research on Mexican families in the US and Mexico, sociologists Manuel Barajas and Elvia Ramirez (2007) critique a simplistic "home-host" dichotomy that constructs the sending society as a site of patriarchal oppression and the host society as the locus of greater equality. Their study reveals that while Mexican women in the US report more extensive familial authority and equality in decision making than do their counterparts in Michoacán, Mexico, they also report greater burdens associated with waged work and household chores. Thus, neither migration, nor employment, nor women's greater authority within the home have altered the traditional division of labor for Mexican immigrant women in the US and in fact they experience a greater "double burden" than do their counterparts in Mexico for whom work and domestic spaces are integrated.

There are also significant differences between gender ideals and practices that vary by age and location, with older women in the US as well as women in Mexico tending to uphold ideas of male dominance to a greater extent than younger cohorts. In the immigrant context, young women, when talking about their parents, drew distinctions between the authority that a mother has over her children and the authority that a husband has over his wife. In the Michoacán context, young women talked about mothers training their children to defer to fathers. The following response illustrates this perspective:

> When I want to go out, I ask my mom, and she says, "Ask your father for permission, and if he lets you go out, well go." Both decide, but first we ask for permission from our dad, and if he lets us go, she also lets us. And if my dad doesn't give us permission, then she won't either.
>
> (Barajas and Ramirez 2007: 377)

Mexican immigrant women in an age cohort between thirty and forty-nine describe more egalitarian and sharing relationships with their spouses. A similar response was characteristic of women in this cohort in Mexico as well. And yet it is here that the differences between ideology and practice are most apparent – people talk the talk of gender equality but in practice men still want to exercise authority. Thus, one woman reporting on those who return to the village for vacations made the following observation: "Even though the women want to order them . . . and the men support women's liberation . . . But [men from the US] are as sexist as those here. When they come, the woman stays inside the home, while they are out in *fiestas* . . . It is the same *machismo*" (p. 377).

Barajas and Ramirez conclude that their research contradicts the assumption that Mexican immigrant women are more liberated from patriarchy than are their counterparts in the Mexico. Instead these changes are more nuanced and vary by age cohort in both places. That said in Michoacán ideals of male dominance are stronger, something that can be correlated with the possibility of men fulfilling their breadwinning roles – access to jobs may be better in the US and hence the articulated ideology may be less necessary to sustain masculinity. Ultimately, these authors suggest their findings "underscore the continuing significance of gender inequality for Mexican families across borders . . . the seeming empowerment of women in the United States is more illusory than substantive" (p. 385). Further, it is important to note that the unequal division of labor within the household is something that is also sustained by American cultural ideologies that accord less value to women's productive and reproductive roles. Immigrant families operate within this context.

Sociologist Cecilia Menjívar (1999), based on her research among Central American immigrant families in California, also challenges the broad notion that waged employment generally empowers women and enhances their status in the family. She views the impacts as uneven and varied between families of indigenous Guatemalan background and those of Ladino Guatemalan or Salvadoran background. Women themselves report that they earn more here but in El Salvador or Guatemala they may have worked less. And even when women are the main providers, this does not necessarily translate to more authority in the household and in some cases it results in negative consequences. Menjívar (1999: 610) quotes one Salvadoran research participant:

> The Salvadoran man continues to be macho here . . . The man becomes dependent on the woman. The woman goes to work, not the man. But men bring machismo with them and the woman takes on more responsibility . . . When men see themselves like that they drink and

that brings a lot of problems home . . . The women end up suffering a lot because the men let their frustrations out by beating the women. I have not seen a family that is in good shape yet.

Menjívar notes that these tensions are not as common in indigenous Guatemalan households where the men view their wives' employment as an opportunity for both of them to get ahead. She also emphasizes that Ladina Guatemalan women aspire to exit the work force once a more secure middle-class status is achieved. To Menjívar they expressed their confusion over why the women who employ them continue to work outside the home. By contrast, the indigenous women viewed work as part of life. They are not working because their husbands are economically vulnerable, but because it is an expectation, part of their understanding of gender relations and responsibilities. As a consequence, Ladina women perceive greater change in the allocation of tasks within the household than do indigenous women whose husbands already helped out at home in their home country.[4]

What is important about this particular study is that it attunes us to class variations in gender ideologies in the home countries; these variations challenge a simple dichotomy between "traditional" and "modern" or "domestic" and "public" – the former the sphere of women, the latter the sphere of men. While in many places men are culturally constructed as the breadwinner, this is not always the case, and certainly in many places the culturally meaningful distinction between household and street (*casa* and *rua*) as gendered spheres has itself undergone transformation prior to an experience of emigration. The "machismo" that has been associated with these gendered differences survives in many parts of Latin America and hence is challenged in the immigrant context, but in other places, machismo is no longer a significant dimension of gender relations, often having changed in association with the spread of evangelical Christianity (Santos 2012).

The issues that are raised in relation to Latino immigrant families in the US are equally characteristic of Asian immigrant families. Korean immigrant women, for example, are beginning to challenge the gender inequality and unequal division of labor within the family, although patriarchal ideologies are sometimes hard if not impossible to transform. In the US, married Korean women have much higher rates of labor force participation than do women in Korea (Min 1998). Many are employed in a family business and work long hours. This inevitably has an impact on domestic life. Sociologist In-Sook Lim (1997) offers four major conclusions regarding gender and family relations within Korean immigrant families. First, husbands feared the challenge to their authority at home, whether it came as a result of their wives being acculturated to American values with regard to gender relations in the home or from their contributions to the economic stability of the family through waged work. Several husbands referred to the greater assertiveness and self-expression of wives. Second, while wives report making some attempt to change male dominance in the home, they also report not wanting to totally subvert family hierarchy. This is best reflected in the following comment by one Korean immigrant wife: "I don't think it is desirable for a woman to henpeck her husband even though she works outside the home. I want men to lead everything in his family. I think the authority of a family head needs to be secure" (Lim 1997: 40). Third, Korean immigrant women who engaged in waged work do ask more of husbands in sharing domestic responsibilities, something that differentiates them from their counterparts in Korea. Lim (1997: 42) refers to this, however, as a "politics of appeal" rather than outright demand. Doing anything to damage a man's self-respect is not, in the view of these immigrant women, in the best interests of the family. Many, especially those of older cohorts, are in fact resigned to the fact that they will always do more work at home despite their major economic contributions outside the home. This resignation is shaped by patriarchal beliefs regarding sacrifice for the family as well as by a desire to avoid marital conflict.[5] It is also often reinforced by the presence of mothers or mothers-in-law in the home who often support the more traditional division of labor within the household. Finally, the reluctance or resistance to domestic labor on the part of men is matched by Korean women who delay or cut corners. Thus one Korean woman said:

In Korea it might have been absurd for me to treat my husband to a humble dish when he came home from work. However, in the US, with the excuse that I am busy, it is natural for me to make my family a simple dinner. Under these circumstances I work as much as my husband does, there is no other way to do this.

(Lim 1997: 48)

Class can be an important factor shaping gender relations in Asian immigrant families. This is quite apparent in the research of sociologist Sheba George (2005) on Indian Christian families from the state of Kerala. Within these families, there are four different patterns for the household division of labor associated with whether the man or the woman is the primary migrant, what kinds of employment they pursue in the US, and what kind of access to alternative childcare is available (George 2005: 77ff.). One pattern involves traditional male-headed households, where men make financial decisions and women remain responsible for all other domestic tasks including childcare. In these families, the men are the primary migrants and have high status in the US labor market. Women have lower or equal status, often stay at home to take care of children, or the children are left in Kerala with relatives or at boarding school. These households have made the fewest changes in relation to lived experience and gender ideologies.

A second pattern is the "forced-participation household" which in many ways is similar to the traditional household but with exceptions. In these families women are the primary migrants and have high status in the US labor market (largely as nurses) and men have lower status relative to their jobs in India or to the jobs of their wives in the US. Couples in these cases often work alternate shifts, and while women continue to do much of the housework, men are forced to contribute to childcare, and some childcare help is available either in the US or in Kerala. Men retain control of financial decision-making. In these households, unlike traditional households, there is a dissonance between gender ideology and practice. Women in these households deal with this dissonance "by adopting the gender strategy of ignoring the reality of their relative economic success. By not knowing how much they made and by not signing their paychecks, these women consciously chose to play down what threatened their traditional ideology and their husbands" (p. 98). As George puts it, they "do gender" in the home to overcompensate for their breadwinner status (p. 115).

A third pattern is the partnership, and relatively egalitarian households. In these households women are the primary migrants and have high status in the US labor market while husbands have lower status relative to their jobs in India and to their wives' jobs in the US. Men participate in housework and childcare, couples work alternate shifts, there is little outside help for childcare, and financial decisions are shared. Men do not claim headship of the household, despite being raised with this ideology in Kerala. George notes that in these households men and women are more dependent on one another, "seem to be better friends" (p. 99), and model their behavior on the US structural and cultural context. These household have made the most change in relation to the fit between lived experience and gender ideologies.

The final pattern, more anomalous, is the female-led household. Here women are the primary migrants and have high status in the US labor market. Men are absent, dependent, or unreliable. Women are mostly alone, perform all household labor, and relatives and the community provide some support for childcare. If a husband is present, relationships are strained and the women reject a gender ideology that does not correspond to their experience. They continue to live "with the contradictions of female-led households, where they were not socially supported and not rewarded for their headship, as were the men in traditional families" (p. 114).

As in many Latino families, the behavior of daughters in Asian immigrant families is more closely monitored – immigrant parenting, in other words, is highly gendered. This gendered parenting is perhaps best articulated in Yen Le Espiritu's (2001) study of Filipino Americans. Espiritu argues that the "virtuous Filipina daughter is partially constructed on the conception of white woman as sexually immoral." This emphasis on female morality (which includes not only sexual restraint but also dedication to family) is one way in which those groups that are dominated politically and economically can define themselves as superior in relation to the dominant group. However, this strategy, in this case promoting Filipina chastity, also serves to reinforce "masculinist and patriarchal power in the name of a greater ideal of national/ethnic self-respect" (p. 417). Young Filipina women experience restrictions in their mobility, independence, and personal decision-making. They are forbidden to date, to stay out late or spend the night with friends, or to go on out-of-town trips. Their behavior is closely monitored while that of their brothers is not. Sometimes this translates into allowing sons to apply to a distant college while daughters are encouraged to apply closer to home if not to also continue living at home rather than on campus. Young Filipina women express both frustration toward and understanding of the "policing" of their bodies. Sometimes they rebel, and sometimes they vow to develop more egalitarian relationships when they marry and have their own families. As one research participant put it:

> I see myself as very traditional in upbringing but I don't see myself as constricting on my children one day and I wouldn't put the gender roles on them. I wouldn't lock them into any particular way of behaving.
>
> (Espiritu 2001: 435)

Masculinity, Intimacy, and Domestic Violence in Immigrant Families

What is most intriguing about the research on immigrants in the US is the effort to link gendered and generational dynamics within the micro-structural context of the family to larger macro-structural factors of culture, race, and class as well as to the institutional contexts of American society. These connections are particularly important for one of the most recent immigrant populations, Somalis. Somalis have the highest poverty rate of any population living in the US (51% living in poverty compared with 13% for the total US population). Somalian families are patriarchal and the household is perceived to be headed by a male breadwinner. But, as sociologist Cawo Mohamed Abdi (2014) points out, based on research among Somalian families in Minnesota, this understanding comes up against welfare and government assistance programs which tend to undermine the economic position of men and generate conflict within the family.[6] Welfare checks are issued to women and this upsets domestic life. As one Somali man put it:

> The person with the highest share of the company is the CEO. If we say each has an equal share, no one will rule. What will that lead to? Chaos! People are depending on a third party. If there is some outside source of income, then there is no respect between the couple. If you are fed and provided for, then your attachment and respect to each other diminishes. The man is told "you don't provide for this family, so don't be arrogant."
>
> (Abdi 2014: 467)

Somali men feel emasculated in the US, describing a situation where the economic and cultural foundations of their authority is undermined by their own precarious employment, by their wives' employment, and/or by public assistance programs directed toward women and children. Welfare, claims Abdi (p. 469), is viewed as a symbolic menace by men but as a necessity by women although they recognize as well that it upsets family hierarchies. Somali men support the perpetuation of traditional and Islamic forms of conflict resolution, and are suspicious of 911 as a "non-Muslim" system that breaks up families and undermines their authority. Somali women often go along with this because they feel pressures from the broader Somali community to accede to patriarchal ideologies. Further, increasing hostilities toward Muslims in the host society turn them inward and result in gender bargains that limit the options Somali women have to resist their subordination in the US.

The challenges to culturally constructed ideas of masculinity and fatherhood that result from menial or under employment, is a topic that has been explored for other immigrant and refugee populations (Austin and Este 2001; Este and Tachble 2009). Deborah

Boehm (2008b) describes the loss of autonomy and erosion of masculinity (if not feminization) that is associated with a transition for Mexican immigrant men from managing their own farm in Mexico to washing dishes and bussing tables in the US. And the masculinity of those who do not migrate is also called into question because migration is what is expected of men. Meanwhile the women who join their husbands in the US are often doing waged work for the first time in their lives and this results in altered family roles and in "many negotiations, controls, conflicts, alliances, strategies and maneuvers that coincide to construct gender subjectivities in a transnational space" (Boehm 2008b: 20).

In a somewhat more nuanced approach, Chad Broughton (2008) discusses the emergence of three different, but not necessarily mutually exclusive, masculine stances toward migration and the changes brought on Mexico by processes of neoliberalism: traditionalist, adventurer, and breadwinner. Broughton describes these as "negotiated, gendered approaches for meeting instrumental and identity goals related to work, family, and place, and they are often deployed strategically at different stages in the life course and in hybridized combinations" (pp. 573–574). The traditionalist view places a high moral priority on family protection and cohesion, commitment to village and nation, abiding by the law, and sustaining a stable identity. The traditionalist tends not to migrate and is concerned about depopulation, declining social mores, and the loss of talented young men. The adventurer view involves more risk taking and is guided by the desire "to elevate ... social status, to test ... courage and virility, and to escape the tedium and tighter moral codes of the rural [Mexican] south" (p. 578). The adventurer emphasizes social mobility and material possessions. Finally, the breadwinner is motivated to migrate in order to provide sustenance, to upgrade housing, to keep his children in school. His is a selfless choice impelled by desperate circumstances.

The masculinity of Iranian immigrant men in the US is also challenged. Iranian families have traditionally been "authoritarian and adult-centered" and in accordance with the values of the Islamic Republic, the husband is the head of the household (Mahdi

1999: 71). Most of the Iranians who have migrated to the US, and especially those who are wealthy and educated, have achieved an economic status equal to or higher than the status they had in Iran. However, women have achieved greater social gains (social and educational skills, a new sense of individuality, autonomy) than men who have lost the authority and many of the privileges they enjoyed in Iran. Many Iranian women have become more liberal in the US context, something that directly contradicts their Iranian male counterparts (Mobasher 2012: 145). Within the immigrant household, however, women still assume the primary responsibility for shopping, cooking, ironing, laundry, caring for children, and chauffeuring, while maintenance of the yard, house, and car are largely in the hands of men. The task that appeared to be shared was financial planning, although by comparison with husbands in Iran, Iranian immigrant men were contributing to more household tasks. The greatest conflicts regarding changes in roles and domestic authority were within the households of lower-class families. Sociologist Ali Mahdi reports that Iranian women often describe their households as a battleground and occasionally the tensions can erupt into violence. Social scientist Mohsen Mobasher (2012: 147) quotes the following observation made by an Iranian woman in Dallas: "Iranian women in the United States live in an inferno and are tormented, torn between individual freedom encouraged by the American culture and familial commitments and expectations cultivated by the Iranian culture."

The "adult-centered" nature of the Iranian family has also been impacted by the immigrant context as children demand more freedom and parents are focused on their children's success. Fathers are more involved in their daughters' lives than in Iran and in general there is a more liberal approach to upbringing. However this is not applied in the same way to sons and daughters. "Girls, whose sexuality and lifestyle have a direct bearing on the family honor and dignity, are sometimes subject to closer supervision and stricter home regulations," although they rarely let this interfere with a desire for their educational and social mobility (Mahdi 1999: 73). Summing up these households, Mahdi (1999: 70) writes:

Lack of family support and a larger kin network reduces the resources available to [Iranian] couples and increases the amount of time they spend with each other. In situations of conflict and crisis, increased interaction in a highly dense relationship multiplies the number of roles each spouse has to play in relation to the other. In the traditional family in Iran, a husband was "a husband" and a wife "a wife". In the new setting each spouse not only has to play the role of intimate other but also, in many cases, the role of an absent father, mother, or brother at times of crises.

These more companionate marriages and the new forms of intimacy associated with them that are described for at least some Iranian families are key dimensions of the Mexican families in Atlanta studied by anthropologist Jennifer Hirsch (2003). Hirsch describes a generational shift from heterosexual relationships that are based on respect (*respeto*) to those based on trust (*confianza*) and explores how this shift impacts courtship, marriage, sexuality, and fertility. Older couples tend to have marriages based on respect while young couples have marriages based on trust. She views the companionate marriage (a marriage characterized by a high degree of sexual intimacy and intense psychological companionship) as something that has emerged not only in migrant families but also in families in Jalisco and Michoacán, Mexico where she also conducted research. Hence, like other researchers she rejects the facile assumption of there (i.e. Mexico) as traditional and here (i.e. the US) as modern. What she views as different between the two contexts is the greater ability among Mexican women in Atlanta to negotiate these changes within the family based on the economic opportunities that are available to them as well as the legal and institutional protections that characterize the US context. Further, while the companionate marriage may offer women more emotional satisfaction, they may also be more fragile. Hirsch argues, for example, that "equal access to intimate companionship is not the same as equal access to power" (p. 156).

Toward the end of her discussion of companionate marriages, Hirsch (2003: 202ff) tells us about being invited to visit a support group for Hispanic battered women in Atlanta. She observes that such a group is an odd context for arguing that Mexican women in the US have more social and economic leverage (are more empowered) than do their counterparts in Mexico. However, many of the women in this group had already left their husbands or were planning to do so and they argued that this option would not have been possible in the home country.

> They spoke about how, with the support of social workers, they had learned to use the law to defend themselves through restraining orders, court-mandated child support, and mandatory batterers' programs for their husbands.
>
> (p. 203)

Not only were there mechanisms to support them in their actions, but they also had the economic wherewithal to stand on their own two feet. They described the domestic violence laws in their own countries as a lot of "blah, blah, blah" because without financial support they were meaningless. Further, they spoke about the anonymity of life in a big city like Atlanta ("nobody gets in your business") making it possible to leave a spouse.

Hirsch's reflections on the issue of domestic violence within immigrant families is representative of a new dimension of gendered immigration research. Sociologists Cecilia Menjívar and Olivia Salcido (2002) opened this discussion by beginning to identify specific factors that exacerbate the already gendered, race, and class vulnerability of immigrant women who confront verbal and physical violence in the home. Among these are limited host-language skills, domestic isolation and dependency, uncertain legal statuses, precarious employment, limited opportunities for alternative living situations, and hence a reluctance to leave an abuser. In many cultural contexts, the family culture discourages a woman from breaking up a marriage. Further, conflicts within the family are considered to be private matters – hence individuals are discouraged from going to the authorities for help. The limited language skills often make it difficult for immigrant women to understand their rights in the country of immigration and/or reach out for help. Host-language deficiencies also restrict access to decent jobs. However, sometimes it is a woman's greater earning power that becomes a source of conflict that can erupt into abuse.

In a more ethnographic study that highlights how some of these issues play out specifically in relation to Hispanics in the United States, Salcido and Adelman (2004) adopt a two-pronged approach. They demonstrate not only how domestic violence (battering) leads to illegality, but also how immigration policies lead to men's battering. In the first case, social scientists who have interviewed female migrants have often discovered that one of the motives for a woman's departure is to escape from a batterer (Arguelles and Rivero 1993) or from gossip that challenges a woman's reputation – a form of verbal abuse (Hart 1997; Brettell 2002; Brennan 2004). Contreras and Griffith (2012) highlight this dimension in their study of Mexican women who have been drawn to North Carolina to work in the Blue Crab industry. The employment opportunities are one draw and seeking them out in order to improve the quality of their children's lives is a motivating factor, but so too is the chance to escape often abusive relationships. By migrating, such relationships can come to an end and women can take control of their own lives.

Domestic violence is also found within Asian immigrant families (Abraham 2000; Mehrotra 1999; Rudrappa 2004; Bhattacharjee 2006). Shamita Das Gupta (1999) has argued that the South Asian community in the United States, in conjunction with the "model minority" image assigned to them by broader American society, has promoted an image of intact and quiescent families where no abuse of women exists. "If any such episode surfaced, [it was] quickly blamed on renegade individuals, particularly pathological relationships, and the working class 'others'" (p. 588). Thus, organizations to address violence against women were slow to emerge within this community and the challenges they have faced are formidable "On the one hand they are struggling against community policing that insistently tries to silence and deny women's reality of abuse, and on the other hand they are striving to empower battered women in the face of a racialized society as well as restrictive immigration and welfare policies" (p. 589). South Asian domestic violence organizations and shelters try to provide a culturally sensitive context where counselors recognize the special concerns of abused women who might not want to reveal their problems to the "whole community" or who have no one and nowhere to turn. As Amita Preisser (1999: 692) observes, among South Asians domestic violence is "not just between a woman and her spouse, but between a woman, her spouse, in-laws, and the community at large." For these women, "obedience to family elders, upholding family honor, fear of losing children, and dictates of religious practices may influence her to suffer in silence rather than to seek help" (p. 692).

Other scholars have taken on issues of sexual abuse, including marital rape, the manipulation of reproductive rights (Abraham 1999), and bride burning (Singh and Unnithan 1999). In South Asia there is no concept of marital rape because a woman is a man's property and marriage is for procreation and hence sexual intercourse is expected to occur with the woman having little right to refuse. In the immigrant context the interplay between these culturally sanctioned sexual rights to a woman's body, combined with discrimination based on ethnic, class, cultural, and structural location of immigrant families (and often the downward mobility experienced by men in particular) may in fact exacerbate sexual abuse (Abraham 1999: 604–605). It is further exacerbated by a perception of American society as sexually permissive and the desire of South Asian men to have as much control as they can over the sexuality of their wives.[7]

So-called "crimes of honor" constitute another dimension of domestic violence within the families of immigrants. In January of 2008, two Dallas area teenage girls, Amina (age eighteen) and Sarah (age seventeen) Said, were killed by their Egyptian Muslim father. He was reported to be a strict father who rarely allowed his daughters to spend time with their friends. Friends of Sarah were reported to have said that when Sarah met a boy at her job she told them that her father would kill her if he found out. The father did not approve of non-Muslim boyfriends, or of boyfriends in general. A cab driver, he drove to a motel in Irving, shot his daughters, left them to die (one called 911 to say she was dying), and disappeared. There were reports of previous abuse;

the girls' great aunt was quoted in the newspaper claiming that the mother had previously fled with her two daughters and that "this was an honor killing" (Eiserer 2008). Services were held in a Christian chapel as well as at the Richardson Mosque – the largest and oldest mosque in the Dallas-Fort Worth (DFW) metropolitan area.

The incident in DFW is not unique. In July of 2008, a Pakistani pizza shop owner in the Atlanta area supposedly killed his daughter to protect family honor. His daughter, whose marriage had been arranged, was seeking a divorce from a husband much older than she and often absent. Her father, it was reported, thought that divorce would bring shame upon the family. He was quoted as saying that his daughter "wasn't being true to her religion or to her husband" (Tarabay 2009). In this case the father admitted to his crime and turned himself in. And in Chicago, Subash Chander, killed his pregnant daughter, son-in-law and 3-year-old grandson "because he disapproved of his daughter's marriage to a lower caste man" (CBS News 2008). And more than a decade earlier an Iranian immigrant in California killed his wife and six children by burning his house down. The reason he gave to law enforcement was that his wife was having "illegitimate relationships with male strangers" (Mahdi 1999: 69). Examples of so-called honor killings in the US extend beyond the Muslim community. Alison Renteln (2004) cites cases among Chinese and Hmong immigrants – men who killed their wives when confronted by adultery or some other indication of wayward female sexuality.

Some scholars have attempted to analyze why this occurs within immigrant communities. Most often, it is linked with a broader literature on domestic violence that we have been discussing here (Narayan 1995; Ayyob 2000; Sheehan et al. 2000). Indeed, sometimes those within Muslim immigrant communities attempt to draw on this discourse in order to turn attention away from Islam itself and from cultural explanations rooted in codes of honor and honor killings, and by extension away from the stigma and racism that may accordingly be directed toward them (Werbner 2005: 32). Turkish sociologist Akpinar (2003) suggests that the immigrant context enhances the role of women as bearers of group identity and that abuse emerges when women violate ideas of acceptable femininity. This happens, because in the immigrant context women may gain more freedom as well as economic responsibility as potential wage earners; correspondingly, men may experience downward social mobility, greater marginalization, and a loss of self-esteem. Immigrant men who feel that they are discriminated against may turn inward and exert patriarchal control over women (wives and daughters) because this is something they still can control. Powerlessness in the public sphere generates a desire to exercise more power in the domestic sphere (Akpinar 2003: 428, 435). Drawing on the work of Baker et al. (1999), Akpinar writes:

> women's increased autonomy and threatened traditional male privilege due to increased acceptance of women's human rights puts men into a potential shameful position ... These individual men may resort to violence, especially in times of economic and/or social stress, towards women – to protect their honour, or in other words not to experience shame.
>
> (p. 427)

The ethnic community becomes an important reference group against which one's own worth is measured. Akpinar (2003: 436) describes how gossip and stigma among Turks living in a Swedish suburb become mechanisms "for the control of women by men as a group, but also among women themselves as a punishment for those who deviate from the norms."[8]

A final observation is worth making, and here I take my inspiration from sociologist Yen Le Espiritu's (2001) work on Filipino immigrants in the United States. Immigrant women, and by extension their daughters, are the ones charged with preserving culture. Thus their bodies are policed, Espiritu suggests, and this is the main means by which immigrant groups who are otherwise defined as economically, socially, politically, and legally inferior can assert their moral superiority. "This rhetoric of moral superiority often leads to patriarchal calls for cultural 'authenticity' that locates family honor and national integrity in the group's female members" (Espiritu 2001: 435).

Transnational Parenthood

The family life of migrants has been significantly impacted by trans-national practices (Abrego 2014). One dimension of this impact is the growing significance of long-distance parenting (Carling, Menjívar, and Schmalzbauer 2012), and particularly of trans-national motherhood that has developed as increasing numbers of women have migrated in response to the growth of the global gendered labor force discussed in Chapter 3. Transnational motherhood refers to the "circuits of affection, caring, and financial support [on the part of mothers] that transcend national borders" (Hondagneu-Sotelo and Avila 1997: 550). As anthropologist Heather Millman (2013:73) has emphasized, the daily lives of transnational mothers "involves the constant negotiation of geographies, economics, and social and familial roles." How can one continue to be both physically absent and a "good" mother or parent?

There are myriad examples of this transnational mothering among immigrant women across the globe who have decided to leave their children with surrogate caregivers or "other mothers," usually a relative and often their own mothers, while they migrate to distant places in search of waged-work (Schmalzbauer 2004).[9] Thus, their own mobility brings grandparents as non-migrants into the activities of the transnational social field. It also serves to reframe conceptualizations of motherhood. As sociologist Umut Erel (2002: 132) has observed, "the separation of mothers and children runs counter to hegemonic discourses on the mother as the primary caretaker of her children, and the emotional, physical and thus geographical closeness that is claimed and naturalized by such discourses." How do transnational mothers react to this situation?

Often, they adjust their ideas about what it means to be a good mother in order to accommodate the decision they have made to live and work apart from their children. Many Latina domestic workers, and particularly those who are serving as live-in nannies in the United States (and hence cannot bring their own children with them), forthrightly reject the notion that they have abandoned their children and concertedly work to minimize estrangement between themselves and their offspring. According to sociologists Pierrette Hondagneu-Sotelo and Ernestine Avila (1997), they convince themselves that their children are better off at home than with them and that their own physical absence does not mean emotional absence. They redefine "motherhood" to encompass their role as breadwinners and they expand their understanding of caregiving to include the wages they earn as domestic workers. Thus, transnational mothers often "juxtapose traditional ideas of physical and emotional nurturing with realities of nurturing from outside of their own domestic sphere, providing physical support that comes from remittances and emotional help through technological mediums such as the internet or over the phone" (Millman 2013: 77). This redefinition of the meaning of motherhood has been documented for a range of societies around the world. For example, Peruvian migrant women in Chile view the abandonment of their children "as part of an exercise of responsible motherhood in that [it] . . . is motivated by the need to secure family welfare. It is because of an almost heroic sense of responsibility and love for her children that a mother undertakes the journey to an unknown country, even if it means separation from her loved ones" (Illanes 2010: 211). Similar ideas about self-sacrifice and responsibility are expressed by Ecuadorian immigrant women in Italy who also articulate a form of "double living" – their bodies are in Italy but their hearts and souls are in Ecuador (Boccagni 2012).

What of the emotional needs, or "embodied distress" (Horton 2009), of mothers themselves who often allude to the pain of separation and to feelings of sadness, regret, guilt, and incompleteness (Illanes 2010: 211)? Anthropologist Sarah Horton explores the compartmentalized lives of mostly undocumented Salvadoran women who are workers in the US and mothers in El Salvador, placing particular emphasis on how separations are negotiated intersubjectively between these women and their children. She observes that the conversations that occur between mothers and children prior to departure result in a sense of "profound moral failure" among mothers who are unable to continue as physical caretakers for their children in order to secure the financial and physical wellbeing of their children by working abroad. "As children challenge their mothers' absence, mothers attempt to situate their migration in a context of continuing love" (Horton 2009: 30).

These transformations in the meaning of mother love are also considered by sociologist Rhacel Parreñas in her work on "mothering from a distance" among Filipina domestic workers in Italy and the United States. Parreñas (2001a: 381) makes reference to a form of "commodified love" based on purchasing things to send to children who have been left behind in the sending country. The mediation of physical absence through commodities which act as "communicative devices expressing social bonds and belonging" has also been identified among Ukranian and Ecuadorian transnational parents in Spain (Leifsen and Tymczuk 2012: 220). And anthropologist Sarah Horton (2009) has found a similar emphasis among the Salvadoran families she studied. Drawing on her interviews with one research participant, Gloria, Horton (2009: 33) writes:

> Gloria and her husband sent their children toys and luxuries they had never before enjoyed – a color TV, a VCR, a freezer, brand-name clothing, jewelry, comforters, and toy cars. As Gloria thinks back on the comforts she provided her children, her face lights up in a smile. She rattles the objects off in a long list, each item punctuated by the phrase "which we never had over there." "Casi todo" ("Almost everything"), she says. Her children wear the bracelets and new clothes to school; they are popular and receive invitations for playdates from friends who wish to share in their good fortune. "Their friends tell them that they have the best mother in the world," she says, laughing with pride.

And yet these mothers also acknowledge the frustrations that their children express regarding their absence. Money and goods are not a total substitute. Thus Horton quotes one child's query to her mother: "You only send me things; you don't visit and you barely call. How can I know you love me?" (p. 34). As Horton observes, this unease regarding the strength of maternal love is aggravated when a mother has other children while abroad, children who can enjoy the daily physical presence of a mother while those left behind cannot.[10]

Sociologist Rhacel Parreñas (2001b) suggests that while the Filipina women she studied work hard at their transnational motherhood, such households are considered "broken" because they diverge from what is considered a normative, cohabiting family with the woman performing the primary childcare responsibilities. This image emerges despite the more egalitarian gender structure in the Philippines (bilateral kinship, women with comparable levels of education to men and a high rate of participation in the labor force). A similar negative image also seems to emerge in Sri Lanka in relation to the families of women who have migrated to the Middle East to work as housemaids on two-year labor contracts, leaving their husbands and children behind. Sri Lankan villagers, as well as local politicians and the national media, have expressed concern about the long-term effects of maternal absence on children. While children do not experience abuse and neglect, they do receive reduce education, and paternal alcohol consumption has increased (Gamburd 2000, 2008). According to anthropologist Michele Gamburd (2000), when women breadwinners return from abroad they face backlash and are subjected to accusations of prostitution and marital infidelity. In short, their reputation and image as wives and mothers is subverted and once back home, they tend to abandon their cosmopolitan identity in order to minimize these accusations and the sometimes violent behavior that accompanies them. But the image of men is also undermined.

Men, bereft of the "breadwinner" role, suffered a challenge to their masculinity. In both villages, migrants reported hearing Arabs speculate that "Sri Lankan men must be donkeys because they send their women abroad to work." Images of uneducated, slothful husbands suggested that men wasted the money their wives earned abroad. Sinhala stereotypes portrayed men turning to alcohol (an exclusively masculine beverage) to drown their troubles: in Muslim stereotypes, men did not drink, but smoked, gambled and womanized like their Sinhala counterparts. Representations of the delinquent, emasculated men appeared in tandem with the images of promiscuous, selfish, pleasure-seeking women who neglected their husbands and children.

(Gamburd 1999: 5)

In the state of Kerala, in southwest India, as in Sri Lanka, Malayali men who are left behind while their wives work in domestic service in Italy also have to contend with emasculating public identities (Gallo 2006). They are known as "waiting men", biding their time until a visa is approved for them or dependent on their wife's remittances. Further, they are made fun of because they have no control of the sexuality of their absent wives who reside within the intimacy of Italian domestic space. They are equally emasculated when they travel to join wives working abroad. Often they are given positions in the same household in work that is perceived as feminizing. And yet Italians often view them as "good south Asians" by contrast with South Asian men from the Punjab who are often in Italy without families. Anthropologist Ester Gallo (2006: 368) sums up the complexities of these transnational gender identities as follows:

Through the rhetoric of Italy as a "feminizing" place, Malayali men in transnational marriages make meaningful and contest their difficult and conflicting experiences of downward mobility and being "dependent husbands" or "displaced householders and fathers." Indeed, men's conjugal ties with women working in Italy and their relationships within the employers' households in turn impact on how Malayali society perceives men with wives in Italy or who migrate following marriage ... Men's transnational marital experiences, through their dependence on women's remittances and sponsorship, are socially constructed as a symbol of lower status. On the other hand ... this rhetoric may assume different meanings across places. Thus, in the highly constrained labour market of central Italy, the feminization of Malayali migrants is used ambiguously to construct respectable male identity in the eyes of Italian society. Men's conjugal status emerges as crucially important in shaping not only their working relations and everyday life, but also their public respectability and legal status.

While transnational motherhood, including its impact on husbands and children left behind, has received a good deal of scholarly attention, the significance of transnational fatherhood and its association with the construction of masculine identities should not be overlooked. Indeed, the long-distance parenting of male migrants is, in some sense, implicit. By this I mean that in many contexts, for example Mexico or Portugal, there is an historically rooted culture of migration that includes the expectation that men will migrate and support their families from afar (Brettell 1986; Cohen 2004). For some time in such places, the father as breadwinner has been equivalent to the father as migrant and both are part of what it means in these contexts to be a good father.

One out of every twenty-five Mexican children has a migrant father in the US (Nobles 2011). Those who are married are more likely to be in involved in the lives of children who remain in Mexico. They visit as much as they can and invest in their education, something that sociologist Jenna Nobles argues is in fact a long-term investment in the development of Mexico. In another study of Mexican families in New Jersey, sociologist Joanna Dreby (2006) has identified three types of transnational families, types that parallel those that I found when working with Portuguese immigrant families in France in the 1970s (Brettell 1995). These types are: fathers who leave their wives and children behind, migrating alone; couples who migrate together leaving minor children in Mexico; and mothers who are unwed mothers or separated or divorced who leave children and migrate alone. Dreby finds that the emotional responses of men and women to being separated from their children differ and she links this to gender ideology in Mexico where a woman's role as mother is "sacralized" while the father's role is tied to financial provisioning. She observes that while a mother's relationship to her children in Mexico is very dependent on being able to show emotional intimacy from a distance, the fathers' relationships are rooted in their success as migrant workers. If a father cannot fulfill his role as a provider, he grows more distant from his children. A father, even one who has had relationships with other women while abroad, maintains his image as a "good" father if he is sending money back to his family. Conversely, if Mexican women do not show dimensions of stress and suffering related to being physically absent from their children, they can be subjected to accusations of being a "bad" mother and abandoning their children. Dreby (2006: 56) concludes as follows:

> Migration does not appear to significantly transform notions of Mexican motherhood and fatherhood even though it does change parenting activities. Fathers' relationships with their children are directly related to their ability to honorably fulfill the role of economic provider for the family. When fathers are successful economically as migrants, they tend to maintain stable and regular relationships with children in Mexico regardless of marital status. In contrast, even though Mexican mothers migrate to work like fathers, their relationships with children once abroad depend on their ability to demonstrate emotional intimacy from a distance.

Thus, a critical question is how fatherhood and masculinity are redefined or reaffirmed in connection with migration. Anthropologist Jason Pribilsky (2012) examines this issue in relation to undocumented Ecuadorian men living in New York City. He describes men who balance their desires for the good things of life in New York with their responsibility to send money back home to their families ("remittance discipline") and hence act as responsible fathers. This requires a mental shift, Pribilsky observes, from a subsistence orientation ("making a living") to a surplus generating orientation ("working for money") so that there is money to remit. The latter means learning how to save and learning how not to spend or consume. Men are drawn into the world of money management, a world dominated by their wives back in Ecuador. One of the most serious consumption dilemmas is what to do about alcohol, something they are routinely used to consuming in Ecuador. Ecuadorian migrant men, as primary breadwinners, tend to forego alcohol in order to save money to support their families. Alcohol no longer defines masculinity; saving money does make these Ecuadorians "more modern" men by comparison with their fathers and with those men who remain behind in Ecuador. Like the Filipina transnational mothers described by Parreñas, these Ecuadorian fathers construct the meaning of good fatherhood in the gifts that they send back to recognize the birthdays and other important events in the lives of their children.

> The act of remitting gifts and the accompanying tasks of shopping, packaging gifts up with letters and receiving family members' reactions to the purchase allowed men to look towards their home communities and produce a coherent identity of themselves as successful migrants, committed husbands and attentive fathers.
>
> (Pribilsky 2012: 336)

Migration not only changes "traditional" gender roles including the division of labor but also alters the meanings of gender categories. Men, especially those who have left their families behind, assume responsibility for their own domestic lives, adopting female roles, and women sometimes are doing what their husbands normally did.

> Beyond "degendering" male and female tasks ... namely removing the assignation of specific behavior to one gender or another, couples must also work in tandem to "learn to exist side by side" (*aprender a convivir*) in order to meet their goals of success in migration. Indeed, what counts as "success" for many migrant households – minimally defined as a couple's ability to "get ahead" (*salir adelante*) with remittances – depends as much or more on wives' ability to work with husbands to orchestrate household affairs and handle remittances as it does on the hard labor of husbands abroad.
>
> (Pribilsky 2004: 316)

As part of an effort to emphasize the more emotional and personal dimensions of the transnational family and transnational fatherhood in particular, sociologist Veronica Montes (2013) explores how men move away from the expected hegemonic masculine identity (being unemotional, non-nurturing, dispassionate, and aggressive) and toward emotional expressions of love and caring. Migrant men express the emotional cost of being separated from family differently from migrant women, often through drug and alcohol use. But some have used the situation of separation to reflect in more demonstrative ways about why they are abroad, how they feel about living apart from their wives and children, and about what their families mean to them. They articulate these feelings in relation to ideas about sacrifice, nostalgia, love, sadness, and anxiety – all fully contrary to the ideas about what it means to be masculine with which they were raised. For example, Montes (2013: 483) offers the following comment from one of her research participants, a man named Daniel:

> One takes the risk to migrate for the love of the offspring, in order to give them a better life. I don't care if I don't get my papers, if I die without papers; what matters is that my children have better opportunities, a better life [crying]. I don't care if I have to go through the same again, risking everything again, as long as my son has the opportunity to achieve what we [my wife and I] did not achieve. My job has not finished yet; my job will finish when I see my son going to college and becoming a good man. That's why I do not go out so much because of the fear of getting deported.

Cultural context is equally important for understanding the impact of transnational families on ideas of masculinity, particularly in situations where women are the migrant breadwinners and their husbands are left behind to assume caregiving and other domestic tasks that were carried out by women prior to their departure. In some contexts men do not openly admit how much housework they are doing for fear that it will undermine their masculinity (Gamburd 2000). In other contexts men call on the assistance of extended family members or older children to avoid becoming primary caregivers for their children. In Vietnam, a context where women are seen as making important economic contributions to the family and where men have always contributed to childcare (Hoang and Yeoh 2011), men with migrant breadwinner wives, and the wives themselves, maintain the idea that the new domestic responsibilities that fall on men left behind is a temporary situation and does not undermine either their masculinity or their role as the head of household and the decision maker. Vietnamese men insist that their wives would not have migrated without their consent.

Others acknowledge that their wives do not always remit money back, but appear to deny that this has an impact on their sense of themselves as men – although beneath the surface it clearly does aggravate some that their wives maintain so much control of the money they earn.

Fathering is an important dimension of masculine identity in Vietnam and hence men step into the role of primary caregiver while their wives are working abroad. However, it is exhausting because at the same time they are working to bring some resources in to the household. The paid work is important to them so that they do not look like "spongers."

> Some men were torn between fathering responsibilities and the sense of masculinity attached to their breadwinner role when their wives decided not to remit her income. Instead of applying pressure on the woman to remit, they worked longer hours (and thus spent less time with and for the children) or borrowed money from other people to pay for daily expenses (if possible). Clearly, one identity contradicts the other in these instances and the men's ability to keep their sense of masculinity intact compromises their efforts to be good fathers. Conversely, other men readjusted their livelihood strategies to accommodate family duties at the expense of their breadwinner status and economic autonomy . . . Women's labor migration has indeed given new meanings to the notion of masculinity, and gender boundaries are shifting along with ongoing global economic restructuring.
>
> (Hoang and Yeoh 2011: 734)

Hoang and Yeoh (2011: 734) argue that the Vietnamese case challenges a universal crisis of masculinities resulting from the migration of women and supports an approach that views gender roles as malleable and flexible in the face of population mobility.

A different transnational family form, described by the term "astronauting," is found in close association with emigrants from some parts of Asia. For example, it is discussed by Pe-Pua, et al. (1996) for Hong Kong immigrants in Sydney, Australia; by Wong (1998) for recent Chinese immigrants in the San Francisco area; by Min (1998) for Korean families in the US, and by Chee (2005) and Chiang (2008) for Taiwanese immigrants in Canada and the

United States. Astronauts are "people who travel, live, and work in different parts of the world as they explore opportunities in the global village (Wong 1998: 87). Some "astronauting" began as an adaptive strategy in relation to the corporate downsizing in the US during the 1990s; in other cases it was simply the inability to find sustained employment abroad. The difference between these families and other transnational families is that the children are left in the country of immigration while one or more parent works in the country of origin. Most commonly it is the father/husband who returns to the home country and commutes back to see his wife and children. The decision is often taken so that children can pursue the advantages of the host country educational system. In these families, the father lives where he can best fulfill his role as breadwinner; the mother often remains in her role as primary care-taker and hence with the children.

Scholars who explore the impact of astronaut and other "split household"[11] transnational family arrangements on women as workers, wives and mothers, and on marital relations, observe that husbands and wives maintain contact in transnational space through fax, telephone, email and travel, all of which reflects their class background and access to economic resources (Chee 2005). Also of interest is the impact on the children and in the context of this research, some researchers have described a variant transnational family form that involves what have come to be termed "parachute kids." Parachute kids are children sent to or left behind with a friend or relative or other caregiver while both parents remain in or return to the home country (Orellana et al. 2001; Tsong and Liu 2009). One study conducted in 1990 estimated a total of 40,000 Taiwanese unaccompanied minors between the ages of eight and eighteen living in the United States with smaller numbers from South Korea and Hong Kong. Another study identified 7,000 unaccompanied Korean minors in elementary and secondary schools in southern California in 1997 (both studies cited in Tsong and Liu 2009: 367). Chiang-Hom (2004), based on research with unaccompanied Chinese adolescents born abroad but living in the US, found that 36 percent were living with a relative (6 percent with a grandparent), 30 percent were with paid caretakers, 5 percent were with siblings only, 5 percent with friends of the family, 4 percent with a cousin, and 3 percent entirely alone.

While the primary motive for this transnational migration strategy is, as mentioned above, to take advantage of primary and secondary education in the host country, and eventually university education, some of the other motivations are highly gendered. Tsong and Liu (2009: 368) point, for example, to the desire of parents in South Korea and Taiwan to avoid compulsory military service for their sons; alternatively they may send their daughters to act as caregivers for younger brothers in the US. Educating children in the US is also a symbol of higher status. Needless to say, much of the research explores the psychological impact of these familial situations on children, identifying feelings of loneliness, homesickness, and depression but also a rapid maturity and sense of responsibility and role reversal – the latter particularly in the case of astronaut families where sons become the "man of the household" (Zhou 1998; Alaggia et al. 2001; Chiang-Hom 2004).

In summary, transnational parents, no matter what their strategy, are operating in both productive and reproductive roles across space. As some researchers have emphasized, "the essence of migrant transnationalism is that physical absence is compatible with social presence and participation" and hence the subject of transnational parenthood places emphasis on "how the parent–child relationship is practiced and experienced within the constraints of physical separation" (Carling et al. 2012: 192).

The Gendered Dimension of Remittances

One of the important transnational mechanisms linking migrants abroad and those who remain in the country of origin is economic remittances. Economic remittances are transfers of money from a foreign worker to the home country. The World Bank has estimated that the flow of remittance funds to the developing countries totaled a little more than 400 billion in 2012 and the expectation for 2014 was that this would rise to 436 billion.

In 2013 the countries receiving the highest volume of officially recorded remittances were India ($71 billion), China ($60 billion), the Philippines ($26 billion), Mexico ($22 billion), Nigeria ($21 billion), and Egypt ($20 billion).[12]

Remittances have played and continue to play a very important role in the economies of developing as well as some developed countries and they certainly impact the lives of individual families.[13] In Portugal in the 1960s and 1970s it was the remittances of male and sometimes female workers abroad that provided the resources to build new houses, what came to be known as "casas francesas" – the homes of Portuguese migrant workers who lived in France (Brettell 1986). Today one sees such houses in China (Chu 2010), in the state of Kerala in India (Kurien 2002), and in many of the small villages of Mexico and other parts of Central and South America. Early studies of the impact of remittances noted that much of the money was spent on conspicuous consumer items (deemed a negative) rather than for economic investment (deemed a positive) that would spur economic development (Rhoades 1978; Gmelch 1980; Gardner 1995). While recent research in places such as Thailand and Mexico (Gullette 2009, 2012, 2013; Cohen 2011) has offered a more positive view of the impact of remittances on local development, anthropologists Sarah Mahler and Patricia Pessar (2006: 45) critique the entire debate about the productive or unproductive (positive versus negative) use of economic remittances as gender-biased. They note that the bulk of remittances goes to women who are demeaned and disciplined by a discourse that undervalues expenditures on family sustenance (food, shelter, clothing, education) by labeling them unproductive. Clearly, there are significant gendered dimensions to remittances but they are rarely considered (Kunz 2008). "Remittances reflect and transmit power" (Mahler and Pessar 2006: 45) and hence knowing who earns the funds, to whom are they sent, on what are they spent, who has control of such expenditures, and whom they ultimately benefit is exceedingly important.

Emphasizing that remittances should be conceptualized as a social process, sociologists Mizanur Rahman and Lian Kwen Fee (2009) have explored the gendered dimensions of funds remitted by Indonesian domestic workers who have migrated to Singapore, Hong Kong, and Malaysia. They find that female domestic workers in general remit a much larger portion of their earnings than do their male counterparts and these funds are most commonly directed to mothers and sisters rather than to brothers, fathers, and husbands.[14] Gender differences are also found in the use of such remittances, with female recipients directing them toward investments in human capital and male recipients investing in physical capital. Through remittances many young women enhance not only their own social status in the sending community but also that of their families.

In the North American context the bulk of remittances is sent by Hispanic (Mexican and Central American) men to their wives left behind in the countries of origin. What do these remittances mean to these women? Sean McKenzie and Cecilia Menjívar (2011) explore the more emotional dimension of remittances for Honduran women who continue to live in their home villages while their husbands and sons are abroad. Many accept the hardship of separation if it results in their ability to build a new home with the money their spouses send home. These resources also open up educational opportunities for their children and provide them with better clothing and nourishment. However, the meaning of remittances, these authors observe, goes well beyond the economic. They describe a seventy-year-old woman whose three sons were working in the US who views remittances as more than increased money for the household to spend: "those home repairs and extra finances meant love, commitment and sacrifice, meanings intimately linked to the social milieu in which they are formed" (McKenzie and Menjívar 2011: 69).

Are remittances a source of empowerment for the women left behind? There is certainly evidence that supports a positive answer to this question. For example, in my own work on Portuguese wives who remained in home villages while their husbands migrated to France in the 1960s and 1970s, I identified any number of cases where these wives assumed the role as heads of household. They managed the continued cultivation of family plots of land and they often oversaw the construction of a new house. They represented the household at village meetings. However, in the Portuguese case, these patterns have deep historical roots that resonate with other dimensions of life in northern rural Portugal including naming and social identity practices, inheritance patterns, patterns of rural employment (particularly day laboring), and high rates of out-of-wedlock births (Brettell 1986).

More recent research on more contemporary migrations has begun to challenge or at least nuance the discussion of whether remittances truly empower women or change gender norms about formal sector work. Economists Catalina Amuedo-Dorantes and Susan Pozo (2006), for example, find that in Mexico remittances do not reduce the male labor supply, but do reduce the female labor supply by ten percent, particularly in rural areas. They suggest that this substantiates the conclusion that women engage in waged-work only when male income is insufficient. Remittances allow a portion of wives left behind to remain in the household. Research in Morocco has found that although the wives of male migrants live more comfortably and securely and assume responsibility for decision-making, many of them view this as a burden (De Haas and van Rooij 2010). This is equally true of Honduran women who claim that male migration has created more work for them and that the additional responsibilities generate stress and anxiety (McKenzie and Menjívar 2011: 76–77). Some of the stress comes from an increased work load and some of it from having to manage the debt created by their husband's migration. Very often remittances first go to pay off these debts and hence the family cannot enjoy the more tangible benefits that remittances might ultimately bring.

In the Moroccan context mentioned above, it is the in-laws with whom the wife lives who most often take responsibility for how remittances are spent. Thus, while changes have occurred recently in the lives and social position of women in rural Morocco, this may be only partially explained by male migration and remittances. The same is true in rural Armenia and Guatemala (Menjívar and Agadjanian 2007). In these locations, women have little control over how money is spent and see little increase in their independence and autonomy, primarily because they are watched by their husband's relatives and by an absent husband who remains in touch via telephone to monitor behavior. Women reported that it was their husbands who decided whether they could work outside the home and who largely remained in control of the money they remitted. In these contexts, a woman working outside the home reflected poorly on the husband, indicating that he was not successful abroad. This observation suggests that the impact of remittances on masculinity is also important to consider.

It is precisely this question that sociologist Hung Cam Thai (2006) addresses. Among transnational Vietnamese families he identifies three types of male economic remitters: status remitters, altruistic remitters, and contract remitters. Here, Thai is building on the work of sociologist Leah Vanwey (2004) who, based on research among rural urban migrants in Thailand, demonstrates that female migrants and poorer migrants are more altruistic in their remittance behavior (that is, sending money to increase the welfare of family members), while male migrants and migrants from wealthier households are more contractual in their remittance behavior (that is, sending money to non-family members to repay a debt, pay for education, or purchase a piece of land, etc.). Thai argues that status remitters "send money for claiming and valorizing social worth in the community of origin" (p. 255). Often the recipients of their remittances are not family members but other individuals with whom they want to retain social ties. Status remitters engage in small-scale conspicuous consumption, and gain deference, recognition, and respect when they return to Vietnam. They gain "importance". Thai (2006: 264) argues that these low wage men are "more likely than women, and more likely than economically privileged Vietnamese immigrants to feel compelled to claim social positions at "home" [because] social positions [are] often denied to them in the country of migration as a result of being low wage racialized men."[15]

The altruistic remitters, usually adult children or siblings of recipients of remittances, direct their money to improving the welfare of their family. These remitters constituted about half the participants in his study. They express the most stress about the burden of sending money home, observing that to cease sending money would mean the termination of ties with family members. They rarely share with these family members the sacrifices they make in the country of immigration in order to send money home. Further, what they can afford to send and what those in the homeland expect them to send are often not the same and their failure to match expectations poses challenges to their masculine identity. To sustain this identity, some send more than they can afford, thus not only going without in the country of immigration but also sometimes into debt.

The contractual remitters, often older men who are the most likely to return to Vietnam, are engaging in reimbursement for past or future expenses associated with their departure. Often, Thai points out, these individuals "enter a remittance relationship because it allows them leverage for taking partial ownership of properties and land that they could take residence upon their visits" (Thai 2006: 255; see also Thai 2005). This is a strategy used in response to laws that make it difficult for Vietnamese abroad to own properties in Vietnam and is an insurance policy in relation to potential return. These remitters experience the least stress and can achieve personal goals that enhance both their social status and their self-worth.

While scholars generally focus on economic remittances, several years ago sociologist Peggy Levitt (1996: 926) formulated the concept of social remittances to refer to "the ideas, behaviors, identities, and social capital that flow from receiving- to sending-country communities" (see also Levitt and Lamba-Nieves 2011). Clearly, social remittances have numerous implications for gender relations and gender ideologies. The critical question is: have these changed as a result of outmigration, transnational connections, and return migration? Some of these changes have already been alluded to but they require further elaboration.

Levitt herself (2001) has discussed the young women from the Dominican village of Miraflores who changed their ideas about the kinds of men they wanted to marry based on ideas they had learned while working abroad. Further, young women who had remained behind in the village noticed that when couples returned to visit they appeared to make more decisions together and the husband was more respectful of his wife. They began to seek the same equality for themselves. Anthropologists working in other regions of Latin America have documented similar changes in ideas and practices. Kimberly Grimes (1998) describes the increasing consumerism that has emerged in Mexican sending communities as well as the impact of mass media and other new technologies on the lives of those who have remained behind. More important to the discussion here is her analysis of the impact of migration on gender relations – the liberal attitudes that are brought back, the attack on the macho image, and the general loosening of gender norms such that returned migrant men often help with household chores and child rearing. Deborah Boehm (2008a) describes Mexican women who increasingly assume the roles previously performed by men – they manage household finances, supervise farm labor, oversee home construction and renovation, and attend community meetings. As a result, new ideas about womanhood as less passive and more independent are emerging. And finally, anthropologist Julia Pauli (2008) describes a traumatic relationship between Mexican wives and their mothers-in-law with whom they live when their husbands depart for the United States. These Mexican wives use the remittances sent by husbands to construct a home of their own so that they can achieve some independence. Pauli suggests that the changes associated with these new patterns of residence are likely to erode the status and security of the elderly population living in these sending villages

The impact of social remittances on gender roles and ideologies is increasingly being documented in international migration flows to other receiving societies around the world. Yemeni migrants who have returned from East Africa bring back an experience of a different gender order – of places where women do not wear a veil, where there is less gender segregation such that men and women socialize more easily, and where there are more educational opportunities for women (Christiansen 2012). Some of these return migrants attempt to position themselves according to these new gendered guides for action and living a life. Similarly, Romanian migrants who return from working in Italy, often as a result of a decision made by a husband, nevertheless begin to challenge gender relations (Vlase 2013). And social analyst Sule Akkoyunlu (2013) argues that Turkish migration to European Union and OECD countries has an impact on people's attitudes and preferences and by extension on the participation of women in politics, measured in this case in relation to their participation in the Turkish Parliament. This author cautions, however, that the nature of social remittances and their impact on gender ideologies may vary depending on the destination country. But what is important about this study in particular is that it reveals the potential of social remittances for changing gender roles and relations not only in the domestic sphere but also in the public sphere – whether in the realm of politics, in the realm of religion, or in the realm of entrepreneurial enterprises. Thus sociologist Peggy Levitt (nd) has observed that Pakistani women become involved in the management of Islamic Centers in the United States and then take these ideas back to their home countries, calling for more collective spaces of prayer for women. And Brazilian women have taken back to Brazil the idea of organization leadership, whether in churches or in other neighborhood groups.

Conclusion

Anthropologist Jennifer Hirsch (2003: 266) astutely points out that a good deal of the theoretical literature on gender and migration is framed in relation to resource theory and hence argues that women's participation in waged work provides the basis for challenges to traditional gender relations within the family. Gender theory, she suggests, emphasizes that even when women have greater access to economic resources through waged work, gender ideologies may in fact limit processes of empowerment. More nuanced research on what is meant by empowerment and how it is differentially constructed and experienced is therefore essential to a full understanding of how migration impacts gender relations within the family. Certainly in some cases greater gender-egalitarianism emerges as a result of women's full-time employment. In other cases men's lives are also changed as a result of chronic or periodic unemployment and the need to assume more domestic responsibilities. Men, in particular, may experience lower self-esteem and challenges to their sense of masculinity as a result of a loss in their traditional breadwinner role within the family. Gender relations within the family may, in all these cases, be renegotiated. But equally, traditional gender hierarchies can be reinforced. Or gender relations may be renegotiated in some contexts but not in others, hence challenging a simple continuum from disempowerment to empowerment.

How migration impacts gender relations in the family (including patriarchal relations) thus varies not only in relation to issues of male and female employment but also in association with factors such as the culture of origin, social class status (and the human capital associated with it), legal status, auspices of migration (male first, female first, as a couple together), and access to resources (extended family, neighbors and compatriots, institutional support) in the country of immigration. Gender relations may also be affected by how a family copes with the inequalities, including racism and discrimination, which it may confront in the broader host society. Further, just as relations between husbands and wives can change, so too do intergenerational relations, resulting often in role reversals where parents come to rely on their children to help them interface with the language and social institutions of the society of immigration. Parental relations with sons may be more lenient than those with daughters, resulting in tensions and conflicts over issues such as choice of friends, dating, college, marriage, and career choices. Commonly, adolescent girls raised in immigrant families have fewer freedoms and less autonomy in making decisions than do their brothers. The gendered and intergenerational tensions that emerge sometimes erupt into domestic violence.

If anything, gender relations for migrant families are fluid and contingent and constantly in a process of formation and reformation, contestation and re-contestation. This is as true in the space of the sending society as it is in the space of the host society. It is equally true of the transnational spaces between. How migrants, men and women, operate within transnational social fields has become fundamental to our understanding of twenty-first-century mobility. Migrant women, in particular, have redefined dimensions of motherhood to accommodate their physical absence; but so too do migrant men, who equally act as fathers from a distance. And for those families that are operating transnationally, with one parent in the society of immigration and another in the sending society, the economic and social remittances that 'travel' can have varying impacts. For some women left behind remittances can enhance their status and autonomy as household decision-makers. In other contexts gender roles and gender ideologies remain unchanged or women become less autonomous and more dependent on resources that flow from outside.

Concluding Thoughts:
A Gendered Theory of Migration

By now, the scholarly literature that explores the relationship between gender and migration is exceedingly rich and suggests that future studies of population mobility must take gender (that is, the social construction and meaning of differences between men and women) into account to understand decisions to migrate, processes of border crossing (where immigration policies and laws come into play), experiences of settling into a new social, economic, and political context in the place(s) of destination, and the transnational practices that sustain associations with a home country. Gender shapes the "reality" of migration, just as it shapes other social realities. Some of the research discussed in this book illustrates, for example, how the meanings of motherhood and fatherhood (and of being a "good mother" or a "good father") are redefined and renegotiated in relation to geographical movement. Globally, families have had to and continue to adapt to the migration process. Non-migrating men are sometimes assuming domestic and caretaking responsibilities that traditionally fell to their now mobile wives. Alternatively, women who remain behind while their husbands migrate take on new tasks as they adapt to the transnational family of which they are now a part.

Women migrants in particular have been moved, analytically and theoretically, out of the category of being solely dependent or associational migrants – that is, individuals who follow a spouse. Indeed, even our understanding of the complexity of "dependent migration" has become more nuanced. As sociolo-

172

gist Shawn Mailai Kanaiaupuni (2000: 1336) observes, "often, in fact, economic motivations are hidden under the pretext of an associational move, which not only represents the 'proper' reason for migration in many social contexts, but also the mode that most facilitates entry into the US." In addition, the research on female migrants has been supplemented in important and insightful ways with research on the gendered dimensions of the male migrant experience and more broadly on gendered relations of power within and beyond the household in places of origin and places of destination. In the context of contemporary mobilities research, it is important to recognize that migration and stasis are not opposing processes but interconnected dimensions of the human experience (Glick Schiller and Salazar 2013). From this perspective, research on migration should focus equally on the constraints on mobility that derive, for example, from a legal context or from "global racializing categories" (Glick Schiller and Salazar 2013: 188), but also those related to gender ideologies that vary from one cultural context to another as well as over time.

A gendered theory of migration must be intersectional in its approach such that gender differences are situated in relation to class, race, and even religion and immigration status. However, there is more work to be done to better understand how "deserving" and "undeserving" or "desirable" and "undesirable" immigrants are constructed in relation to their intersectional positionality. Among other things, such constructions are apparent within labor markets, in relation to legislation affecting economic migrants as well as those seeking political asylum, as dimensions of civic engagement, and as attributes of transnational practices. Sociologist Kanaiaupuni (2000: 1337), for example, has argued that educated Mexican women may be more likely to migrate internationally than internally because they face "great[er] gender discrimination and fewer occupational rewards" in their home country than they do abroad. On the other hand, both male and female migrants will confront labor market segmentation to greater or lesser degrees depending on their class position and on the gendered biases inherent in immigration policies and the broader society.

Another example of the gendered and class dimensions of migration is provided by anthropologist Andrew Gardner's (2010) research on immigrants from India who are living in Bahrain. Gardner distinguishes between proletarian transnationalists and diasporic elites. The former refers to the "Indian foreign laborers in the working class, usually men, alone, with families behind in India. Their gaze remains fixed on their home in India, and they are transnational in the sense that their social fields, collectively and individually, are spread between two nations but free of neither" (Gardner 2010:25). The diasporic elite are composed of middle and upper-class Indians who are professionals, skilled workers, educators, and merchants who bring their families with them to Bahrain. These migration patterns are gendered differently in relation to class positionality. Legal scholar Kitty Calavita (2006: 125) has therefore rightfully argued that "only by taking class variation seriously can the intersection of class, race and gender – an intersection that is often talked about but rarely traveled – be explored from all sides and the full complexity of immigrants' realities accounted for."

Theoretically, the research on gender and migration also needs to move toward more interdisciplinary and comparative approaches, and it needs to operate on multiple and interacting scales of analysis from micro, to meso, to macro. While the emphasis in this book has been on the US immigrant experience, of the past and at present, I have occasionally drawn on research from other destination countries to point to some critical areas of similarity and difference. For example, scholars have written about transnational motherhood or fatherhood as a characteristic of myriad migration flows around the world including those to the US; we need to begin to compile and compare (rather than simply add another study) these examples to help determine what drives variations in experience – distance traveled, gender ideologies in sending and/or receiving areas, labor markets, immigration/emigration policies, etc. Economists, sociologists, anthropologists, and political scientists working together, and at the scales of analysis with which they are most adept, can emerge with a more comprehensive theoretical understanding of this dimension of the contemporary immigrant experience. We could argue similarly for a more sophisticated approach to the relationship between gender and citizenship.

And in conclusion, if I were to identify some additional areas for future investigation, I would point to the need for more research on: (1) the gendered dimensions of political incorporation, political activism and resistance in local, national, and especially transnational contexts; (2) the gendered dimensions of immigrant health; (3) the intersections of gender, sexuality, and migration, including the experiences of LGBT immigrants; and (4) the gendered and intersectional differences among second-generation immigrants.

Notes

Introduction: Engendering the Study of Immigration

1 By now this topic is by no means understudied. The literature is vast, as are the number of review or overview articles and edited volumes on the subject. See, for example, Buijs 1993; Hondagneu-Sotelo 1999; Kelson and DeLaet 1999; Knorr and Meier 2000; Boyd and Grieco 2003; Pessar 2003; Sinke 2006a; Piper 2008; Lutz 2010; Pearce, Clifford and Tandon 2011; Brettell 2012.

1 The Gendered Demography of US Immigration History

1 See Halter (1993) on Cape Verdeans in the US.
2 See Reeve (2009) on the Portuguese role in the textile industry of southeastern New England.
3 See Lamphere (1987) for further discussion.
4 Gabaccia and Zanoni (2012: 213) argue that globally in 1830 females were approximately 28 percent of outgoing migrants. By 1920 this proportion "had increased to 38 percent (compared to 34 percent among incoming migrants worldwide and closer to 40 percent for the United States)."
5 Demographers who address the gendered dimensions of migration refer to either the sex ratio or the gender ratio. The sex ratio is the ratio of males to females in a population but it is generally a measure of the proportion of males to females at birth – in a normal population, 105 males/100 females. The gender ratio has been used to measure the actual number of men and women in a society, hence reflecting social conditions. In discussing the participation of men versus women in migration flows it seems most appropriate to talk about the gender ratio since migration in human populations is a social phenomenon not a natural one.
6 See also Houston et al. 1984. Donato et al. (2011) offer a more subtle age-

standardized analysis than is offered here. This alters some of the trends and reduces some of the divergence across decades apparent in Table 1.2.

7 Gordon (2005) points to gender selectivity in refugee populations as an important factor of variation. Placing the US into a global context, Gabaccia and Zanoni (2012: 208) emphasize that male-predominant and even heavily male migration streams were common during the nineteenth century. Donato et al. (2011: 513) demonstrate that despite regional and national origin variations, migration flows worldwide have become increasingly female since 1960, with the exception of emigration from African countries and from Mexico to the US.

8 See also Jackson 1984.

9 In Portugal, these women left behind were known as "widows of the living" (Brettell 1986).

10 For an explanation of this theory see Massey et al. 1993.

11 The next highest ratio was for Saudi Arabian immigrants (208 males/100 females).

12 For further discussion of African immigrants in the US see Capps et al. 2012.

13 These figures are provided in Donato et al. 2011: 512.

2 The Gendering of Law, Policy, Citizenship, and Political Practice

1 For further details see Harzig (2003).

2 Often identified as the first major federal law restricting immigration to the US, and promulgated to respond to growing anti-Chinese sentiment in the country, the Chinese Exclusion Act prohibited the immigration of all Chinese laborers for a decade. It resulted in a virtual halt to all Chinese immigration and also made it impossible for Chinese immigrants in the US to become naturalized citizens. Chinese laborers already in the US who left the country had to secure certifications for reentry. Few Chinese men in the US had any chance of reuniting with their wives or starting a family. The Chinese Exclusion Act did, however, provide Chinese merchants with the ability to enter the US with their wives, children and domestic servants. This Act was renewed in 1892 and remained in place in some form until 1943.

3 The 2013 film "The Immigrant" starring Marion Cotillard depicts just such a scenario at Ellis Island.

4 As Yuval Davis (1997: 12) observes: "In Britain, women lost their citizenship during Victorian times when they got married; they continued to lose it if they got married to 'foreigners' until 1948 and it was not until 1981 that they got the independent right to transfer their citizenship to their children."

5 Gardner (2005: 139) describes the impact directly: "While the Cable Act had provided that white or black women who married men ineligible for citizenship could regain their citizenship upon termination of their

marriage, it did not include women who themselves were racially ineligible to citizenship. These women could never regain their citizenship." However, this act did not extend to American women the ability to pass their citizenship on to their children. This only occurred in 1934 with passage of the Equal Nationality Act.

6 The Dillingham Commission, an early twentieth-century congressional committee that was charged with investigating the "immigration problem", addressed the picture bride issue and concluded that "a large majority of the women coming in this way are intended for purposes of prostitution" (Immigration Commission 1911: 69). See also Gardner (2005: 37–45).

7 Lee (2013) argues that principles of family reunification have a much deeper history in US immigration policy.

8 This is a system that qualifies individuals for entry as a federal skilled worker. Points are accorded for education, experience, age, English and/or French language skills, etc. Individuals must accumulate at least 67 points to qualify. It is important to consider this system since there are those who hold it up as a model for one direction for US immigration reform.

9 These issues have extended to the use of DNA testing to prove kinship relationships in the context of family reunification. See Heinemann (2015).

10 The figure for California was 27 percent and for New York 14 percent.

11 As of late July 2015 the Obama administration put new policies in place – a priority enforcement program. Under this program, the majority of unauthorized immigrants will not be the focus of deportation and will have "a degree of protection" to remain in the US. Instead, deportations will focus on immigrants who are national security threats, gang members, convicted felons and recent border crossers. Other priorities include repeat offenders with lesser crimes and individuals who entered the US illegally or were ordered deported after January 1, 2014 (Rosenblum 2015).

12 For a broad discussion of these impacts see Human Rights Watch (2007).

13 See Bowen (2007) for a discussion of the headscarf issue in the French context.

14 I have not done full justice here to Catherine Raissiguier's complex analysis. For another analysis of gender bias in European Union immigration policies related to irregular or illegal migrants see Askola (2010).

15 Talia Inlender (2009: 357) defines gender specific persecution as that which "can be suffered only by women, for example, forced pregnancy and female genital cutting." Gender-based forms refer "to persecution motivated by particular beliefs about gender, for example, laws that mandate severe punishments for violations of governing mores related to women's proper dress and social status."

16 In Germany, until January 2000, citizenship was based purely on ethnic (*jus sanquinis*) grounds. Thus non-residents of German origin could claim citizenship while all non-Germans, even if they were residing in Germany,

did not have this right. The new citizenship law is based on *jus domicilis* – beginning in January of 2000 children born in Germany can claim citizenship if one of the parents has been living in Germany for eight years and has a secure residence status. In Britain, birth on the territory, including former colonial territory, extended access to British citizenship. Ireland, by means of a law passed in 2004, moved away from birthright citizenship.

17 See Bloemraad (2013) for further discussion. This issue emerged strongly during the summer and fall of 2015 once Donald Trump entered the race for President of the United States. For commentaries at the time see Law (2015) and Fix (2015).

18 This law established that a person born in Ireland on or after January 1, 2005 is entitled to be an Irish citizen if at least one of his/her parents is an Irish citizen (or someone entitled to be an Irish citizen); a British citizen; a resident of the Island of Ireland who is entitled to reside in either the Republic or in Northern Ireland without any time limit on that residence; or a legal resident of Ireland for three out of the four years preceding the child's birth (with time spent as a student or asylum seeker not counting).

19 The first Act, among other things, mandated the deportation of legal permanent residents and illegal immigrants for relatively minor crimes, limited judicial review for immigrants facing deportation and raised the hardship standards to avoid deportation, raised the barriers on reentering the country, raised the minimum income requirement on legal immigrants who wanted to sponsor relatives to enter the country, and added a number of other obligations for support. The second Act, among other things, barred most immigrants from supplemental security income (SSI) and food stamps as well as barring them for five years from federal means-tested benefits like TANF (Temporary Assistance for Needy Families) and Medicaid and CHIP (Child Health Insurance Program). The USA Patriot Act expanded the categories of individuals who could be targeted for deportation.

20 Cultural citizenship has been defined by Rosaldo and Flores (1997: 57) as "the right to be different (in terms of race, ethnicity, or native language) with respect to the norms of the dominant national community, without compromising one's right to belong, in the sense of participating in the nation-state's democratic processes." Citizenship from this perspective is not just about relations to the state, but also about relations among fellow citizens within public spaces, work spaces, institutional spaces and/or organizational spaces. Cultural citizenship is also about a sense of belonging on one's own terms, having a voice, and being heard regardless of one's legal status as a citizen.

21 For another example see Cranford's (2007) discussion of a Justice for Janitors campaign in Los Angeles. Over half of these janitors are women and many are single, breadwinning mothers. Everyone involved is "engaging in political practice not as legal residents but as workers" (p. 321). See also

Raissiguier (2010) for a discussion of gendered differences in civic protest among the *sans papiers* in France.

22 I have omitted a discussion of the ramifications of immigration law for other gendered issues such as the sponsorship of same sex partners. This is a subject for future research. See Simmons (2008) for an analysis of the European context. See Luibheid (2007) for a discussion of the homophobic surveillance of US female border crossers.

3 Gendered Labor Markets

1 Readers should consult this article directly. Here I simplify the arguments a good deal.

2 For further information on characteristics of women in the US labor force see www.dol.gov/ub/stats/recentfacts.htm.

3 These data come from a news release on the labor force characteristics of foreign born workers issued by the Bureau of Labor Statistics. See www.bls.gov/news-release/pdf/forbrn.pdf. For another report, based on 2010 data, see Singer (2012).

4 By the 1990s and into the present, the sweatshops of New York have received media attention. See Barnes (1998) and Bechman (2012). For scholarly studies of Chinatown see Kwong (1996) and Zhou (1992).

5 Also valuable is the much earlier film *The Global Assembly Line* (1986) and Miriam Louie's *Sweatshop Warriors* (2001).

6 For studies on this phenomenon from around the world see Friese 1995; Aymer 1997; Chin 1998; Menjívar 1999; Momsen 1999; Andall 2000; Anderson 2000; Chang 2000; Hondagneu-Sotelo 2001; Parreñas 2001b; Ehrenreich and Hochschild 2002; Litt and Zimmerman 2003; Constable 2007. For a report on the Live-in Caregiver Program in Canada see Dorow and Cassiano 2015.

7 See also Repak's (1995) study of Central American domestic servants in Washington, DC. Many of these women have migrated on their own without a male partner, father, or brother.

8 For further information see "I Already Bought You": Abuse and Exploitation of Female Migrant Domestic Workers in the United Arab Emirates. *Human Rights Watch*, 2014.

9 For other studies of domestic workers in Middle Eastern settings see Frantz (2008) and Raijman et al. (2003).

10 See Walton-Roberts (2012) on the development of the nursing profession in Kerala.

11 See, for example, Bonacich and Modell 1980; Min 1988; Tseng 1995; Wong 1998; Min and Bozorgmehr 2000; Kloosterman and Rath 2003. See also Brettell and Alstatt 2007.

12 A recent book by Zulema Valdez (2011) significantly helps to correct this lacuna.

13 The intensity of this debate is captured, at least from one perspective, in Weitzer 2007. See also Pickup 1998; Doezema 2000; Zhang 2009; and Palmary 2010.

4 Gender and the Immigrant Family

1 For other discussions of transnational families see: Pessar 1999; Mahler and Pessar 2001, 2006; Bryceson and Vuorela 2002; Parreñas 2005; Zontini 2010; Coe 2011; Mazzucato et al. 2015.

2 The literature on transnationalism and transborder activities and interactions is vast. See, for example, Levitt 2001, 2003; Gardner and Grillo 2002; Tsuda 2003; England 2006; FitzGerald 2008; Chu 2010; Gardner 2010.

3 For further discussion of how immigrant families interface with the law see Coleman (2007).

4 Class is also discussed in Denise Segura's (2007) comparison of Mexican immigrant and Chicana women's attitudes toward work and motherhood. Mexican immigrant women have a model of the corporate family in which all members contribute to the common good. Chicanas adhere to a patriarchal structure centered on the middle-class value of the stay-at-home mother.

5 Min (1998) records surprise at the extent of marital conflict within Korean immigrant families in New York City, particularly within dual worker families.

6 The parallels between the case of Somalians and that of Cambodians (Ong 1996) should be noted.

7 While the topic of domestic violence among South Asians has been widely studied, this is less so for the Vietnamese. Nazli Kibria (1993) addresses it briefly, emphasizing primarily that women who are the objects of domestic abuse are generally reluctant to report it because they are hesitant to have the law intervene in family life. Sociologists Hoan Bui and Merry Morash (1999) found a similar reluctance in their research. The rate of wife abuse within Korean immigrant families is among the highest for Asian American populations and correlates with male dominance within these families, high levels of alcohol intake among Korean men, and the stress of adjusting to living in US society (Rhee 1997).

8 For an additional example see Mirdal (2006). See Parla (2001) for a discussion of the role of the modern Turkish state in "surveilling" the chastity of women. In the absence of the state, it makes sense that an immigrant ethnic community might assume this role. For discussion of the significance of honor and shame among Pakistani immigrants in Britain see Werbner (2005).

9 See, for example, Nicholson 2006; Moran-Taylor 2008; Horton 2008; Zontini 2010; Akesson et al. 2012; Boccagni 2012; Leifsen and Tymczuk 2012; and Madziva and Zontini 2012.

10 See Parreñas (2005) for a discussion of the perspectives of children.

11 The term "split-household transnational families" is used by Yeoh, Huang and Lam (2005).

12 For further information on global remittances see the website for the World Bank: web.worldbank.org.

13 For an excellent summary of the literature on motives to remit see Peter (2010). See also Goldring (2004).

14 Some of the remittance literature demonstrates that female migrants on average remit more than do male migrants (Chant 1992; Vanwey 2004). However, there are variations across different immigration streams and in relation to the differential earnings of men and women in the immigrant context (Semyonov and Gorodzeisky 2005). More recently, some scholars have documented that gendered differences in the likelihood of remitting endure into the second generation (Lee 2007).

15 See Peter (2010) for additional discussion of the association between remittances and social status.

References

Abdi, Cawo Mohamed. 2014. Threatened Identities and Gendered Opportunities: Somali Migration to America. *Signs* 5 (2): 459–483.

Abraham, Margaret. 1999. Sexual Abuse in South Asian Immigrant Marriages. *Violence Against Women* 5 (6): 591–618.

———. 2000. *Speaking the Unspeakable: Marital Violence among South Asian Immigrants in the United States.* New Brunswick: Rutgers University Press.

Abrams, Kerry. 2005. Polygamy, Prostitution, and the Federalization of Immigration Law. *Columbia Law Review* 105 (3): 641–716.

Abrego, Leisy J. 2014. *Sacrificing Families: Navigating Laws, Labor, and Love Across Borders.* Stanford: Stanford University Press.

Adepoju, Aderanti. 2004a. Trends in International Migration in and From Africa. In *International Migration; Prospects and Policies in a Global Market*, Douglass S. Massey and J. Edward Taylor, eds., pp. 59–76. Oxford: Oxford University Press.

———. 2004b. Changing Configurations of Migration in Africa. Migration Policy Institute. *Migration Information Source*, September 1.

Agathangalou, Anna M. and L. H. M. Ling. 2003. Desire Industries: Sex Trafficking, UN Peacekeeping, and the Neo Liberal World Order. *Brown Journal of World Affairs* 10 (1): 133–148.

Agustin, Laura. 2006. The Disappearing of a Migration Category: Migrants Who Sell Sex. *Journal of Ethnic and Migration Studies* 32 (1): 29–47.

Akesson, Lisa A., Jorgen Carling, and Heike Drotbohm. 2012. Mobility, Moralities and Motherhood: Navigating the Contingencies of Cape Verdean Lives. *Journal of Ethnic and Migration Studies* 38 (2): 237–260.

Akkoyunlu, Sule. 2013. Migration-Induced Women's Empowerment: The Case of Turkey. European University Institute, Working Papers. http://cadmus.eui.eu/bitstream/handle/1814/28360/RSCAS_2013_77.pdf?sequence=1 (accessed February 22, 2015).

References

Akpinar, Aylin. 2003. The Honor/Shame Complex Revisited: Violence Against Women in the Migrant Context. *Women's Studies International Forum* 26 (5): 425–442.

Alaggia, R., S. Chau, and K. T. Tsang. 2001. Astronaut Asian Families: Impact of Migration on Family Structure from the Perspectives of the Youth. *Journal of Social Work Research* 2 (2): 295–306.

Alexander, J. Trent and Annemarie Steidl. 2012. Gender and the "Laws" of Migration: A Reconsideration of Nineteenth-Century Patterns. *Social Science History* 36 (2): 223–241.

Amuedo-Dorantes, Catalina and Susan Pozo. 2006. Migration, Remittances, and Male and Female Employment Patterns. *American Economic Review* 96 (2): 222–226.

Andall, Jacqueline. 2000. *Gender, Migration and Domestic Service: The Politics of Black Women in Italy*. Sydney: Ashgate.

Anderson, Bridget. 2000. *Doing the Dirty Work? The Global Politics of Domestic Labour*. London: Zed Books.

Andrijasevic, Rutvica. 2003. The Difference Borders Make: (Il)legality, Migration and Trafficking in Italy among Eastern European Women in Prostitution. In *Uprootings/ Regroundings: Questions of Home and Migration*, Sara Ahmed, Claudia Casteneda, Anne-Marie Fortier, and Mimi Sheller, eds., pp. 251–272. Oxford: Berg Publishers.

——. 2007. Beautiful Dead Bodies: Gender, Migration and Representation in Anti-trafficking Campaigns. *Feminist Review* 86: 24–44.

Antin, Mary. 1912. *The Promised Land*. New York: Houghton Mifflin Co.

Arguelles, Lourdes and Anne M. Rivero. 1993. Gender/Sexuality Orientation, Violence and Transnational Migration: Conversations with Some Latinas We Think We Know. *Urban Anthropology* 22: 259–275.

Askola, Heli. 2010. Illegal Migrants', Gender and Vulnerability: The Case of the EU's Returns Directive. *Feminist Legal Studies* 18: 159–178.

Austin, Christopher and David Este. 2001. The Working Experiences of Underemployed Immigrant and Refugee Men. *Canadian Social Work Review* 18 (2): 213–229.

Aymer, Paula. 1997. *Uprooted Women: Migrant Domestics in the Caribbean*. New York: Praeger Press.

Ayyob, Ruksana. 2000. Domestic Violence in the South Asian Muslim Immigrant Population in the US. *Journal of Social Distress and Homelessness* 9 (3): 237–248.

Baker, Nancy V., Peter R. Gregware, and Margery A. Cassidy. 1999. Family Killing Fields. Honor Rationales in the Murder of Women. *Violence Against Women* 5(2): 164–184.

Barajas, Manuel and Elvia Ramirez. 2007 Beyond Home-Host Dichotomies: A Comparative Examination of Gender Relations in a Transnational Mexican Community. *Sociological Perspectives* 50 (3): 367–392.

References

Barker, Kim. 2014. Behind Closed Doors: Abuse of Domestic Workers. *The New York Times*, October 9.

Barnes, Edward. 1998. Slaves of New York. *Time*, November 9 (http://content.time.com/time/world/article/0,8599,2053983,00.html0).

Batalova, Jeanne. 2009. Immigrant Women in the United States. Migration Policy Institute (www.migrationpolicy.org/article/immigrant-women-united-states).

Batnitzky, Adina, Linda McDowell, and Sarah Dyer. 2008. A Middle-Class Global Mobility? The Working Lives of Indian Men in a West London Hotel. *Global Networks* 8 (1): 51–70.

Bayor, Ronald H. 2014. *Encountering Ellis Island: How European Immigrants Entered America*. Baltimore: The Johns Hopkins University Press.

Bechman, Leah. 2012. A Brief Visit to Designer Alexander Wang's Alleged Chinatown Sweatshop. *Gawker*, March 9 (http://gawker.com/5892011/a-brief-visit-to-designer-alexander-wangs-alleged-chinatown-sweatshop).

Bhabha Jacqueline. 2009. The "Mere Fortuity of Birth?": Children, Borders, and the Right to Citizenship. In *Migrations and Mobilities: Citizenship, Borders, and Gender*, Seyla Benhabib and Judith Resnick, eds., pp. 187–227. New York: New York University Press.

Bhachu, Parminder. 1988. Apni Marzi Kardhi Home and Work: Sikh Women in Britain. In *Enterprising Women*, Sallie Westwood and Parminder Bhachu, eds., pp. 76–102. London: Routledge.

Bhattacharjee, Anannya. 2006. The Public/Private Mirage: Mapping Homes and Undomesticating Violence Work in the South Asian Immigrant Community. In *The Anthropology of the State*, Aradhana Sharma and Akhil Gupta, eds., pp. 337–355. Oxford: Blackwell Publishing.

Bhimji, Fazila. 2010. Struggles, Urban Citizenship, and Belonging: The Experience of Undocumented Street vendors and Food Truck Owners in Los Angeles. *Urban Anthropology and Studies of Cultural Systems and World Economic Development* 39 (4): 455–492.

Blackwelder, Julia Kirk. 1997. *New Hiring. The Feminization of Work in the United States, 1900–1995*. College Station: Texas A & M Press.

Bloemraad, Irene. 2013. Being American/Becoming American: Birthright Citizenship and Immigrants' Membership in the United States. *Studies in Law, Politics, and Society* 60:55–84.

Boccagni, Paolo. 2012. Practising Motherhood at a Distance: Retention and Loss in Ecuadorian Transnational Families. *Journal of Ethnic and Migration Studies* 38 (2): 261–277.

Boehm, Deborah A. 2008a. "For My Children:" Constructing Family and Navigating the State in the US-Mexico Transnation. *Anthropological Quarterly* 81 (4): 777–802.

———. 2008b. "Now I am a Man and a Woman!": Gendered Moves and Migrations in a Transnational Mexican Community. *Latin American Perspectives* 35 (1): 16–30.

References

Bonacich, Edna. 1973. A Theory of Middleman Minorities. *American Sociological Review* 38: 583–594.

Bonacich, Edna and John Modell. 1980. *The Economic Basis of Ethnic Solidarity: Small Business in the Japanese American Community*. Berkeley: University of California Press.

Bonacich, Edna and Richard Appelbaum. 2000. *Behind the Label: Inequality in the Los Angeles Apparel Industry*. Berkeley: University of California Press.

Bowen, John R. 2007. *Why the French Don't Like Headscarves: Islam, the State, and Public Space*. Princeton: Princeton University Press.

Boyd, Monica. 2013. Recruiting High Skill Labour in North America: Policies, Outcomes and Futures. *International Migration* 52 (3): 40–54.

Boyd, Monica and Elizabeth Grieco. 2003. Women and Migration: Incorporating Gender into International Migration Theory. *Migration Information Source*, March 1. Migration Policy Institute (www.migrationinformation.org/Feature/display.cfm?id=106).

Boyd, Monica and Deanna Pikkov. 2008. Finding a Place in Stratified Structures: Migrant Women in North America. In *New Perspectives on Gender and Migration: Livelihood, Rights and Entitlements*, Nicola Piper, ed., pp. 19–58. New York: Routledge.

Brabeck, Kalina and Qingwen Xu. 2010. The Impact of Detention and Deportation on Latino Immigrant Children and Families: A Quantitative Exploration. *Hispanic Journal of Behavioral Sciences* 32 (3): 341–361.

Brah, Avtar and Ann Phoenix. 2004. "Ain't I a Woman": Revisiting Intersectionality. *Journal of International Women's Studies* 5 (3): 75–86.

Brault, Gerard J. 1986. *The French-Canadian Heritage in New England*. Hanover: University Press of New England.

Bredbenner, Candice Lewis. 1998. *A Nationality of Her Own: Women, Marriage, and the Law of Citizenship*. Berkeley: University of California Press.

Brennan, Denise. 2004. Women Work, Men Sponge, and Everyone Gossips: Macho Men and Stigmatized/ing Women in a Sex Tourism Town. *Anthropological Quarterly* 77 (4): 705–733.

——. 2005. Methodological Challenges in Research with Trafficked Persons: Tales from the Field. *International Migration* 43 (1/2): 35–54.

Brettell, Caroline B. 1986. *Men Who Migrate, Women Who Wait: Population and History in a Portuguese Parish*. Princeton: Princeton University Press.

——. 1995. *We Have Already Cried Many Tears: The Stories of Three Portuguese Migrant Women*. Prospect Heights: Waveland Press. (Originally 1982 Schenkman Publishing Company).

——. 2002. The Individual/Agent and Culture/Structure in the History of the Social Sciences. *Social Science History* 26 (3): 429–445.

——. 2007. Immigrant Women in Small Business: Biographies of Becoming Entrepreneurs. In *Handbook of Research on Ethnic Minority Entrepreneurs*,

References

Leo-Paul Dana, ed., pp. 83–98. Cheltenham, UK and Northampton, MA: Edward Elgar.

——. 2012. Migration, Gender, and Family. In *The Oxford Handbook of the Politics of International Migration*, Marc R. Rosenblum and Daniel J. Tichenor, eds., pp. 478–508. Oxford: Oxford University Press.

Brettell, Caroline and Kristoffer Alstatt. 2007. The Agency of Immigrant Entrepreneurs: Biographies of the Self Employed in Ethnic and Occupational Niches of the Urban Labor Market. *Journal of Anthropological Research* 63: 383–397.

Brettell, Caroline B. and Deborah Reed-Danahay. 2012. *Civic Engagements: The Citizenship Practices of Indian and Vietnamese Immigrants*. Stanford: Stanford University Press.

Broughton, Chad. 2008. Migration as Engendered Practice: Mexican Men, Masculinity, and Northward Migration. *Gender and Society* 22 (5): 568–589.

Browne, Colette V. and Kathryn L. Braun. 2008. Globalization, Women's Migration and the Long-Term-Care Workforce. *The Gerontolotist* 48 (1): 16–24.

Bryceson, Deborah and Ulla Vuorela, eds. 2002. *The Transnational Family: New European Frontiers and Global Networks*. Oxford and New York: Berg Publishers.

Buechler, Hans and Judith Maria Buechler. 1981. *Carmen: The Autobiography of a Spanish Galician Woman*. Cambridge: Schenkman Publishing Company.

Bui, Hoan N. and Merry Morash. 1999. Domestic Violence in the Vietnamese Immigrant Community: An Exploratory Study. *Violence Against Women* 5: 769–795.

Buijs, Gina, ed. 1993. *Migrant Women: Crossing Boundaries and Changing Identities*. Oxford and Washington, DC: Berg Publishers.

Bun, Chan Kwok and Ong Jin Hui. 1995. The Many Faces of Immigrant Entrepreneurship. In *The Cambridge Survey of World Migration*, Robin Cohen, ed., pp. 523–531. Cambridge: Cambridge University Press.

Bustamante, Jorge A. 1983. Maquiladoras: A New Face of International Capitalism on Mexico's Northern Frontier. In *Women, Men, and the International Division of Labor*, June Nash and Maria Patricia Fernandez-Kelly, eds., pp. 224–256. Albany: State University of New York Press.

Busza, Joanna. 2004. Sex Work and Migration: The Dangers of Oversimplification: A Case Study of Vietnamese Women in Cambodia. *Health and Human Rights* 7 (2): 231–249.

Cairoli, M. Laetitia. 1998. Factor as Home and Family: Female Workers in the Moroccan Garment Industry. *Human Organization* 57 (2): 181–189.

Calavita, Kitty. 2006. Gender, Migration and Law: Crossing Borders and Bridging Disciplines. *International Migration Review* 40 (1): 104–132.

Camarillo, Albert. 2007. Mexico. In *The New Americans: A Guide to Immigration since 1965*. Mary C. Waters and Reed Ueda, eds., pp. 504–517. Cambridge, MA: Harvard University Press.

References

Cameron, Ardis. 1993. *Radicals of the Worst Sort: Laboring Women in Lawrence, Massachusetts, 1860–1912.* Urbana and Chicago: University of Illinois Press.

Capps, Randy, Kristen McCabe and Michael Fix. 2012. *Diverse Streams: African Migration to the United States.* Migration Policy Institute: National Center on Immigrant Integration Policies.

Carling, Jorgen. 2005. Trafficking in Women from Nigeria to Europe. *Migration Information Source,* July 2. www.migrationpolicy.org/article/trafficking-women-nigeria-europe.

Carling, Jorgen, Cecilia Menjívar, and Leah Schmalzbauer. 2012. Central Themes in the Study of Transnational Parenthood. *Journal of Ethnic and Migration Studies* 38 (2): 191–217.

Caroli, Betty Boyd. 1973. *Italian Repatriation from the United States, 1900–1914.* New York: Center for Migration Studies.

Castles, Stephen, and Mark Miller. 2009. *The Age of Migration: International Population Movements in the Modern World.* New York: Palgrave-Macmillan.

CBS News. 2008. "Cops: Arson and Murder, By Way of India" www.cbsnews.com/stories/2008/01/03/national/main3669575.shtml.

Chai, Alice Yun. 1987a. Adaptive Strategies of Recent Korean Immigrant Women in Hawaii. In *Beyond the Public/Domestic Dichotomy: Contemporary Perspectives on Women's Public Lives,* Janet Shristanian, ed., pp. 65–100. New York: Greenwood Press.

——. 1987b. Freed from the Elders but Locked into Labor: Korean Immigrant Women in Hawaii. *Women's Studies* 13: 223–233.

Chang, Grace. 2000. *Disposable Domestics; Immigrant Women Workers in the Global Economy.* Cambridge, MA: South End Press.

Chant, Sylvia (ed.). 1992. *Gender and Migration in Developing Countries.* New York: Belhaven Press.

Chant, Sylvia and Kathy McIlwaine. 1995. Gender and Export Manufacturing in the Philippines: Continuity or Change in Female Employment? *Gender, Place and Culture* 2 (2): 147–176.

Chantler, Khatidja. 2010. Women Seeking Asylum in the UK: Contesting Conventions. In *Gender and Migration: Feminist Interventions,* Ingrid Palmary, Erica Burman, Khatidja Chantler, and Peace Kuguwa, eds., pp. 104–118. London: Zed Books.

Chapkis, Wendy. 2003. Trafficking, Migration, and the Law: Protecting Innocents, Punishing Immigrants. *Gender and Society* 17 (6): 923–937.

Chavez, Leo. 2007. A Glass Half Empty: Latina Reproduction and Public Discourse. In *Women and Migration in the US-Mexico Borderlands: A Reader,* Denise A. Segura and Patricia Zavella, eds., pp. 67–91. Durham: Duke University Press.

——. 2008. *The Latino Threat.* Stanford: Stanford University Press.

References

Chee, Maria W. L. 2005. *Taiwanese American Transnational Families: Women and Kin Work.* New York: Routledge.

Chiang, Lan-Hung Nora. 2008. Astronaut Families: Transnational Lives of Middle Class Taiwanese Married Women in Canada. *Social and Cultural Geography* 9: 505–518.

Chiang-Hom, Christy. 2004. Transnational Cultural Practices of Chinese Immigrant Youth and Parachute Kids. In *Asian American Youth: Culture, Identity and Ethnicity*, J. Lee and Min Zhou, eds., pp. 143–158. New York: Routledge.

Chin, Christine. B. N. 1998. *In Service and Servitude: Foreign Female Domestic Workers and the Malaysian "Modernity" Project.* Ithaca, NY: Cornell University Press.

Chishti, Muzaffar and Claire Bergeron. 2011. DHS Announces End to Controversial Post-9/11 Immigrant Registration and Tracking Program. *Migration Information Source*, May 11. Washington, DC: Migration Policy Institute.

Chock, Phyllis Pease. 1995. Ambiguity in Policy Discourse: Congressional Talk about Immigration. *Policy Sciences* 28 (2): 165–184.

Choy, Catherine. 2003. *Empire of Care: Nursing and Migration in Filipino American History.* Durham, NC: Duke University Press.

Christiansen, Connie. 2012. Gender and Social Remittances: Return Migrants to Yemen from East Africa. *Arabian Humanities.*(http://cy.revues.org/1869; accessed February 22, 2015)

Chu, Julie Y. 2010. *Cosmologies of Credit: Transnational Mobility and the Politics of Destination in China.* Durham, NC: Duke University Press.

Coe, Cati. 2011. What is the Impact of Transnational Migration on Family Life? Women's Comparisons of Internal and International Migration in a Small Town in Ghana. *American Ethnologist* 38 (1): 148–163.

Cohen, Jeffrey H. 2004. *The Culture of Migration in Southern Mexico.* Austin: University of Texas Press.

———. 2011. Migration, Remittances and Household Strategies. *Annual Review of Anthropology* 40: 103–114.

Cohen, Miriam. 1992. *Workshop to Office: Two Generations of Italian Women in New York City, 1900–1950.* Ithaca: Cornell University Press.

Coleman, Doriane Lambelet. 2007. The Role of the Law in Relationships with Immigrant Families: Traditional Parenting Practices in Conflict with American Concepts of Maltreatment. In *Immigrant Families in Contemporary America*, Jennifer E. Lansford, Kirby Deater-Deckard, and Marc H. Bornstein, eds., pp. 287–303. New York: The Guilford Press.

Coll, Kathleen. 2010. *Remaking Citizenship: Latina Immigrants & New American Politics.* Stanford: Stanford University Press.

Connell, John. 1984. Status or Subjugation? Women, Migration and Development in the South Pacific. *International Migration Review* 18 (1): 964–983.

References

Constable, Nicole. 1997. Sexuality and Discipline among Filipina Domestic Workers in Hong Kong. *American Ethnologist* 24 (3): 539–558.

——. 2007. *Maid to Order in Hong Kong*. Ithaca: Cornell University Press.

Contreras, Ricardo and David Griffith. 2012. Managing Migration, Managing Motherhood: The Moral Economy of Gendered Migration. *International Migration* 50 (4): 51–66.

Cott, Nancy. 1998. Marriage and Women's Citizenship in the United States, 1830–1934. *The American Historical Review* 103: 1440–74.

Cranford, Cynthia. 2007 "Aqui estamos y no nos vamos! Justice for Janitors in Los Angeles and New Citizenship Claims. In *Women and Migration in the US–Mexico Borderlands: A Reader*, Denise A. Segura and Patricia Zavella, eds., pp. 306–324. Durham: Duke University Press.

Dallalfar, Arlene. 1994. Iranian Women as Immigrant Entrepreneurs. *Gender and Society* 8 (4): 541–561.

Das Gupta, Monisha. 2006. *Unruly Immigrants – Rights, Activism and Transnational South Asian Politics in the United States*. Durham, NC: Duke University Press.

Das Gupta, Shamita. 1999. Guest Editor's Introduction. *Violence Against Women* 5 (6): 587–590.

Degiuli, Francesca. 2007. A Job with no Boundaries: Home Eldercare Work in Italy. *European Journal of Women's Studies* 14 (3): 193–207.

De Haas, Hein and Aleida van Rooij. 2010. Migration as Emancipation? The Impact of Internal and International Migration on the Position of Women Left Behind in Rural Morocco. *Oxford Development Studies* 38 (1): 43–62.

Dhaliwal, Amarpal. 1995. Gender at Work: The Renegotiation of Middle-Class Womanhood in a South Asian-Owned Business. In *Reviewing Asian America: Locating Diversity*, Wendy L. Ng, Soo-Young Chin, James S. Moy and Gary Y. Okihiro, eds., pp. 75–86. Pullman, WA: Washington State University Press.

Dhingra, Pawan. 2012. *Life Behind the Lobby: Indian American Motel Owners and the American Dream*. Stanford: Stanford University Press.

Diner, Hasia. 1983. *Erin's Daughters in America: Irish Women in the Nineteenth Century*. Baltimore: Johns Hopkins University Press.

Doezema, Jo. 2000. Loose Women or Lost Women? The Re-emergence of White Slavery in Contemporary Discourses of Trafficking in Women. *Gender Issues* (Winter): 23–50.

Dolnick, Sam. A. 2011. Post-9/11 Registration Effort Ends, but Not Its Effects. *The New York Times*, May 30.

Donato, Katharine M. 1992. Understanding US Immigration: Why Some Countries Send Women and Others Send Men. In *Seeking Common Ground: Female Immigration to the United States*, Donna Gabaccia, ed., pp. 159–184. Westport, CT: Greenwood.

——. 2010. US Migration from Latin America: Gendered Patterns and Shifts.

References

The Annals of the American Academy of Political and Social Science 630: 78–92.

——. 2012a Introduction: Variation in Gender Composition of Migrant Populations. *Social Science History* 36 (2): 191–195.

——. 2012b. Gender, Immigration and the US Labor Market. In *Transforming America: Perspectives on US Immigration*, Michael C. LeMay, ed., pp. 131–150. New York, Praeger.

Donato, Katherine. M., Donna Gabaccia, Jennifer Holdaway, Martin Manalansan IV, and Patricia R. Pessar. 2006. A Glass Half Full? Gender in Migration Studies. *International Migration Review* 40 (1): 3–26.

Donato, Katharine M., Joseph T. Alexander, Donna R. Gabaccia, and Johanna Leinonen. 2011. Variations in the Gender Composition of Immigrant Populations: How and Why They Matter. *International Migration Review* 45 (3): 495–526.

Donato, Katharine M. and Donna Gabaccia. 2015. *Gender and International Migration*. New York: Russell Sage Foundation.

Dorow, Sara and Marcella S. Cassiano. 2015. Live-in Caregivers in Fort McMurray: A Socioeconomic Footprint. On the Move Partnership Report (www.onthemovepartnership.ca). accessed January 31, 2015.

Dreby, Joanna. 2006. Honor and Virtue: Mexican Parenting in the Transnational Context. *Gender and Society* 20 (1): 32–59.

Durand, Jorge, and Douglas S. Massey. 1992. Generalizations about Mexico–US migration: A Critical Review. *Latin American Research Review* 27 (2): 3–42.

Ehrenreich, Barbara and Arlie Russell Hochschild. 2002. *Global Woman: Nannies, Maids, and Sex Workers in the New Economy*. New York: Henry Holt & Company.

Eiserer, Tanya. 2008 "Slain Lewisville Sisters Mourned at Christian, Muslim Services" *Dallas Morning News*, January 6 (http://www.dallasnews.com/sharedcontent/dws/dn/latestnews/stories/010608dnmetfunerals).

England, Sarah. 2006. *Afro Central Americans in New York City: Garifuna Tales of Transnational Movements in Racialized Space*. Gainesville: University Press of Florida.

Erdem, Esra and Monika Mattes, M. 2003. Gendered Policies/Gendered Patterns: Female Labour Migration from Turkey to Germany from the 1960s to the 1990s. In *European Encounters, Migrants, Migrations and European Societies since 1945*, Rainer Ohliger, Karen Schönwälder, and Triadafilos Triadafilopoulos, eds., pp. 167–185. Aldershot: Ashgate.

Erel, Umut. 2002. Reconceptualizing Motherhood: Experiences of Migrant Women from Turkey Living in Germany. In *The Transnational Family: New European Frontiers and Global Networks*, Deborah Bryceson and Ulla Vuorela, eds., pp. 127–146. New York: Berg Publishers.

Espiritu, Yen Le. 1995. *Filipino American Lives*. Philadelphia: Temple University Press.

References

——. 1999. Gender and Labor in Asian Immigrant Families. *American Behavioral Scientist* 42 (4): 628–647.

——. 2001. "We Don't Sleep Around like White Girls Do": Family, Culture and Gender in Filipina American Lives. *Signs: Journal of Women in Culture and Society* 26 (2): 415–440.

Este, David C. and Admasu A. Tachble. 2009. The Perceptions and Experiences of Russian Immigrant and Sudanese Refugee Men as Fathers in an Urban Center in Canada. *Annals of the American Academy of Political and Social Science* 624: 139–155.

Ewen, Elizabeth. 1985. *Immigrant Women in the Land of Dollars: Life and Culture on the Lower East Side, 1890–1925*. New York: Monthly Review Press.

Fernandez-Kelly, Maria Patricia. 1983. *For We are Sold, I and My People: Women and Industry in Mexico's Frontier*. Albany: SUNY Press.

FitzGerald, David. 2008. Colonies of the Little Motherland: Membership, Space and Time in Mexican Migrant Hometown Associations. *Comparative Studies in Society and History* 50 (1): 145–169.

——. 2009. *A Nation of Emigrants: How Mexico Manages Its Migration*. Berkeley: University of California Press.

Fix, Michael. 2015. *Repealing Birthright Citizenship: The Unintended Consequences*. Washington, DC: Migration Policy Institute Commentary, August 21.

Fix, Michael and Wendy Zimmerman. 2001. All Under One Roof: Mixed-Status Families in an Era of Reform. *International Migration Review* 35 (2): 397–419.

Foner, Nancy. 1999. Immigrant Women and Work in New York City, Then and Now. *Journal of American Ethnic History* 18 (3): 95–113.

——. 2009. Gender and Migration: West Indians in Comparative Perspective. *International Migration* 47 (1): 3–29.

Ford, Michele and Nicola Piper. 2007. Southern Sites of Female Agency: Informal Regimes and Female Migrant Labour Resistance in East and Southeast Asia. In *Everyday Politics of the World Economy*, John M. Hobson and Leonard Seabrooke, eds., pp. 63–80. Cambridge: Cambridge University Press.

Frantz, Elizabeth. 2008. Of Maids and Madams: Sri Lankan Domestic Workers and their Employers in Jordan. *Critical Asian Studies* 40 (4): 609–638.

Freedman, Jane. 2012. Taking Gender Seriously in Asylum and Refugee Policies. In *Global Migration: Challenges in the Twenty-First Century*, Kavita R. Khory, ed., pp. 45–64. New York: Palgrave-Macmillan.

Friedman, Marilyn. 2005. *Women and Citizenship*. Oxford: Oxford University Press.

Friedman-Kasaba, Kathie. 1996. *Memories of Migration: Gender, Ethnicity, and Work in the Lives of Jewish and Italian Women in New York, 1870–1924*. Albany: State University of New York Press.

Friese, Marianne. 1995. East European Women as Domestics in Western Europe:

New Social Inequality and Division of Labour among Women. *Journal of Area Studies* 3 (6): 194–202.

Fry, Richard. 2006. *Gender and Migration.* Pew Hispanic Center Report (www. pewhispanic.org/2006/07/05/gender-and-migration).

Gabaccia, Donna R., ed. 1992. *Seeking Common Ground: Multidisciplinary Studies of Immigrant Women in the United States:* Westport, CT: Greenwood Press.

——. 1994. *From the Other Side: Women, Gender, and Immigrant Life in the US, 1820–1990.* Bloomington: Indiana University Press.

Gabaccia, Donna and Elizabeth Zanoni. 2012. Transitions in Gender Ratios among International Migrants, 1820–1930. *Social Science History* 36(2): 197–221.

Gallo, Ester. 2006. "Italy is Not a Good Place for Men": Narratives of Places, Marriage, and Masculinity among Malayali Migrants. *Global Networks* 6 (4): 357–372.

Gamburd, Michel Ruth. 1999. Class Identity and the International Division of Labor: Sri Lanka's Migrant Housemaids. *Anthropology of Work Review* 19 (3): 3–8.

——. 2000. *The Kitchen Spoon's Handle: Transnationalism and Sri Lanka's Migrant Housemaids.* Ithaca: Cornell University Press, 2000.

——. 2008. Milk Teeth and Jet Planes: Kin Relations in Families of Sri Lanka's Transnational Domestic Servants. *City and Society* 20 (1): 5–31.

Gardner, Andrew M. 2010. *City of Strangers: Gulf Migration and the Indian Community in Bahrain.* Ithaca: Cornell University Press.

Gardner, Katy. 1995. *Global Migrants, Local Lives: Travel and Transformation in Rural Bangladesh.* Oxford: Clarendon Press.

Gardner, Katy and Ralph Grillo. 2002. Transnational Households and Ritual: An Overview. *Global Networks* 2 (3): 179–190.

Gardner, Martha. 2005. *The Qualities of a Citizen: Women, Immigration and Citizenship, 1870–1965.* Princeton: Princeton University Press.

George, Sheba. 2005. *When Women Come First: Gender and Class in Transnational Migration.* Berkeley: University of California Press.

Gilbertson, Greta A. 1995. Women's Labor and Enclave Employment: The Case of Dominican and Colombian Women in New York City. *International Migration Review* 29: 657–670.

Gjerde, Jon. 1985. *From Peasants to Farmers: The Migration from Balestrand, Norway, to the Upper Midwest.* Cambridge: Cambridge University Press.

Glick, Jennifer. 2010. Connecting Complex Processes: A Decade of Research on Immigrant Families. *Journal of Marriage and the Family* 72: 498–515.

Glick Schiller, Nina, Linda Basch, and Cristina Szanton Blanc. 1992. Transnationalism: A New Analytical Framework for Understanding Migration. In *Towards a Transnational Perspective on Migration: Race, Class, Ethnicity, and Nationalism Reconsidered,* Nina Glick Schiller, Linda Basch, and Cristina

References

Szanton Blanc, eds., pp. 1–24. New York: Annals of the New York Academy of Sciences.

Glick Schiller, Nina and Noel B. Salazar. 2013. Regimes of Mobility across the Globe. *Journal of Ethnic and Migration Studies* 39 (2): 183–200.

Gmelch, George. 1980. Return Migration. *Annual Review of Anthropology* 9: 135–159.

Goldring, Luin. 2004 Family and Collective Remittances to Mexico: A Multi-Dimensional Typology. *Development and Change* 35 (4): 799–840.

Gordon, Linda W. 2005. Trends in the Gender Ratio of Immigrants to the United States. *International Migration Review* 39 (4): 796–818.

Gould, Chandré. 2010. The Problem of Trafficking. In *Gender and Migration: Feminist Interventions*, Ingrid Palmary, Erica Burman, Khatidja Chantler and Peace Kuguwa, eds., pp. 31–49. London: Zed Books.

Gozdziak, Elzbieta M. and Elizabeth A. Collett. 2005. Research on Human Trafficking in North America: A Review of Literature. *International Migration* 43 (1/2): 99–128.

Grasmuck, Sherri and Patricia R. Pessar. 1991. *Between Two Islands: Dominican International Migration*. Berkeley: University of California Press.

Grassi, Marzia and Jeanne Vivet. 2014. *Fathering and Conjugality in Transnational Patchwork Families: The Angola/Portugal Case*. TL Network e-Working Papers. European Science Foundation (www.tlnetwork.ica.ul.pt).

Green, Nancy L. 1996. Women and Immigrants in the Sweatshop: Categories of Labor Segmentation Revisited. *Comparative Studies in Society and History* 38 (3): 411–433.

Grieco, Elizabeth. 2003. Sex Ratios of the Foreign Born in the United States. *Migration Information Source*, March 1. Migration Policy Institute (www.migrationpolicy.org/article/sex-ratios-foreign-born-united-states).

Grimes, Kimberley. 1998. *Crossing Borders: Changing Social Identities in Southern Mexico*. Tucson: The University of Arizona Press.

Gulcur, Leyla and Pincar Ilkkaracan. 2002. The "Natasha" Experience: Migrant Sex Workers from the Former Soviet Union and Eastern Europe in Turkey. *Women's Studies International Forum* 25 (4): 411–421.

Gullette, Gregory S. 2009. Transnational Participatory Development: Economic and Cultural Flows in Oaxaca, Mexico. *Urban Anthropology* 38 (3–4): 235–267.

———. 2012. State Tourism, Labour Mobilities, and Remittance Potentials within Huatulco, Oaxaca. *International Journal of Tourism Anthropology* 2 (4): 299–317.

———. 2013. The Role of Urbanity, Status and Identity on Migrant Remittance Management and Rural Development Potentials in Thailand. *Human Organization* 72 (2): 132–143.

Gunewardena, Nandini. 2007. Disrupting Subordination and Negotiating Belonging: Women Workers in the Transnational Production Sites of Sri

References

Lanka. In *The Gender of Globalization: Women Navigating Cultural and Economic Marginalities,* Nandini Gunewardena and Ann Kingsolver, eds., pp. 35–60. Santa Fe: School for Advanced Research Press.

Gutiérrez, Elena R. 2008. *Fertile Matters: The Politics of Mexican-Origin Women's Reproduction.* Austin: University of Texas Press.

Hagan, Jacqueline Maria. 1994. *Deciding to be Legal: A Maya Community in Houston.* Philadelphia: Temple University Press.

Hagan, Jacqueline, Karl Eschbach, and Nestor Rodriguez. 2008. US Deportation Policy, Family Separation, and Circular Migration. *International Migration Review* 42 (1): 64–88.

Hagan, Jacqueline, Nester Rodriguez, and Brianna Castro, 2011. Social Effects of Mass Deportations by the United States Government, 2000–2010. *Ethnic and Racial Studies* 34: 1374–1391.

Halter, Marilyn. 1993. *Between Race and Ethnicity: Cape Verdean American Immigrants, 1860–1965.* Urbana and Chicago: University of Illinois Press.

Hampton, Maricar C. P. 2010. Filipino Health Workers Struggle in Filling Eldercare Gap. New American Media, Philippine News (http://www.new americanmedia.org/2010/06/filipino-health-workers-struggle-in-fillingelder care-gap.php); accessed January 22, 2015.

Hardy-Fanta, Carol. 1993. *Latina Politics, Latino Politics: Gender, Culture, and Political Participation in Boston.* Philadelphia: Temple University Press.

Hareven, Tamara K. 1982. *Family Time and Industrial Time.* Cambridge: Cambridge University Press.

Hart, Dianne Walta. 1997. *Undocumented in LA.* Lanham, MD: Rowman and Littlefield.

Hartford, William F. 1990. *Working People of Holyoke: Class and Ethnicity in a Massachusetts Mill Town, 1850–1960.* New Brunswick, NJ: Rutgers University Press.

Harzig, Christiane. 1997. Creating a Community: German–American Women in Chicago. In *Peasant Maids, City Women: From the European Countryside to Urban America,* Christiane Harzig, ed., pp. 185–222. Ithaca: Cornell University Press.

——. 2003. Immigration Policies: A Gendered Historical Comparison. In *Crossing Borders and Shifting Boundaries,* Mirjana Morokvasic, U. Erel, and K. Shinozaki, eds., pp. 35–58. Opladen: VS Verlag.

Hedberg, Charlotta and Katarina Peterson. 2012. Disadvantage, Ethnic Niching or Pursuit of a Vision? *International Migration and Integration* 13 (4): 423–440.

Heinemann, Torsten (ed.). 2015. *Suspect Families: DNA Analysis, Family Reunification and Immigration Policy.* Surrey, UK: Ashgate.

Hernández, Ramona and Francisco Rivera-Batiz. 2003. *Dominicans in the United States: A Socio-Economic Profile.* New York: Dominican Research Monographs. CUNY: Dominican Studies Institute.

References

Hewson, Jack. 2014. Hong Kong's Domestic Worker Abuse. *Al Jazeera*, January 19.

Higham, John. 1955. *Strangers in the Land: Patterns in American Nativism 1860–1925*. New Brunswick, NJ: Rutgers University Press.

Hirata, Lucie Cheng. 1979. Free, Indentured, Enslaved: Chinese Prostitutes in Nineteenth-Century America. *Signs* 5 (1): 3–29.

Hirsch, Jennifer S. 2003. *A Courtship After Marriage: Sexuality and Love in Mexican Transnational Families*. Berkeley: University of California Press.

Hoang, Lan Anh and Brenda Yeoh. 2011. Breadwinning Wives and "Left-Behind" Husbands: Men and Masculinities in the Vietnamese Transnational Family. *Gender & Society* 25 (6): 717–39.

Hofman, Erin Trouth and Cynthia J. Buckley. 2013. Global Changes and Gendered Responses: The Feminization of Migration from Georgia. *International Migration Review* 47 (3): 508–538.

Hondagneu-Sotelo, Pierrette (ed.). 1999. *Gender and US Immigration: Contemporary Trends*. Berkeley: University of California Press.

——. 2001. *Domestica: Immigrant Workers, Cleaning and Caring in the Shadows of Affluence*. Berkeley: University of California Press.

——. 2011. Gender and Migration Scholarship: An Overview from a 21st Century Perspective. *Migraciones Internacionales* 6 (1): 219–233.

Hondagneu-Sotelo, Pierrette and Ernestine Avila. 1997. "I'm here, but I'm there": The Meanings of Latina Transnational Motherhood. *Gender and Society* 11 (5): 548–571.

Hondagneu-Sotelo, Pierrette and Cynthia Crawford, 1999. Gender and Migration. In *Handbook of the Sociology of Gender*, Janet Saltzman Chafetz, ed., pp. 105–126. New York: Kluwer/Plenum Publishers.

Horton, Sarah. 2008. Consuming Childhood: "Lost" and "Ideal" Childhood as a Motivation for Migration. *Anthropological Quarterly* 81 (4): 925–943.

——. 2009. A Mother's Heart is Weighted Down with Stones: A Phenomenological Approach to the Experience of Transnational Motherhood. *Culture, Medicine and Psychiatry* 33 (1): 21–40.

Houston, Marion F., Roger G. Kramer, and Joan M. Barrett. 1984. Female Predominance in Immigration to the United States since 1930: A First Look. *International Migration Review* 18 (4): 908–63.

Huang, Shirlena, Brenda S. Yeoh, and M. Toyota. 2012. Caring for the Elderly: The Embodied Labour of Migrant Care Workers in Singapore. *Global Networks* 12: 195–215.

Human Rights Watch. 2007. *Forced Apart: Families Separated and Immigrants Harmed by United States Deportation Policy*. (hrw.org/reports/2007/us0707/).

Ibarra, Maria. 2002. Emotional Proletarians in a Global Economy. Mexican Immigrant Women and Elder Carework. *Urban Anthropology* 31 (3–4): 317–350.

——. 2003. The Tender Trap: Mexican Immigrant Women and the Ethics of Elder Care Work. *Atzlan* 28 (2): 87–113.

——. 2007. Mexican Immigrant Women and the New Domestic Labor. In *Women and Migration in the US-Mexico Borderlands: A Reader,* Denise A. Segura and Patricia Zavella, eds., pp. 286–305. Durham: Duke University Press.

Illanes, Javiera Cienfuegos. 2010. Migrant Mothers and Divided Homes: Perceptions of Immigrant Peruvian Women about Motherhood. *Journal of Comparative Family Studies* 41 (2): 205–224.

Immigration Commission. 1911. *Importation and Harboring of Women for Immoral Purposes.* Reports of the Immigration Commission presented to Mr. Dillingham, Volume 19. Washington, DC: United States Senate, 61st Congress, 3rd Session.

Inlender, Talia. 2009. Status Quo or Sixth Ground? Adjudicating Gender Asylum Claims. In *Migrations and Mobilities: Citizenship, Borders, and Gender,* Seyla Benhabib and Judith Resnik, eds., pp. 356–379. New York: New York University Press.

International Labor Organization (ILO). 1998. *Labor and Social Issues Relating to Export-Processing Zones. Technical Background.* Paper for the International Tripartite Meeting of Export-Processing Zones Operating Countries. Geneva.

Iredale, Robyn. 2005. Gender, Immigration Policies and Accreditation: Valuing the Skills of Professional Women Migrants. *Geoforum* 36: 155–166.

Jackson, Pauline. 1984. Women in Nineteenth-Century Irish Emigration. *International Migration Review* 18 (4): 1004–1020.

Jaggar, Alison M. 2005. Arenas of Citizenship: Civil Society, the State, and the Global Order. In *Women and Citizenship*, Marilyn Friedman, ed., pp. 91–110. Oxford: Oxford University Press.

Jamal, Amaney. 2005. Mosques, Collective Identity, and Gender Differences among Arab Americans. *Journal of Middle East Women's Studies* 1 (1): 53–78.

Jones-Correa, Michael. 1998. Different Paths: Gender, Immigration and Political Participation. *International Migration Review* 32 (2): 326–49.

Joseph, Samuel. 1914. *Jewish Immigration to the United States from 1881 to 1910.* New York: Arno Press.

Josephides, Sasha. 1988. Honour, Family, and Work: Greek Cypriot Women Before and After Migration. In *Enterprising Women,* Sallie Westwood and Parminder Bhachu, eds., pp. 34–57. London: Routledge.

Kanaiaupuni, Shawn Malia. 2000. Reframing the Migration Question: An Analysis of Men, Women, and Gender in Mexico. *Social Forces* 78 (4): 1311–1347.

Kang, Miliann. 2003. The Managed Hand: The Commercialization of Bodies and Emotions in Korean Immigrant-Owned Nail Salons. *Gender and Society* 17 (6): 820–839.

Katzman, David M. 1978. *Seven Days a Week: Women and Domestic Service in Industrializing America.* New York: Oxford: Oxford University Press.

References

Kelson, Gregory A. and Debra L. DeLaet, eds. 1999. *Gender and Immigration*. New York: New York University Press.

Kerber, Linda K. 2009. The Stateless as the Citizen's Other: A View from the United States. In *Migrations and Mobilities: Citizenship, Borders, and Gender*, Seyla Benhabib and Judith Resnik, eds., pp. 76–123. New York: New York University Press.

Kessner, Thomas and Betty Boyd Caroli. 1978. New Immigrant Women at Work: Italians and Jews in New York City, 1880–1905. *Journal of Ethnic Studies* 5: 19–32.

Kibria, Nazli. 1993. *Family Tightrope: The Changing Lives of Vietnamese Americans*. Princeton: Princeton University Press.

Kilkey, Majella, Diane Perrons and Ania Plomien. 2013. *Gender, Migration and Domestic Work: Masculinities, Male Labour and Fathering in the UK and USA*. New York: Palgrave Macmillan.

Kingma, Mireille. 2006. *Nurses on the Move: Migration and the Global Health Care Economy*. Ithaca: Cornell University Press.

Kloosterman, Robert and Jan Rath. 2003. *Immigrant Entrepreneurs: Venturing Abroad in the Age of Globalization*. London: Bloomsbury Academic.

Knorr, Jacqueline and Barbara Meier, eds. 2000. *Women and Migration: Anthropological Perspectives*. New York: St Martin's Press.

Kofman, Eleonore. 1999. "Birds of Passage" a Decade later: Gender and Immigration in the European Union. *International Migration Review* 33 (2): 269–299.

Kunz, Rahel. 2008. "Remittances are Beautiful?" Gender Implications of the New Global Remittances Trend. *Third World Quarterly* 29 (7): 1389–1409.

Kurien, Prema A. 2002. *Kaleidoscopic Ethnicity: International Migration and the Reconstruction of Community Identities in India*. New Brunswick, NJ: Rutgers University Press.

Kwong, Peter. 1996. *The New Chinatown*. New York: Hill and Wang.

Lamphere, Louise. 1987. *From Working Daughters to Working Mothers: Immigrant Women in a New England Industrial Community*. Ithaca: Cornell University Press.

Lan, Pei-Chia. 2003. Maid or Madam? Filipina Migrant Workers and the Continuity of Domestic Labor. *Gender and Society* 17: 187–208.

Law, Anna O. 2015. Trump things that being born in the US shouldn't make you a citizen. Changing that would be very hard. (www.washingtonpost.com/blogs/money-cage/wp/2015/08/21trump-thinks-that-being).

Lee, Catherine. 2013. *Fictive Kinship: Family Reunification and the Meaning of Race and Nation in American Immigration*. New York: Russell Sage.

Lee, Helen. 2007. Transforming Transnationalism: Second Generation Tongans Overseas. *Asian and Pacific Migration Journal* 16 (2): 157–178.

Leifsen, Esben and Alexander Tymczuk. 2012. Care at a Distance: Ukranian and Ecuadorian Transnational Parenthood from Spain. *Journal of Ethnic and Migration Studies* 38 (2): 219–236.

Leonard, Karen Isaksen. 1997. *The South Asian Americans*. Westport, CT: Greenwood Press.

Levitt, Peggy. nd. *Social Remittances – Culture as a Development Tool* (http://idbdocs.iadb.org/wsdocs/getdocument.aspx?docnum=561717).

——. 1996. Migration-Driven Local-Level Forms of Cultural Diffusion. *International Migration Review* 32 (4): 926–948.

——. 2001. *The Transnational Villagers*. Berkeley: University of California Press.

——. 2003. "You know, Abraham was really the first immigrant": Religion and Transnational Migration. *International Migration Review* 37: 847–874.

Levitt, Peggy and Deepak Lamba-Nieves. 2011. Social Remittances Revisited. *Journal of Ethnic and Migration Studies* 37 (1): 1–22.

Lien, Pei-te, M. Margaret Conway, and Janelle Wong. 2004. *The Politics of Asian Americans: Diversity and Community*. New York: Routledge.

Light, Ivan. 1972. *Ethnic Enterprise in America*. Berkeley: University of California Press.

Light, Ivan and Edna Bonacich. 1988. *Immigrant Entrepreneurs*. Berkeley: University of California Press.

Lim, In-Sook. 1997. Korean Immigrant Women's Challenge to Gender Inequality at Home: The Interplay of Economic Resources, Gender, and Family. *Gender and Society* 11 (1): 31–51.

Lister, Ruth. 1997a. *Citizenship: Feminist Perspectives*. London: Macmillan.

——. 1997b. Citizenship: Towards a Feminist Synthesis. *Feminist Review* 57: 28–48.

——. 2001. Citizenship and Gender. In *The Blackwell Companion to Political Sociology*. K. Nash and A. Scott, eds., pp. 323–332. Oxford: Blackwell Publishers.

Litt, Jacquelin S. and Mary K. Zimmerman. 2003. Global Perspectives on Gender and Carework: An Introduction. *Gender and Society* 17 (2): 156–165.

Louie, Miriam Ching Yoon. 2001. *Sweatshop Warriors: Immigrant Women Workers Take on the Global Factory*. Cambridge, MA: South End Press.

Lowell, B. Lindsay, Susan Martin and Robyn Stone. 2010. Ageing and Care Giving in the United States: Policy Contexts and the Immigrant Workforce. *Population Ageing* 3: 59–82.

Luibheid, Eithne. 2002. *Entry Denied: Controlling Sexuality at the Border*. Minneapolis: University of Minnesota Press.

——. 2004. Childbearing against the State? Asylum Seeker Women in the Irish Republic. *Women's Studies International Forum* 27: 335–349.

——. 2007. "Looking Like a Lesbian": The Organization of Sexual Monitoring at the United States–Mexican Border. In *Women and Migration in the US-Mexico Borderlands: A Reader*, Denise A. Segura and Patricia Zavella, eds., pp.106–133. Durham: Duke University Press.

References

Lum, Kathryn. 2012. *Indian Diversities in Italy: Italian Case Study.* CARIM-India Research Report 2012/02, Developing a Knowledge Base for Policy Making on India-EU Migration.

Lutz, Helma. 1997. The Limits of European-ness. Immigrant Women in Fortress Europe. *Feminist Review* 57: 93–111.

———. 2010. Gender in the Migratory Process. *Journal of Ethnic and Migration Studies* 36 (10): 1647–1663.

Madziva, Roda and Elisabetta Zntini. 2012. Transnational Mothering and Forced Migration: Understanding the Experiences of Zimbabwean Mothers in the UK. *European Journal of Women's Studies* 19 (4): 428–443.

Mageean, Deirdre. 1997. To Be Matched or to Move: Irish Women's Prospects in Munster. In *Peasant Maids, City Women: From the European Countryside to Urban America*, Christiane Harzig, ed., pp. 57–98. Ithaca: Cornell University Press.

Mahdi, Ali Akbar. 1999. Trading Places: Changes in Gender Roles within the Iranian Immigrant Family. *Critique: Critical Middle Eastern Studies* 8 (15): 51–75.

Mahler, Sarah J. and Patricia R. Pessar. 2001. Gendered Geographies of Power: Analyzing Gender across National Spaces. *Identities: Global Studies in Culture and Power* 7 (4): 441–450.

———. 2006. Gender Matters: Ethnographers Bring Gender from the Periphery toward the Core of Migration Studies. *International Migration Review* 40 (1): 27–63.

Malarek, Victor. 2003. *The Natashas: Inside the New Global Sex Trade.* New York: Arcade Publishing.

Man, Guida. 2004. Gender, Work and Migration: Deskilling Chinese Immigrant Women in Canada. *Women's Studies International Forum* 27: 135–148.

Martin, Philip. Manolo Abella, and Christiane Kuptsch. 2006. *Managing Labor Migration in the Twenty-first Century.* New Haven: Yale University Press.

Massey, Douglas S., Joaquin Arango, Graeme Hugo, Ali Kovaouci, Adela Pelegrino, and J. Edward Taylor. 1993. Theories of International Migration: A Review and an Appraisal. *Population and Development Review* 19 (3): 431–466.

Massey, Douglas S., Jorge Durand, and Nolan J. Malone. 2002. *Beyond Smoke and Mirrors: Mexican Immigration in an Era of Economic Integration.* New York: Russell Sage Foundation.

Massey, Douglas S., Mary J. Fischer, and Chiara Capoferro. 2006. International Migration and Gender in Latin America: A Comparative Analysis. *International Migration* 44 (5): 63–91.

Matovic, Margareta. 1997. Embracing a Middle-Class Life: Swedish-American Women in Lake View. In *Peasant Maids, City Women: From the European Countryside to Urban America*, Christiane Harzig, ed., pp. 261–298. Ithaca: Cornell University Press.

References

Mazzucato, Valentina, Djamila Schans, Kim Caarls, and Cris Beauchemin. 2015. Transnational Families Between Africa and Europe. *International Migration Review* 49 (1): 142–172.

McCabe, Kristen. 2011. Caribbean Immigration in the United States. *Migration Information Source*, Migration Policy Institute (April 7).

McCall, Leslie. 2005. The Complexity of Intersectionality. *Signs* 36 (3): 1771–1800.

McIlwaine, Cathy. 2008. *Subversion or Subjugation: Transforming Gender Ideologies among Latin American Migrants in London.* Department of Geography, Queen Mary University, London (http://www.geog.qmul.ac.uk/docs/staff/6313.pdf).

McKay, Steven. 2007. Filipino Sea Men: Constructing Masculinities in an Ethnic Labour Niche. *Journal of Ethnic and Migration Studies* 33 (4): 617–632.

McKenzie, Sean and Cecilia Menjívar. 2011. The Meanings of Migration, Remittances and Gifts: Views of Honduran Women who Stay. *Global Networks* 11 (1): 63–81.

Mehrotra, Meeta. 1999. The Social Construction of Wife Abuse: Experiences of Asian Indian Women in the United States. *Violence against Women* 5 (6): 619–40.

Melnick, Jeffrey. 2007. Immigration and Race Relations. In *The New Americans: A Guide to Immigration Since 1965.* Mary C. Waters and Reed Ueda, eds., pp. 255–273. Cambridge, MA: Harvard University Press.

Menjívar, Cecilia. 1999. The Intersection of Work and Gender: Central American Immigrant Women and Employment in California. *American Behavioral Scientist* 42 (4): 601–617.

Menjívar, Cecilia and Olivia Salcido. 2002. Immigrant Women and Domestic Violence: Common Experiences in Different Countries. *Gender and Society* 16 (6): 898–920.

——. 2013. *Gendered Paths to Legal Status: The Case of Latin American Immigrants in Phoenix.* Washington, DC: Immigration Policy Center, Special Report.

Menjívar, Cecilia and Victor Agadjanian. 2007. Men's Migration and Women's Lives: Views from Rural Armenia and Guatemala. *Social Science Quarterly* 88 (5): 1243–1262.

Middleton, Julie. 2010. Barriers to Protection: Gender-related Persecution and Asylum in South Africa. In *Gender and Migration: Feminist Interventions*, Ingrid Palmary, Erica Burman, Khatidja Chantler, and Peace Kuguwa, eds., pp. 67–85. London: Zed Books.

Millman, Heather L. 2013. Mothering from Afar: Conceptualizing Transnational Motherhood. *Totem: The University of Western Ontario Journal of Anthropology* 21 (1): 72–82.

Min, Pyong Gap. 1988. *Ethnic Business Enterprise: Korean Small Business in Atlanta.* Staten Island, NY: Center for Migration Studies.

——. 1998. *Changes and Conflicts: Korean Immigrant Families in New York.* Needham Heights, MA: Allyn and Bacon.

Min, Pyong Gap and Mehdi Bozorgmehr. 2000. Immigrant Entrepreneurship and Business Patterns: A Comparison of Koreans and Iranians in Los Angeles. *International Migration Review* 34: 682–706.

——. 2003. United States: The Entrepreneurial Cutting Edge. In *Immigrant Entrepreneurs: Venturing Abroad in the Age of Globalization*, Robert Kloosterman and Jan Rath, eds., pp. 17–37. Oxford: Berg.

Mirdal, Gretty M. 1984. Stress and Distress in Migration: Problems and Resources of Turkish Women in Denmark. *International Migration Review* 18 (1): 984–1003.

——. 2006. Changing Idioms of Shame; Experiences of Disgrace and Dishonour in the Narratives of Turkish Women Living in Denmark. *Culture and Psychology* 12 (4): 395–414.

Mobasher, Mohsen. 2012. *Iranians in Texas: Migration, Politics, and Ethnic Identity.* Austin; University of Texas Press.

Moloney, Deirdre. 2012. Strangers in the Land: Gendered Immigration Policy. *The Journal of the Gilded Age and the Progressive Era* 11 (2): 270–276.

Momsen, Janet Henshall (ed.). 1999. *Gender, Migration and Domestic Service.* London: Routledge.

Montes, Veronica. 2013. The Role of Emotions in the Construction of Masculinity: Guatemalan Migrant Men, Transnational Migration, and Family Relations. *Gender and Society* 27 (4): 469–490.

Moran-Taylor, Michelle J. 2008. When Mothers and Fathers Migrate North: Caretakers, Children, and Child Rearing in Guatemala. *Latin American Perspectives* 35 (4): 79–95.

Morokvasic, Mirjana. 1984. "Birds of Passage are Also Women . . ." *International Migration Review*, Special Issue: *Women in Migration* 18 (4): 887.

Morrison, Andrew, Maurice Schiff, and Mirja Sjoblom. 2008. *The International Migration of Women.* Washington: The World Bank and Palgrave-Macmillan.

Moya, José C. 2012. Gender and Migration: Searching for Answers to Basic Questions. *Social Science History* 36 (2): 269–274.

Narayan, Uma. 1995. "Male-Order" Brides: Immigrant Women, Domestic Violence and Immigration Law. *Hypatia* 10 (1): 104–119.

Nash, June C. and Maria Patricia Fernandez-Kelly (eds.). 1984. *Women, Men, and the International Division of Labor.* Albany: State University of New York Press.

National Domestic Worker Alliance. 2012. *The Invisible and Unregulated World of Domestic Work.* Center for Urban Economic Development, University of Illinois-Chicago Data Center. (http://www.domesticworkers.org/homeeconomics/key-findings, consulted January 19, 2015).

References

Newman, Barry. 2006. Who Will Care for US Elderly If Border Closes? *The Wall Street Journal*, July 26, p. B1.

Nicholson, Melanie. 2006. Without their Children: Rethinking Motherhood among Transnational Migrant Women. *Social Text* 24 (3): 13–33.

Nicolosi, Ann Marie. 2001. "We Do Not Want our Girls to Marry Foreigners: Gender, Race and American Citizenship. *NWSA Journal* 13 (3): 1–21.

Nobles, Jenna. 2011. Parenting from Abroad: Migration, Nonresident Father Involvement, and Children's Education in Mexico. *Journal of Marriage and Family* 73 (4): 729–746.

Nolan, Janet A. 1989. *Ourselves Alone: Women's Emigration from Ireland, 1885–1920*. Lexington: University of Kentucky Press.

Nowak, Joanne. 2009. Gendered Perceptions of Migration among Skilled Female Ghanaian Nurses. *Gender and Development* 17 (2): 269–280.

Nwosu, Chiamaka and Jeanne Batalova. 2014. Immigrants from the Dominican Republic in the United States. *Migration Information Source*, July 18 (www.migration.policy.org/article/foreign-bron-dominican-republic-united-states).

Ojong, Vivian Besem. 2007. Entrepreneurship among Ghanaians in South Africa. In *Handbook of Research on Ethnic Minority Entrepreneurs*, Leo-Paul Dana, ed., pp. 707–719. Cheltenham, UK and Northampton, MA: Edward Elgar.

Ong, Aihwa. 1987. *Spirits of Resistance and Capitalist Discipline: Factory Women in Malaysia*. Albany: State University of New York Press.

——. 1996. Cultural Citizenship as Subject-making: Immigrants Negotiate Racial and Cultural Boundaries in the United States. *Current Anthropology* 37 (5): 737–762.

Orellana, M. F., B. Thorne, B., A. Chee, and W. S. E. Lam. 2001. Transnational Childhoods: The Participation of Children in Processes of Family Migration. *Social Problems* 48 (4): 572–591.

Orsi, Robert Anthony. 1985. *The Madonna of 115th Street: Faith and Community in Italian Harlem, 1880–1950*. New Haven: Yale University Press.

Palmary, Ingrid. 2010. Sex, Choice and Exploitation: Reflections on Anti-trafficking Discourse. In *Gender and Migration: Feminist Interventions*, Ingrid Palmary, Erica Burman, Khatidja Chantler and Peace Kiguwa, eds., pp. 50–66. London: Zed Books.

Pande, Amrita. 2012. From "Balcony Talk" and "Practical Prayers" to Illegal Collectives: Migrant Domestic Workers and Meso-Level Resistances in Lebanon. *Gender and Society* 26 (3): 382–405.

——. 2013. "The Paper that You Have in Your Hand is My Freedom": Migrant Domestic Work and the Sponsorship (Kafala) System in Lebanon. *International Migration Review* 47 (2): 414–441.

Pantoja, Adrian D. and Sarah Allen Gershon. 2006. Political Orientations and Naturalization Among Latino and Latina Immigrants. *Social Science Quarterly* 87 (5): 1171–1187.

References

Parla, Ayse. 2001. The "Honor" of the State: Virginity Examinations in Turkey. *Feminist Studies* 27 (1): 65–88.

Parrado, Emilio A. and Chenua A. Flippen. 2005. Migration and Gender among Mexican Women. *American Sociological Review* 70 (4): 606–632.

Parreñas, Rhacel. 2001a. Mothering from a Distance: Emotions, Gender and Intergenerational Relations in Filipino Transnational Families. *Feminist Studies* 27 (2): 361–390.

——. 2001b. *Servants of Globalization: Women, Migration, and Domestic Work*. Stanford: Stanford University Press.

——. 2005. *Children of Global Migration: Transnational Families and Gendered Woes*. Stanford: Stanford University Press.

——. 2011. *Illicit Flirtations: Labor, Migration, and Sex Trafficking in Tokyo*. Stanford: Stanford University Press.

Passell, Jeffrey and Paul Taylor. 2010. *Unauthorized Immigrants and Their US-Born Children*. Pew Hispanic Center, August 11 (www.pewhispanic.org/files/reports/125.pdf).

Pauli, Julia. 2008. A Home of One's Own: Gender, Migration and Residence in Rural Mexico. *American Ethnologist* 35 (1): 171–187.

Pearce, Susan C., Elizabeth J. Clifford, and Reena Tandon. 2011. *Immigration and Women: Understanding the American Experience*. New York: New York University Press.

Pessar, Patricia R. 1995. *A Visa for a Dream: Dominicans in the United States*. Boston: Allyn and Bacon.

——. 1999. Engendering Migration Studies: The Case of New Immigrants in the United States. *The American Behavioral Scientist* 42 (4): 577–600.

——. 2001. Women's Political Consciousness and Empowerment in Local, National, and Transnational Contexts: Guatemalan Refugees and Returnees. *Identities* 7 (4): 461–500.

——. 2003. Anthropology and the Engendering of Migration Studies. In *American Arrivals: Anthropology Engages the New Immigration*, Nancy Foner, ed., pp. 75–98. Santa Fe, NM: School of American Research Press.

Pessar, Patricia and Sarah J. Mahler. 2003. Transnational Migration; Bringing Gender In. *International Migration Review* 37: 812–846.

Pe-Pua, Rogelia, C. Mitchell, Robyn Iredale, and Stephen Castles. 1996. *Astronaut Families and Parachute Children: The Cycle of Migration between Hong Kong and Australia*. Canberra: Australian Government Public Service.

Peter, Kankonde Bukasa. 2010. Transnational Family Ties, Remittance Motives, and Social Death among Congolese Migrants: A Socio-Anthropological Analysis. *Journal of Comparative Family Studies* 41 (2): 225–243.

Phizacklea, Annie (ed.). 1983. *One Way Ticket: Migration and Female Labour*. London: Routledge, Kegan and Paul.

Pickup, Francine. 1998. More Words but No Action? Forced Migration and Trafficking of Women. *Gender and Development* 6 (1): 44–51.

References

Pine, Barbara and Diane Drachman. 2005. Effective Child Welfare Practice with Immigrant and Refugee Children and their Families. *Child Welfare* 84 (5): 537–562.

Pio, Edwina. 2007. Enterprising Indian Women in New Zealand. In *Handbook of Research on Ethnic Minority Entrepreneurs*, Leo-Paul Dana, ed., pp. 744–753. Cheltenham, UK and Northampton, MA: Edward Elgar.

Piper, Nicola. 2006. Gendering the Politics of Migration. *International Migration Review* 40 (1): 133–164.

Piper, Nicola (ed.). 2008. *New Perspectives on Gender and Migration: Livelihood, Rights and Entitlements*. New York: Routledge.

Preisser, Amita Bhandari. 1999. Domestic Violence in South Asian Communities in America. *Violence Against Women* 5 (6): 684–699.

Preston, Julia. 2015. Judge Orders Immigrant Children and Mothers Released from Detention. *The New York Times*, July 25, p. A14.

Pribilsky, Jason. 2004. "Aprendemos a Convivir": Conjugal Relations, Co-Parenting, and Family Life among Ecuadorian Transnational Migrants in New York City and the Ecuadorian Andes. *Global Networks* 4 (3): 313–334.

——. 2012. Consumption Dilemmas: Tracking Masculinity, Money and Transnational Fatherhood Between the Ecuadorian Andes and New York City. *Journal of Ethnic and Migration Studies* 38 (2): 323–343.

Raghuram, Parvati. 2004a. The Difference that Skills Make: Gender, Family Migration Strategies and Regulated Labour Markets. *Journal of Ethnic and Migration Studies* 30 (2): 303–321.

Raghuram, Parvati. 2004b. Migration, Gender and the IT Sector: Intersecting Debates. *Women's Studies International Forum* 27: 163–176.

Rahman, Mizanur and Lian Kwen Fee. 2009. Gender and the Remittance Process: Indonesian Domestic Workers in Hong Kong, Singapore, and Malaysia. *Asian Population Studies* 5 (2): 103–125.

Raijman, Rebeca, Silvina Schammah-Gesser and Adriana Kemp. 2003. International Migration, Domestic Work, and Care Work: Undocumented Latina Migrants in Israel. *Gender and Society* 17 (5): 727–749.

Raissiguier, Catherine. 2010. *Reinventing the Republic: Gender, Migration and Citizenship in France*. Stanford: Stanford University Press.

Ramirez, Hernan and Pierrette Hondagneu-Sotelo. 2009. Mexican Immigrant Gardeners: Entrepreneurs or Exploited Workers. *Social Problems* 56 (1): 70–88.

Ravenstein, Ernest George. 1885. The Laws of Migration. *Journal of the Statistical Society of London* 48: 167–235.

Reeder, Linda. 2003. *Widows in White: Migration and the Transformation of Rural Italian Women, Sicily, 1880–1920*. Toronto: University of Toronto Press.

Reeve, Penn. 2009. Portuguese Labor Activism in Southeastern Massachusetts. In *Community, Culture and the Makings of Identity: Portuguese Americans along*

References

the Eastern Seabord, Kimberly DaCosta Holden and Andrea Klimt, eds., pp. 337–356. North Dartmouth, MA: University of Massachusetts at Dartmouth.

Renteln, Alison Dundes. 2004. *The Cultural Defense.* Oxford: Oxford University Press.

Repak, Terry. 1995. *Waiting on Washington: Central American Workers in the Nation's Capital.* Philadelphia: Temple University Press.

Rhee, Siyon. 1997. Domestic Violence in the Korean Immigrant Family. *Journal of Sociology and Social Welfare* 24 (1): 63–77.

Rhoades, Robert E. 1978. Intra-European Migration and Rural Development: Lessons from the Spanish Case. *Human Organization* 37: 136–147.

Rodriguez, Robyn M. 2008. The Labor Brokerage State and the Globalization of Filipina Care Workers. *Signs* 33 (4): 794–800.

Rosaldo, Michelle and Louise Lamphere. 1974. *Woman, Culture and Society.* Stanford: Stanford University Press.

Rosaldo, Renato and William V. Flores. 1997. Identity, Conflict, and Evolving Latino Communities; Cultural Citizenship in San Jose, California. In *Latino Cultural Citizenship: Claiming Identity, Space and Rights,* William V. Flores and Rina Benmayor, eds., pp. 57–96. Boston: Beacon Press.

Rosenblum, Marc. 2015. *Understanding the Potential Impact of Executive Action on Immigration Enforcement.* Washington, DC: Migration Policy Institute, July 23.

Rudrappa, Sharmila. 2004. Radical Caring in an Ethnic Shelter: South Asian American Women Workers at Apna Ghar, Chicago. *Gender and Society* 18 (5): 588–609.

Salcido, Olivia and Madelaine Adelman. 2004. "He has me tied with the blessed and damned papers": Undocumented-Immigrant Battered Women in Phoenix, Arizona." *Human Organization* 63 (2): 162–172.

Salcido, Olivia and Cecilia Menjívar. 2012. Gendered Paths to Legal Citizenship: The Case of Latin-American Immigrants in Phoenix, Arizona. *Law and Society Review* 46 (2): 335–368

Santos, José Leonardo. 2012. *Evangelicalism and Masculinity: Faith and Gender in El Salvador.* Lanham, MD: Lexington Books.

Schauer, Edward J. and Elizabeth M. Wheaton. 2006. Sex Trafficking Into the United States: A Literature Review. *Criminal Justice Review* 31 (2): 146–169.

Schmalzbauer, Leah. 2004. Searching for Wages and Mothering from Afar: The Case of Honduran Transnational Families. *Journal of Marriage and the Family* 66 (5): 1317–1331.

Scott, James C. 1985. *Weapons of the Weak: Everyday Forms of Peasant Resistance.* New Haven: Yale University Press.

Segura, Denise. 2007. Working at Motherhood: Chicana and Mexican Immigrant Mothers and Employment. In *Women and Migration in the US-Mexico Borderlands: A Reader,* Denise A. Segura and Patricia Zavella, eds., pp. 368–387. Durham: Duke University Press.

References

Seif, Hinda. 2008. Wearing Union T-Shirts: Undocumented Women Farm Workers and Gendered Circuits of Political Power. *Latin American Perspectives* 35 (1): 78–103.

Seller, Maxine ed., 1981. *Immigrant Women*. Philadelphia: Temple University Press.

Semyonov, Moshe and Anastasia Gorodzeisky. 2005. Labor Migration, Remittances and Household Income: A Comparison between Filipino and Filipina Overseas Workers. *International Migration Review* 39 (1): 45–69.

Serrão, Joel. 1974. *Emigração Portuguesa*. Lisbon: Livros Horizonte.

Sharma, Rashmi. 2011. Gender and International Migration: The Profile of Female Migrants from India. *Social Scientist* 39 (3/4): 37–63.

Sheehan, Helen E., Rafael A. Javier, and Theresa Thanajan. 2000. Introduction to the Special Issue on Domestic Violence in the South Asian Community. *Journal of Social Distress and Homelessness* 9 (3): 167–171.

Simon, Rita J. and Caroline B. Brettell eds., 1986. *International Migration: The Female Experience*. Totowa, NJ: Rowman and Allan held.

Simmons, Tracy. 2008. Sexuality and Immigration: UK Family Reunion Policy and the Regulation of Sexual Citizens in the European Union. *Political Geography* 27: 213–230.

Singer, Audrey. 2012. *Immigrant Workers in the US Labor Force*. Washington, DC: The Brookings Institution.

Singh, Raghu N. and N. Prabha Unnithan. 1999. Wife Burning: Cultural Cues for Lethal Violence against Women among Asian Indians in the United States. *Violence Against Women* 5 (6): 641–653.

Sinke, Suzanne. 2006a. Gender and Migration: Historical Perspectives. *International Migration Review* 40 (1): 82–103.

——. 2006b. Gender and Migration. In *A Companion to American Immigration*, Reed Ueda, ed., pp. 289–308. Oxford: Blackwell Publishing.

Smith, Angele. 2008. The Irish Citizenship Referendum (2004): Motherhood and Belonging in Ireland. In *Citizenship, Political Engagement, and Belonging: Immigrants in Europe and the United States*, Deborah Reed-Danahay and Caroline B. Brettell, eds., pp. 60–77. Brunswick, NJ: Rutgers University Press.

Smith, Michael Peter and Matt Bakker. 2008. *Citizenship Across Borders: The Political Transnationalism of El Migrante*. Ithaca: Cornell University Press.

Snodgrass, Michael. 2011. The Bracero Program. In *Beyond the Border: The History of Mexican-US Migration*, Mark Overmyer-Velazquez, ed., pp. 79–102. New York. Oxford University Press.

Solari, Cinzia. 2007. Professionals and Saints: How Immigrant Careworkers Negotiate Gender Identities at Work. In *Citizenship and Immigrant Incorporation: Comparative Perspectives on North America and Western Europe*, Gokce Yurdakul and Y. Michal Bodemann, eds., pp. 185–212. New York, Palgrave-Macmillan.

Stephen, Lynn. 2003. Cultural Citizenship and Labor Rights for Oregon Farm

References

Workers: The Case of Pineros y Campesinos Unidos del Noroeste (PCUN). *Human Organization* 62: 27–39.

Storey, Sierra and Jeanne Batalova. 2013. Filipina Immigrants in the United States. *Migration Information Source*, June 5. Washington, DC: Migration Policy Institute.

Su, Julie A and Chanchanit Martorell. 2001. Exploitation and Abuse in the Garment Industry: The Case of the Thai Slave-Labor Compound in El Monte. In *Asian and Latino Immigrants in a Restructuring Economy: The Metamorphosis of Southern California*, Maria Lopez-Garza and David R. Diaz, eds., pp. 21–45. Stanford: Stanford University Press.

Tarabay, Jamie. 2009. "Man Accused of Killing Daughter for Family Honor." National Public Radio, April 20 (http//www.npr.org/templates/story/story. php?storyId=99616128).

Tastsoglou, Evangelia and Alexandra Z. Dobrowolsky. 2006. *Women, Migration and Citizenship: Making Local, National and Transnational Connections.* London: Ashgate.

Thai, Hung Cam. 2005. Globalization as Gender Strategy: Respectability, Masculinity, and Convertibility across the Vietnamese Diaspora. In *Critical Globalization Studies*, Richard P. Appelbaum and William I. Robinson, eds., pp. 313–322. New York: Routledge.

——. 2006. Money and Masculinity among Low Wage Vietnamese Immigrants in Transnational Families. *International Journal of Sociology of the Family* 32 (2): 247–271.

Thronson, David B. 2008. Creating Crisis: Immigration Raids and the Destabilization of Immigrant Families. *Wake Forest Law Review* 43: 391–418.

Tseng, Yen-fen. 1995. Beyond Little Taipei: The Development of Taiwanese Immigrant Businesses in Los Angeles. *International Migration Review* 29: 34–45.

Tsong, Yuying and Yuli Liu. 2009. Parachute Kids and Astronaut Families. In *Asian Americn Psychology: Current Perspectives*, Nita Tewari and Alvin N. Alvarez, eds., pp. 365–379. New York: Taylor and Francis Group.

Tsuda, Takeyuchi. 2003. *Strangers in the Ethnic Homeland: Japanese Return Migration in Transnational Perspective.* New York: Columbia University Press.

Tung, Charlene. 2000. Cost of Caring: the Social Reproductive Labor of Filipina Live-in Home Health Caregivers. *Frontiers: A Journal of Women's Studies* 21 (1–2): 61–82.

Tyner, James. 1999. The Global Context of Gendered Labor Migration from the Philippines to the United States. *American Behavioral Scientist* 42 (4): 671–689

Tyree, Andrea and Katharine Donato. 1985. The Sex Composition of Legal Immigrants to the United States. *Sociology and Social Research* 69 (4): 577–584.

United Nations Population Fund. 2006. *State of World Population 2006: A*

References

Passage to Hope; Women and International Migration (www.unfpa.org/swp/2006/pdf/en_sowp06.pdf).

Valdez, Zulema. 2011. *The New Entrepreneurs: How Race, Class and Gender Shape American Enterprise*. Stanford: Stanford University Press.

Valji, Nahla, Lee Anne de la Hunt, and Helen Moffett. 2003. Where are the Women? Gender Discrimination in Refugee Policies and Practices. *Agenda: Empowering Women for Gender Equity* 55: 61–72.

Vanwey, Leah K. 2004 Altruistic and Contractual Remittances between Male and Female Migrants and Households in Rural Thailand. *Demography* 41 (4): 739–756.

Varma, Roli and Everett M. Rogers. 2004. Indian Cyber Workers in US. *Economic and Political Weekly* 39 (52): 5645–5652.

Vertovec, Steven. 2010. Introduction: New Directions in the Anthropology of Migration and Multiculturalism. In *Anthropology of Migration and Multiculturalism: New Directions*, Steven Vertovec, ed., pp. 1–18. New York and London: Routledge.

Vlase, Ionela. 2013. Women's Social Remittances and Their Implications at Household Level: A Case Study of Romanian Migration to Italy. *Migration Letters* 10 (1): 81–90.

Volery, Thierry. 2007. Ethnic Entrepreneurship: A Theoretical Framework. In *Handbook of Research on Ethnic Minority Entrepreneurs*, Leo-Paul Dana, ed., pp. 30–41. Cheltenham, UK and Northampton, MA: Edward Elgar.

Walter, Nicholas, Philippe Bourgois, and H. Margarita Loinaz. 2004. Masculinity and Undocumented Labor Migration: Injured Latino Day Laborers in San Francisco. *Social Science and Medicine* 59: 1159–1168.

Walton-Roberts, Margaret 2004. Rescaling Citizenship: Gendering Canadian Immigration Policy. *Political Geography* 23: 265–281.

——. 2012. Contextualizing the Global Nursing Care Chain: International Migration and the Status of Nursing in Kerala, India. *Global Networks* 12 (2): 175–194.

Walton-Roberts, Margaret and I. S. Rajan. 2013. Nurse Emigration from Kerala: Brain Circulation or Trap? *India Migration Report 2013*. New Delhi: Routledge.

Weitzer, Ronald. 2007. The Social Construction of Sex Trafficking: Ideology and Institutionalization of a Moral Crusade. *Politics and Society* 35 (3): 447–475.

Werbner, Pnina. 2005. Honor, Shame and the Politics of Sexual Embodiment among South Asian Muslims in Britain and Beyond: An Analysis of Debates in the Public Sphere. *International Social Science Review* 6 (1): 25–47.

Whatley, Monica and Jeanne Batalova. 2011. Indian Immigrants in the United States. *Migration Information Source*, August 21. Washington, DC: Migration Policy Institute (www.migrationpolicy.org/article/indian-immigrants-united-states).

References

Wollstonecraft, Mary. 1792. *A Vindication of the Rights of Woman*. London: J. Johnson.

Wong, Bernard. 1998 *Ethnicity and Entrepreneurship: The New Chinese Immigrants in the San Francisco Bay*. Boston: Allyn and Bacon.

Wright, M. 1997. Crossing the Factory Frontier: Gender, Place and Power in Mexican Maquiladoras. *Antipode* 29 (3): 278–302.

Yans-McLaughlin, Virginia. 1973. Patterns of Work and Family Organization; Buffalo's Italians. In *The American Family in Social-Historical Perspective*, Michael Gordon, ed., pp. 136–151. New York: St. Martin's Press.

Yeoh, Brenda S. A., Shirlena Huang and Theodora Lam. 2005. Transnationalizing the "Asian" Family: Imaginaries, Intimacies, and Strategic Intents. *Global Networks* 5 (4): 307–315.

Yesierska, Anzia. 1925. *Bread Givers*. New York: Doubleday and Co.

Yung, Judy. 1995. *Unbound Feet: A Social History of Chinese Women in San Francisco*. Berkeley: University of California Press.

Yuval-Davis, Nira. 1997. Women, Citizenship and Difference. *Feminist Review* 57: 4–27.

Zentgraff, Kristine M. 2001. Through Economic Restructuring, Recession, and Rebound: The Continuing Importance of Latina Immigrant Labor in the Los Angeles Economy. In *Asian and Latino Immigrants in a Restructuring Economy*, Marta Lopez-Garza and David Diaz, eds., pp. 46–74. Stanford: Stanford University Press.

Zhang, Sheldon X. 2009. Beyond the "Natasha" Story: A Review and Critique of Current Research on Sex Trafficking. *Global Crime* 10 (3): 178–195.

Zhou, Min. 1992. *Chinatown: The Socioeconomic Potential of an Urban Enclave*. Philadelphia: Temple University Press.

———. 1998. "Parachute Kids" in Southern California: The Educational Experience of Chinese Children in Transnational Families. *Educational Policy* 12: 682–704.

Zlotnik, Hania. 2003. The Global Dimensions of Female Migration. *Migration Information Source* (March). Washington, DC: Migration Policy Institute (www.migrationinformation.org).

Zontini, Elisabetta. 2010. *Transnational Families, Migration and Gender: Moroccan And Filipino Women in Bologna And Barcelona*. New York: Berghahn Books.

Index

Index

Index

Index

Illegal Immigration Reform and
Immigrant Responsibility Act
(IIRIRA) (1996) 67, 179
Immigrant Women in Science 76
Immigration Act (1917) 44
Immigration and Nationality Act
(1965) *see* Hart-Cellar Act
Immigration and Naturalization
Service 47
Immigration Nursing Relief Act
(1989) 103
Immigration (or Expatriation) Act
(1907) 40–42
Immigration Reform and Control Act
(1986) 20, 50, 51, 55–56, 178
India 163, 174
Indian migrants
division of labor 114
in hospitality sector 109
in the Middle East 28
as nurses 102, 104–105
skilled professionals 84
in US 19, 22–23, 35
Indonesian migrants 164
Inlender, Talia 58
International Labor Organization
(ILO) 98
*International Migration: The Female
Experience* (Simon and Brettell) 2
International Migration Review 2, 6
Iran 27
Iranian migrants 113–114, 143–145
Iraq 27, 28
Ireland 65–66
Irish migrants 17, 90, 91, 92
Irish Nationality Law (2004) 65,
66–67
Italian migrants 18–19, 92–93, 128,
129–131, 155
Italy 28, 96, 106, 118, 120, 152,
168

Jamaican migrants 25–26
Jamal, Amaney 69, 74
Japan 120, 121
Japanese migrants 42–3, 44, 45,
107–108

Jewish migrants 17–18, 19, 45,
92–93, 128–129
Johnson-Reed Act (National Origins
Quota Act) (1924) 14, 44, 46, 94
Jones-Correa, Michael 70–72, 77

Kanaiaupuni, Shawn Mailai 172–173
Kang, Miliann 114
Kerala, southwest India 23, 24,
104–105, 139, 163
Kilkey, Majella 110
Kingma, Mireille 103
Kofman, Eleonore 32
Korean migrants 104, 112–113,
137–139

labor market
Bracero Program 94–97
care work 84–85
class differentiations 84
day laborers 108–109
domestic service 91–3
eldercare workers 105–107, 115
employment visas 46
family business/immigrant
entrepreneur 112–116
farming 90
female perspective 85–107, 147
gardeners 107–108
gastarbeiter (guest-worker) program
95–97
gender participation 82, 84–85,
89–94, 122–123
hospitality sector 110
host-language deficiences 146
IT workers 110–111
kafala system 101, 102
male perspective 107–111
models of migration 83–85
nannies/domestic servants 97,
99–102
native-born/foreign-born
participation 85–89
nurses/ 23–24, 25, 27, 102–105
occupational niches 97–107
opportunities in 81–82
segmentation 90–94

Index